Junior
Worldmark
Encyclopedia of
World Cultures

Junior Worldmark Encyclopedia of

World Cultures

VOLUME 7

Norway to Russia

AN IMPRINT OF GALE

DETROIT · LONDON

JUNIOR WORLDMARK ENCYCLOPEDIA OF WORLD CULTURES

U•X•L Staff

Jane Hoehner, *U•X•L Senior Editor*
Carol DeKane Nagel, *U•X•L Managing Editor*
Thomas L. Romig, *U•X•L Publisher*
Mary Beth Trimper, *Production Director*
Evi Seoud, *Assistant Production Manager*
Shanna Heilveil, *Production Associate*
Cynthia Baldwin, *Product Design Manager*
Barbara J. Yarrow, *Graphic Services Supervisor*
Pamela A. E. Galbreath, *Senior Art Director*
Margaret Chamberlain, *Permissions Specialist (Pictures)*

Copyright © 1999
U•X•L
An Imprint of Gale

Library of Congress Cataloging-in-Publication Data
Junior worldmark encyclopedia of world cultures / Timothy L. Gall and
  Susan Bevan Gall, editors.
    p. cm.
  Includes bibliographical references and index.
  Summary: Arranges countries around the world alphabetically,
subdivides these countries into 250 culture groups, and provides
information about the ethnology and human geography of each group.
    ISBN 0-7876-1756-X (set : alk. paper)
    1. Ethnology--Encyclopedias, Juvenile. 2. Human geography-
-Encyclopedias, Juvenile. [1. Ethnology--Encyclopedias. 2. Human
geography--Encyclopedias.] I. Gall, Timothy L. II. Gall, Susan B.
GN307.J85 1999
306' .03--dc21   98-13810
                                   CIP
                                   AC

ISBN 0-7876-1756-X (set)
ISBN 0-7876-1757-1 (vol. 1)   ISBN 0-7876-1758-X (vol. 2)   ISBN 0-7876-1759-8 (vol. 3)
ISBN 0-7876-1760-1 (vol. 4)   ISBN 0-7876-1761-X (vol. 5)   ISBN 0-7876-1762-8 (vol. 6)
ISBN 0-7876-1763-6 (vol. 7)   ISBN 0-7876-1764-4 (vol. 8)   ISBN 0-7876-2761-5 (vol. 9)

Printed in the United States of America
10 9 8 7 6 5 4 3 2

Contents
Volume 7

Cumulative Contents vi
Contributors xi
Reader's Guide xv

Norway 1
   Norwegians 1
   Sami 9

Oman 17
   Omanis 17

Pakistan 25
   Pakistanis 25
   Baluchi 35
   Brahui 41
   Punjabis 46

Panama 57
   Panamanians 57
   Cunas 64

Papua New Guinea 71
   Melanesians 71
   Iatmul 79
   Melpa 84
   Motu 89

Paraguay 93
   Paraguayans 93
   Guaranís 98

Peru 105
   Peruvians 105
   Asháninka............................. 113
   Quechua 119

Philippines 125
   Filipinos 125
   Hiligaynon 136
   Ilocanos 142

Poland 149
   Poles 149

Portugal 157
   Portuguese 157

Qatar 165
   Qataris 165

Romania 171
   Romanians............................. 171
   Roma 178

Russia 187
   Russians 187
   Chechens 199
   Chukchi 206
   Mordvins 211
   Nentsy 216
   Tatars................................. 221

Glossary............................ 229
Index 233

Cumulative Contents

Volume 1

Afghanistan **3**
    Afghanis...3
    Hazaras...10
    Pashtun...13
Albania **19**
    Albanians 19
Algeria **27**
    Algerians 27
Andorra **35**
    Andorrans 35
Angola **39**
    Angolans 39
Antigua and Barbuda.............................**49**
    Antiguans and Barbudans 49
Argentina **57**
    Argentines 57
Armenia...**65**
    Armenians 65
Australia **73**
    Australians 73
    Australian Aborigines 80
Austria..**87**
    Austrians 87
Azerbaijan **95**
    Azerbaijanis 95
Bahamas **101**
    Bahamians..101
Bahrain..**107**
    Bahrainis 107
Bangladesh..**113**
    Bangladeshis 113
    Bengalis 121
    Chakmas...127
Barbados **133**
    Barbadians 133
Belarus...**139**
    Belarusans..139
Belgium **145**
    Belgians 145
    Flemings...151
    Walloons 155
Belize...**159**
    Belizeans 159
    Garifuna 166
Benin **173**
    Beninese...173
Bhutan...**179**
    Bhutanese...179

Bolivia **185**
    Bolivians..185
    Aymara 193
Bosnia and Herzegovina **201**
    Bosnians 201

Volume 2

Brazil...**1**
Brazilians **1**
    Afro-Brazilians 11
    Kayapos 17
    Xavante 22
Bulgaria..**31**
    Bulgarians 31
Burkina Faso **39**
    Burkinabe 39
    Mossi 43
Burundi **51**
    Burundians 51
    Tutsi..57
Cambodia...**61**
    Khmer 61
    Hill Tribespeople 70
Cameroon...**77**
    Cameroonians 77
Canada **83**
    Canadians 83
    French Canadians 89
    Inuit 94
Cape Verde..**101**
    Cape Verdeans 101
Central African Republic.........................**105**
    Central Africans 105
Chad...**113**
    Chadians 113
Chile **119**
    Chileans 119
    Araucanians 126
China **131**
    Chinese 132
    Dong 141
    Han 148
    Man (Manchus) 153
    Miao 157
    Tibetans 163
    Uighurs 168
    Zhuang..173

CUMULATIVE CONTENTS

Colombia **177**
    Colombians 177
    Páez 183
Congo, Democratic Republic of the **189**
    Congolese 189
    Azande 197
    Efe and Mbuti 201
Congo, Republic of the **209**
    Congolese 209
    Aka 215
    Bakongo 221

Volume 3

Costa Rica **1**
    Costa Ricans 1
Cote d'Ivoire **7**
    Ivoirians 7
Croatia **13**
    Croats 13
Cuba **21**
    Cubans 21
Cyprus **29**
    Greek Cypriots 29
Czech Republic **37**
    Czechs 37
Denmark **43**
    Danes 43
Djibouti **51**
    Djiboutians 51
Dominica **57**
    Dominicans 57
Dominican Republic **63**
    Dominicans 63
Ecuador **69**
    Ecuadorans 69
    Jivaro 77
Egypt **83**
    Egyptians 83
El Salvador **91**
    Salvadorans 91
Equatorial Guinea **99**
    Equatorial Guineans 99
Eritrea **107**
    Eritreans 107
Estonia **113**
    Estonians 113
Ethiopia **121**
    Ethiopians 121
    Amhara 133
    Oromos 141
    Tigray 149

Fiji **157**
    Fijians 157
    Indo-Fijians 163
Finland **167**
    Finns 167
France **175**
    French 175
    Bretons 181
    French Guianans 185
Gabon **189**
    Gabonese 189
The Gambia **195**
    Gambians 195
Georgia **205**
    Georgians 205
    Abkhazians 214
    Adjarians 218

Volume 4

Germany **1**
    Germans 1
Ghana **9**
    Ghanaians 9
Greece **17**
    Greeks 17
Grenada **25**
    Grenadians 25
Guatemala **31**
    Guatemalans 31
Guinea **39**
    Guineans 39
    Fulani 46
Guyana **51**
    Guyanans 51
Haiti **57**
    Haitians 57
Honduras **67**
    Hondurans 67
Hungary **75**
    Hungarians 75
Iceland **81**
    Icelanders 81
India **87**
    Indians 88
    Andhras 96
    Gonds 102
    Gujaratis 107
    Marathas 112
    Oriya 117
    Rajputs 122

CUMULATIVE CONTENTS

Indonesia.................................129
   Indonesians 129
   Asmat 139
   Balinese......................................143
   Javanese 149
   Sundanese 155
Iran 161
   Iranians.......................................161
Iraq 169
   Iraqis..169
   Ma'dan (Marsh Arabs)....................176
Ireland 181
   Irish 181
Israel 189
   Israelis..189
   Palestinians 198
Italy 207
   Italians..207
Jamaica 215
   Jamaicans....................................215

Liberia 159
   Malinke 159
Libya 167
   Libyans 167
Liechtenstein 175
   Liechtensteiners 175
Lithuania 181
   Lithuanians 181
Luxembourg 189
   Luxembourgers 189
Macedonia 193
   Macedonians 193
Madagascar 199
   Malagasy 199
Malawi 205
   Chewa and other Maravi Groups 205
Malaysia 213
   Malays 213
Mali 221
   Malians 221
   Songhay 227

Volume 5

Japan 1
   Japanese 1
   Ainu 14
Jordan 21
   Jordanians 21
Kazakhstan 29
   Kazaks 29
Kenya 39
   Kenyans 39
   Gikuyu 50
   Gusii 60
   Kalenjin.......................................67
   Luhya 74
   Luo 81
Korea, Republic of....................91
   South Koreans 91
Kuwait 99
   Kuwaitis 99
Kyrgyzstan 107
   Kyrgyz 107
Laos 115
   Lao 115
   Kammu 125
Latvia...................................133
   Latvians.......................................133
Lebanon.................................139
   Lebanese 139
   Maronites 145
Lesotho 149
   Sotho 149

Volume 6

Mauritania 1
   Mauritanians 1
Mexico...................................7
   Mexicans 7
   Maya 13
Micronesia 21
   Micronesians 21
Moldova 25
   Moldovans 25
Monaco 33
   Monégasques 33
Mongolia 39
   Mongols 39
   Ewenki 46
Morocco 53
   Moroccans 53
Mozambique 61
   Mozambicans 61
Myanmar 67
   Burman 67
   Karens 75
   Shans 83
Namibia 91
   Namibians 91
Nepal 99
   Nepalis 99
   Sherpas 107

CUMULATIVE CONTENTS

The Netherlands......................................115
    Netherlanders 115
    Frisians..122
New Zealand 127
    New Zealanders 127
    Maori..133
    Polynesians 139
Nicaragua 145
    Nicaraguans 145
    Sumu and Miskito 152
Niger..157
    Nigeriens 157
    Tuareg 164
Nigeria..171
    Nigerians 171
    Hausa 176
    Igbo 181
    Yoruba 186

Volume 7

Norway 1
    Norwegians 1
    Sami 9
Oman..17
    Omanis 17
Pakistan 25
    Pakistanis 25
    Baluchi 35
    Brahui 41
    Punjabis 46
Panama 57
    Panamanians 57
    Cunas 64
Papua New Guinea 71
    Melanesians 71
    Iatmul 79
    Melpa 84
    Motu 89
Paraguay 93
    Paraguayans 93
    Guaranís 98
Peru 105
    Peruvians...105
    Asháninka 113
    Quechua 119
Philippines 125
    Filipinos 125
    Hiligaynon 136
    Ilocanos 142
Poland 149
    Poles..149

Portugal 157
    Portuguese 157
Qatar...165
    Qataris 165
Romania 171
    Romanians 171
    Roma 178
Russia 187
    Russians..187
    Chechens 199
    Chukchi 206
    Mordvins 211
    Nentsy..216
    Tatars...221

Volume 8

Rwanda 1
    Rwandans 1
    Hutu 7
St. Kitts and Nevis...............................11
    Kittitians and Nevisians 11
St. Lucia...17
    St. Lucians 17
St. Vincent and the Grenadines.................23
    St. Vincentians 23
San Marino..29
    Sammarinese 29
Saudi Arabia...33
    Saudis 33
    Bedu 41
Senegal..49
    Senegalese 49
    Wolof..56
Seychelles 61
    Seychellois 61
Sierra Leone 67
    Creoles of Sierra Leone 67
Slovakia 73
    Slovaks 73
Slovenia 81
    Slovenes 81
Somalia 87
    Somalis 87
South Africa 93
    Afrikaners 93
    Cape Coloreds 100
    English 105
    Xhosa...110
    Zulu 117
Spain 125
    Spaniards 125
    Andalusians 132

Basques 138
Castilians 144
Catalans... 150
Galicians 155
Sri Lanka **161**
Sinhalese 161
Tamils 169
Sudan **175**
Sudanese 175
Dinka... 181
Suriname **185**
Surinamese 185
Swaziland **189**
Swazis 189
Sweden... **195**
Swedes 195
Switzerland **205**
Swiss 205
Syria **213**
Syrians 213
Druze.. 219

Volume 9

Tajikistan **1**
Tajiks 1
Pamiri 7
Tanzania **13**
Tanzanians 13
Chagga 19
Maasai 25
Nyamwezi 34
Shambaa.. 39
Swahili 45
Thailand **51**
Thai 51
Trinidad and Tobago **59**
Trinidadians and Tobagonians............. 59
Tunisia.. **65**
Tunisians... 65

Turkey **71**
Turks... 71
Kurds 78
Turkmenistan................................... **85**
Turkmens 85
Uganda... **91**
Ugandans 91
Baganda 98
Banyankole 105
Ukraine... **111**
Ukrainians 111
United Arab Emirates **117**
Emirians 117
United Kingdom............................... **123**
English 123
Scots 130
Welsh 136
Uruguay.. **143**
Uruguayans.. 143
Uzbekistan **147**
Uzbeks 147
Karakalpaks 153
Vanuatu **159**
Ni-Vanuatu 159
Venezuela.. **163**
Venezuelans 163
Guajiros 170
Pemon 174
Vietnam **181**
Vietnamese 181
Cham 191
Western Samoa................................ **197**
Samoans 197
Yemen **201**
Yemenis... 201
Zambia **209**
Zambians 209
Bemba... 215
Tonga.. 221
Zimbabwe **227**
Zimbabweans 227

Contributors

Editors: Timothy L. Gall and Susan Bevan Gall

Senior Editor: Daniel M. Lucas

Contributing Editors: Himanee Gupta, Jim Henry, Kira Silverbird, Elaine Trapp, Rosalie Wieder

Copy Editors: Deborah Baron, Janet Fenn, Jim Henry, Patricia M. Mote, Deborah Ring, Kathy Soltis

Typesetting and Graphics: Cheryl Montagna, Brian Rajewski

Cover Photographs: Cory Langley

Data Input: Janis K. Long, Cheryl Montagna, Melody Penfound

Proofreaders: Deborah Baron, Janet Fenn

Editorial Assistants: Katie Baron, Jennifer A. Spencer, Daniel K. Updegraft

Editorial Advisors

P. Boone, Sixth Grade Teacher, Oak Crest Middle School, San Antonio, Texas

Jean Campbell, Foothill Farms Middle School, Sacramento, California

Kathy Englehart, Librarian, Hathaway Brown School, Shaker Heights, Ohio

Catherine Harris, Librarian, Oak Crest Middle School, San Antonio, Texas

Karen James, Children's Services, Louisville Free Public Library, Louisville, Kentucky

Contributors to the Gale Edition

The articles presented in this encyclopedia are based on entries in the *Worldmark Encyclopedia of Cultures and Daily Life* published in 1997 by Gale. The following authors and reviewers contributed to the Gale edition.

ANDREW J. ABALAHIN. Doctoral candidate, Department of History, Cornell University.

JAMAL ABDULLAH. Doctoral candidate, Department of City and Regional Planning, Cornell University.

SANA ABED-KOTOB. Book Review Editor, Middle East Journal, Middle East Institute.

MAMOUD ABOUD. Charge d'Affaires, a.i., Embassy of the Federal and Islamic Republic of the Comoros.

JUDY ALLEN. Editor, Choctaw Nation of Oklahoma.

HIS EXCELLENCY DENIS G. ANTOINE. Ambassador to the United States, Embassy of Grenada.

LESLEY ANN ASHBAUGH. Instructor, Sociology, Seattle University.

HASHEM ATALLAH. Translator, Editor, Teacher; Fairfax, Virginia.

HECTOR AZEVES. Cultural Attaché, Embassy of Uruguay.

VICTORIA J. BAKER. Associate Professor of Anthropology, Anthropology (Collegium of Comparative Cultures), Eckerd College.

POLINE BALA. Doctoral candidate, Asian Studies, Cornell University.

MARJORIE MANDELSTAM BALZER. Research Professor; Coordinator, Social, Regional, and Ethnic Studies Sociology, and Center for Eurasian, Russian, and East European Studies.

JOSHUA BARKER. Doctoral candidate, Department of Anthropology, Cornell University.

IGOR BARSEGIAN. Department of Sociology, George Washington University.

IRAJ BASHIRI. Professor of Central Asian Studies, Department of Slavic and Central Asian Languages and Literatures, University of Minnesota.

DAN F. BAUER. Department of Anthropology, Lafayette College.

JOYCE BEAR. Historic Preservation Officer, Muscogee Nation of Oklahoma.

SVETLANA BELAIA. Byelorussian-American Cultural Center, Strongsville, Ohio.

HIS EXCELLENCY DR. COURTNEY BLACKMAN. Ambassador to the United States, Embassy of Barbados.

BETTY BLAIR. Executive Editor, Azerbaijan International.

ARVIDS BLODNIEKS. Director, Latvian Institute, American Latvian Association in the USA.

ARASH BORMANSHINOV. University of Maryland, College Park.

HARRIET I. BRADY. Cultural Anthropologist (Pyramid Lake Paiute Tribe), Native Studies Program, Pyramid Lake High School.

MARTIN BROKENLEG. Professor of Sociology, Department of Sociology, Augustana College.

REV. RAYMOND A. BUCKO, S.J. Assistant Professor of Anthropology, LeMoyne College.

JOHN W. BURTON. Department of Anthropology, Connecticut College.

CONTRIBUTORS

DINEANE BUTTRAM. University of North Carolina-Chapel Hill.

RICARDO CABALLERO. Counselor, Embassy of Paraguay.

CHRISTINA CARPADIS. Researcher/Writer, Cleveland, Ohio.

SALVADOR GARCIA CASTANEDA. Department of Spanish and Portuguese, The Ohio State University.

SUSANA CAVALLO. Graduate Program Director and Professor of Spanish, Department of Modern Languages and Literatures, Loyola University, Chicago.

BRIAN P. CAZA. Doctoral candidate, Political Science, University of Chicago.

VAN CHRISTO. President and Executive Director, Frosina Foundation, Boston.

YURI A. CHUMAKOV. Graduate Student, Department of Sociology, University of Notre Dame.

J. COLARUSSO. Professor of Anthropology, McMaster University.

FRANCESCA COLECCHIA. Modern Language Department, Duquesne University.

DIANNE K. DAEG DE MOTT. Researcher/Writer, Tucson, Arizona.

MICHAEL DE JONGH. Professor, Department of Anthropology, University of South Africa.

GEORGI DERLUGUIAN. Senior Fellow, Ph.D., U. S. Institute of Peace.

CHRISTINE DRAKE. Department of Political Science and Geography, Old Dominion University.

ARTURO DUARTE. Guatemalan Mission to the OAS.

CALEB DUBE. Department of Anthropology, Northwestern University.

BRIAN DU TOIT. Professor, Department of Anthropology, University of Florida.

LEAH ERMARTH. Worldspace Foundation, Washington, DC.

NANCY J. FAIRLEY. Associate Professor of Anthropology, Department of Anthropology/Sociology, Davidson College.

GREGORY A. FINNEGAN, Ph.D. Tozzer Library, Harvard University.

ALLEN J. FRANK, Ph.D.

DAVID P. GAMBLE. Professor Emeritus, Department of Anthropology, San Francisco State University.

FREDERICK GAMST. Professor, Department of Anthropology, University of Massachusetts, Harbor Campus.

PAULA GARB. Associate Director of Global Peace and Conflict Studies and Adjunct Professor of Social Ecology, University of California, Irvine.

HAROLD GASKI. Associate Professor of Sami Literature, School of Languages and Literature, University of Tromsø.

STEPHEN J. GENDZIER.

FLORENCE GERDEL.

ANTHONY P. GLASCOCK. Professor of Anthropology; Department of Anthropology, Psychology, and Sociology; Drexel University.

LUIS GONZALEZ. Researcher/Writer, River Edge, New Jersey.

JENNIFER GRAHAM. Researcher/Writer, Sydney, Australia.

MARIE-CÉCILE GROELSEMA. Doctoral candidate, Comparative Literature, Indiana University.

ROBERT GROELSEMA. MPIA and doctoral candidate, Political Science, Indiana University.

MARIA GROSZ-NGATÉ. Visiting Assistant Professor, Department of Anthropology, Northwestern University.

ELLEN GRUENBAUM. Professor, School of Social Sciences, California State University, Fresno.

N. THOMAS HAKANSSON. University of Kentucky.

ROBERT HALASZ. Researcher/Writer, New York, New York.

MARC HANREZ. Professor, Department of French and Italian, University of Wisconsin-Madison.

ANWAR UL HAQ. Central Asian Studies Department, Indiana University.

LIAM HARTE. Department of Philosophy, Loyola University, Chicago.

FR. VASILE HATEGAN. Author, *Romanian Culture in America.*

BRUCE HEILMAN. Doctoral candidate, Department of Political Science, Indiana University.

JIM HENRY. Researcher/Writer, Cleveland, Ohio.

BARRY HEWLETT. Department of Anthropology, Washington State University.

SUSAN F. HIRSCH. Department of Anthropology, Wesleyan University.

MARIDA HOLLOS. Department of Anthropology, Brown University.

HALYNA HOLUBEC. Researcher/Writer, Cleveland, Ohio.

YVONNE HOOSAVA. Legal Researcher and Cultural Preservation Officer, Hopi Tribal Council.

HUIQIN HUANG, Ph.D. Center for East Asia Studies, University of Montreal.

ASAFA JALATA. Assistant Professor of Sociology and African and African American Studies, Department of Sociology, The University of Tennessee, Knoxville.

STEPHEN F. JONES. Russian Department, Mount Holyoke College.

THOMAS JOVANOVSKI, Ph.D. Lorain County Community College.

A. KEN JULES. Minister Plenipotentiary and Deputy Head of Mission, Embassy of St. Kitts and Nevis.

GENEROSA KAGARUKI-KAKOTI. Economist, Department of Urban and Rural Planning, College of Lands and Architectural Studies, Dar es Salaam, Tanzania.

EZEKIEL KALIPENI. Department of Geography, University of Illinois at Urbana-Champaign.

CONTRIBUTORS

DON KAVANAUGH. Program Director, Lake of the Woods Ojibwa Cultural Centre.

SUSAN M. KENYON. Associate Professor of Anthropology, Department of History and Anthropology, Butler University.

WELILE KHUZWAYO. Department of Anthropology, University of South Africa.

PHILIP L. KILBRIDE. Professor of Anthropology, Mary Hale Chase Chair in the Social Sciences, Department of Anthropology, Bryn Mawr College.

RICHARD O. KISIARA. Doctoral candidate, Department of Anthropology, Washington University in St. Louis.

KAREN KNOWLES. Permanent Mission of Antigua and Barbuda to the United Nations.

IGOR KRUPNIK. Research Anthropologist, Department of Anthropology, Smithsonian Institution.

LEELO LASS. Secretary, Embassy of Estonia.

ROBERT LAUNAY. Professor, Department of Anthropology, Northwestern University.

CHARLES LEBLANC. Professor and Director, Center for East Asia Studies, University of Montreal.

RONALD LEE. Author, *Goddam Gypsy, An Autobiographical Novel.*

PHILIP E. LEIS. Professor and Chair, Department of Anthropology, Brown University.

MARIA JUKIC LESKUR. Croatian Consulate, Cleveland, Ohio.

RICHARD A. LOBBAN, JR. Professor of Anthropology and African Studies, Department of Anthropology, Rhode Island College.

DERYCK O. LODRICK. Visiting Scholar, Center for South Asian Studies, University of California, Berkeley.

NEIL LURSSEN. Intro Communications Inc.

GREGORIO C. MARTIN. Modern Language Department, Duquesne University.

HOWARD J. MARTIN. Independent scholar.

HEITOR MARTINS. Professor, Department of Spanish and Portuguese, Indiana University.

ADELINE MASQUELIER. Assistant Professor, Department of Anthropology, Tulane University.

DOLINA MILLAR.

EDITH MIRANTE. Project Maje, Portland, Oregon.

ROBERT W. MONTGOMERY, Ph.D. Indiana University.

THOMAS D. MORIN. Associate Professor of Hispanic Studies, Department of Modern and Classical Literatures and Languages, University of Rhode Island.

CHARLES MORRILL. Doctoral candidate, Indiana University.

CAROL A. MORTLAND. Crate's Point, The Dalles, Oregon.

FRANCIS A. MOYER. Director, North Carolina Japan Center, North Carolina State University.

MARIE C. MOYER.

NYAGA MWANIKI. Assistant Professor, Department of Anthropology and Sociology, Western Carolina University.

KENNETH NILSON. Celtic Studies Department, Harvard University.

JANE E. ORMROD. Graduate Student, History, University of Chicago.

JUANITA PAHDOPONY. Carl Perkins Program Director, Comanche Tribe of Oklahoma.

TINO PALOTTA. Syracuse University.

ROHAYATI PASENG.

PATRICIA PITCHON. Researcher/Writer, London, England.

STEPHANIE PLATZ. Program Officer, Program on Peace and International Cooperation, The John D. and Catherine T. MacArthur Foundation.

MIHAELA POIATA. Graduate Student, School of Journalism and Mass Communication, University of North Carolina at Chapel Hill.

LEOPOLDINA PRUT-PREGELJ. Author, *Historical Dictionary of Slovenia.*

J. RACKAUSKAS. Director, Lithuanian Research and Studies Center, Chicago.

J. RAKOVICH. Byelorussian-American Cultural Center, Strongsville, Ohio.

HANTA V. RALAY. Promotions, Inc., Montgomery Village, Maryland.

SUSAN J. RASMUSSEN. Associate Professor, Department of Anthropology, University of Houston.

RONALD REMINICK. Department of Anthropology, Cleveland State University.

BRUCE D. ROBERTS. Assistant Professor of Anthropology, Department of Anthropology and Sociology, University of Southern Mississippi.

LAUREL L. ROSE. Philosophy Department, Carnegie-Mellon University.

ROBERT ROTENBERG. Professor of Anthropology, International Studies Program, DePaul University.

CAROLINE SAHLEY, Ph.D. Researcher/Writer, Cleveland, Ohio.

VERONICA SALLES-REESE. Associate Professor, Department of Spanish and Portuguese, Georgetown University.

MAIRA SARYBAEVA. Kazakh-American Studies Center, University of Kentucky.

DEBRA L. SCHINDLER. Institute of Arctic Studies, Dartmouth College.

KYOKO SELDEN, Ph.D. Researcher/Writer, Ithaca, New York.

ENAYATULLAH SHAHRANI. Central Asian Studies Department, Indiana University.

ROBERT SHANAFELT. Adjunct Lecturer, Department of Anthropology, The Florida State University.

TUULIKKI SINKS. Teaching Specialist for Finnish, Department of German, Scandinavian, and Dutch, University of Minnesota.

JAN SJÅVIK. Associate Professor, Scandinavian Studies, University of Washington.

CONTRIBUTORS

MAGDA SOBALVARRO. Press and Cultural Affairs Director, Embassy of Nicaragua.

MICHAEL STAINTON. Researcher, Joint Center for Asia Pacific Studies, York University.

RIANA STEYN. Department of Anthropology, University of South Africa.

PAUL STOLLER. Professor, Department of Anthropology, West Chester University.

CRAIG STRASHOFER. Researcher/Writer, Cleveland, Ohio.

SANDRA B. STRAUBHAAR. Assistant Professor, Nordic Studies, Department of Germanic and Slavic Languages, Brigham Young University.

VUM SON SUANTAK. Author, *Zo History*.

MURAT TAISHIBAEV. Kazakh-American Studies Center, University of Kentucky.

CHRISTOPHER C. TAYLOR. Associate Professor, Anthropology Department, University of Alabama, Birmingham.

EDDIE TSO. Office of Language and Culture, Navajo Division of Education.

DAVID TYSON. Foreign Broadcast Information Service, Washington, D.C.

NICOLAAS G. W. UNLANDT. Assistant Professor of French, Department of French and Italian, Brigham Young University.

GORDON URQUHART. Professor, Department of Economics and Business, Cornell College.

CHRISTOPHER J. VAN VUUREN. Professor, Department of Anthropology, University of South Africa.

DALIA VENTURA-ALCALAY. Journalist, London, England.

CATHERINE VEREECKE. Assistant Director, Center for African Studies, University of Florida.

GREGORY T. WALKER. Associate Director, Office of International Affairs, Duquesne University.

GERHARD WEISS. Department of German, Scandinavian, and Dutch, University of Minnesota.

PATSY WEST. Director, The Seminole/Miccosukee Photographic Archive.

WALTER WHIPPLE. Associate Professor of Polish, Germanic and Slavic Languages, Brigham Young University.

ROSALIE WIEDER. Researcher/Writer, Cleveland, Ohio.

JEFFREY WILLIAMS. Professor, Department of Anthropology, Cleveland State University.

GUANG-HONG YU. Associate Research Fellow, Institute of Ethnology, Academia Sinica.

RUSSELL ZANCA. Department of Anthropology, College of Liberal Arts and Sciences, University of Illinois at Urbana-Champaign.

Reader's Guide

Junior Worldmark Encyclopedia of World Cultures contains articles exploring the ways of life of over 290 culture groups worldwide. Arranged alphabetically by country in nine volumes, this encyclopedia parallels the organization of its sister set, *Junior Worldmark Encyclopedia of the Nations*. Whereas the primary purpose of *Nations* is to provide information on the world's nations, this encyclopedia focuses on the traditions, living conditions, and personalities of many of the world's culture groups.

Defining groups for inclusion was not an easy task. Cultural identity is shaped by such factors as history, geography, nationality, ethnicity, race, language, and religion. Sometimes the distinctions are subtle, but important. Most chapters in this encyclopedia begin with an article on the people of the country as a nationality group. For example, the chapter on Kenya begins with an article entitled "Kenyans." This article explores the national character shared by all people living in Kenya. However, there are separate articles on the Gikuyu, Kalenjin, Luhya, and Luo—four of the largest ethnic groups living in the country. They are all Kenyans, but each group is distinct. Many profiled groups—like the Kazaks—inhabit lands that cross national boundaries. Although profiled in the chapter on Kazakstan, Kazaks are also important minorities in China, Uzbekistan, and Turkmenistan. In such cases, cross-references direct the student to the chapter where the group is profiled.

The photographs that illustrate the articles show a wonderfully diverse world. From the luxury liners docked in the harbor at Monaco to the dwellings made of grass sheltering the inhabitants of the rain forest, people share the struggles and joys of earning a living, bringing children into the world, teaching them to survive, and initiating them into adulthood. Although language, customs, and dress illustrate our differences, the faces of the people pictured in these volumes reinforce our similarities. Whether on the streets of Tokyo or the mountains of Tibet, a smile on the face of a child transcends the boundaries of nationality and cultural identity to reveal something common in us all. Photographer Cory Langley's images on pages 93 and 147 in Volume 6 serve to illustrate this point.

The picture of the world this encyclopedia paints today will certainly differ from the one painted in future editions. Indigenous people like the Jivaro in Ecuador (Volume 3, page 77) are being assimilated into modern society as forest lands are cleared for development and televisions and VCRs are brought to even the most remote villages. As the global economy expands, traditional diets are supplemented with Coke, Pepsi, and fast food; traditional storytellers are replaced by World Cup soccer matches and American television programs; and cultural heroes are overwhelmed by images of Michael Jordan and Michael Jackson. Photographer Cynthia Bassett was fortunate to be among a small group of travelers to visit a part of China only recently opened to Westerners. Her image of Miao dancers (Volume 2, page 161) shows a people far removed from Western culture . . . until one looks a little closer. Behind the dancers, in the upper corner of the photograph, is a basketball hoop and backboard. It turns out that Miao teenagers love basketball!

ORGANIZATION

Within each volume the chapters are arranged alphabetically by country. A cumulative table of contents for all volumes in the set follows the table of contents to each volume.

Each chapter covers a specific country. The contents of the chapter, listing the culture group articles, follows the chapter title. An overview of the composition of the population of the country appears after the contents list. The individual articles follow, and are organized according to a standard twenty-heading outline explained in more detail below. This structure allows for easy comparison between cultures and enhances the accessibility of the information.

Articles begin with the **pronunciation** of the group's name, a listing of **alternate names** by which the group is known, the group's **location** in the world, its **population**, the **languages** spoken, and the **religions** practiced. Articles are illustrated with maps showing the primary location of the group and photographs of the culture group being profiled. The twenty standard headings by which the articles are organized are presented below.

1 ● INTRODUCTION: A description of the group's historical origins provides a useful background for understanding its contemporary affairs. Information relating to migration helps explain how the group arrived at its present location. Political conditions and governmental structure(s) that affect members of the profiled ethnic group are also discussed.

2 ● LOCATION: The population size of the group is listed. This information may include official census data from various countries and/or estimates. Information on the size of a group's population located outside the traditional homeland may also be included, especially for those groups with large scattered populations. A description of the homeland includes information on location, topography, and climate.

3 ● LANGUAGE: Each article lists the name(s) of the primary language(s) spoken by members. Descriptions of linguistic origins, grammar, and similarities to other languages may also be included. Examples of common words, phrases, and proverbs are listed for many of the profiled groups, and some include examples of common personal names and greetings.

4 ● FOLKLORE: Common themes, settings, and characters in the profiled group's traditional oral and/or literary mythology are highlighted. Many entries include a short excerpt or synopsis of one of the group's noteworthy myths, fables, or legends. Some entries describe the accomplishments of famous heroes and heroines or other prominent historical figures.

5 ● RELIGION: The origins of traditional religious beliefs are profiled. Contemporary religious beliefs, customs, and practices are also discussed. Some groups may be closely associated with one particular faith (especially if religious and ethnic identification are interlinked), while others may have members of diverse faiths.

6 ● MAJOR HOLIDAYS: Celebrations and commemorations typically recognized by the group's members are described. These holidays commonly fall into two categories: secular and religious. Secular holidays often include an independence day and/or other days of observance recognizing important dates in history that affected the group as a whole. Religious holidays are typically the same as those honored by people of the same faith worldwide. Some secular and religious holidays are linked to the lunar cycle or to the change of seasons. Some articles describe customs practiced by members of the group on certain holidays.

7 ● RITES OF PASSAGE: Formal and informal events that mark an individual's procession through the stages of life are profiled. These events typically involve rituals, ceremonies, observances, and procedures associated with birth, childhood, the coming of age, milestones in education or religious training, adulthood, and death.

8 ● RELATIONSHIPS: Information on greetings, body language, gestures, visiting customs, and dating practices is included. The extent of formality to which members of a certain ethnic group treat others is also addressed, as some groups may adhere to customs governing interpersonal relationships more or less strictly than others.

9 ● LIVING CONDITIONS: General health conditions typical of the group's members are cited. Such information includes life expectancy, the prevalence of various diseases, and access to medical care. Information on urbanization, housing, and access to utilities is also included. Transportation methods typically utilized by the group's members are also discussed.

10 ● FAMILY LIFE: The size and composition of the family unit is profiled. Gender roles common to the group are also discussed, including the division of rights and responsibilities relegated to male and female group members. The roles that children, adults, and the elderly have within the group as a whole may also be addressed.

11 ● CLOTHING: Many entries include descriptive information (design, color, fabric, etc.) regarding traditional clothing (or national costume) for men and women, and indicate the frequency of its use in contemporary life. A description of typical clothing worn in modern daily life is also provided, especially if traditional clothing is no longer the usual form of dress. Distinctions between formal and work attire and descriptions of clothing preferences of young people are described for many groups as well.

12 ● FOOD: Descriptions of items commonly consumed by members of the group are listed. The frequency and occasion for meals is also described, as are any unique customs regarding eating and drinking, special utensils and furniture, and the role of food and beverages in ritual ceremonies. Many entries include a recipe for a favorite dish.

13 ● EDUCATION: The structure of formal education in the country or countries of residence is discussed, including information on primary, secondary, and higher education. For some groups, the role of informal education is also highlighted. Some articles include information regarding the relevance and importance of education among the group as a whole, along with parental expectations for children.

14 ● CULTURAL HERITAGE: Since many groups express their sense of identity through art, music, literature, and dance, a description of prominent styles is included. Some articles also cite the contributions of famous individual artists, writers, and musicians.

15 ● EMPLOYMENT: The type of labor that typically engages members of the profiled group is discussed. For some groups, the formal wage economy is the primary source of earnings, but for other groups, informal agriculture or trade may be the usual way to earn a living. Working conditions are also highlighted.

16 ● SPORTS: Popular sports that children and adults play are listed, as are typical spectator sports. Some articles include a description and/or rules to a sport or game.

17 ● RECREATION: Listed activities that people enjoy in their leisure time may include structured pastimes (such as public musical and dance performances) or informal get-togethers (such as meeting for conversation). The role of popular culture, movies, theater, and television in everyday life is also discussed where it applies.

18 ● CRAFTS AND HOBBIES: Entries describe arts and crafts commonly fabricated according to traditional methods, materials, and style. Such objects may often have a functional utility for everyday tasks.

19 ● SOCIAL PROBLEMS: Internal and external issues that confront members of the profiled group are described. Such concerns often deal with fundamental problems like war, famine, disease, and poverty. A lack of human rights, civil rights, and political freedom may also adversely affect a group as a whole. Other problems may include crime, unemployment, substance abuse, and domestic violence.

20 ● BIBLIOGRAPHY: References cited include works used to compile the article, benchmark publications often recognized as authoritative by scholars, and other reference sources accessible to middle school researchers. Website addresses are provided for researchers who wish to access the World Wide Web. The website citation includes the author and title of the website (if applicable). The address begins with characters that follow "http://" in the citation; the address ends with the character preceding the comma and date. For example, the citation for the website of the German embassy appears as follows:

German Embassy, Washington, D.C. [Online]
    Available http://www.germany-info.org/, 1998.

To access this site, researchers type:
    www.germany-info.org

A glossary and an index of groups profiled appears at the end of each volume.

ACKNOWLEDGMENTS

The editors express appreciation to the members of the U•X•L staff who were involved in a number of ways at various stages of development of the *Junior Worldmark Encyclopedia of World Cultures.*

SUGGESTIONS ARE WELCOME: We appreciate any suggestions that will enhance future editions. Please send comments to:

Editors
*Junior Worldmark Encyclopedia
of World Cultures*
U•X•L
27500 Drake Road
Farmington Hills, MI 48331-3535
(800) 877-4253

Norway

■ NORWEGIANS 1
■ SAMI 9

The people of Norway are called Norwegians. The population is nearly all of the same ethnicity—generally tall and fair-skinned, with blue eyes. Minority communities include some 20,000 Sami (Lapps) and 7,000 descendants of Finnish immigrants.

Norwegians

PRONUNCIATION: nohr-WEE-juhns

LOCATION: Norway

POPULATION: 4.3 million

LANGUAGE: Norwegian in two forms: Bokmål and Nynorsk

RELIGION: Evangelical Lutheran Church of Norway; small numbers of Roman Catholics, Greek Orthodox, Methodists, Baptists, Anglicans, Muslims, and Jews

1 ● INTRODUCTION

Norway is part of the region known as Scandinavia. Scandinavia includes Norway together with its neighbors Denmark and Sweden, as well as Finland and Iceland. Norway is bounded on the west by the Atlantic Ocean for most of the country's length, on the southwest by the North Sea, and directly to the south by the Skagerrak, an arm of the North Sea. To the east, Norway shares a long border with Sweden, and for a short distance in the north with Finland and Russia.

Most Norwegians live within a few miles (kilometers) of the sea, which has played a pivotal role in their country's history. Norway's great Viking era took place during the ninth century AD, when the Vikings (Norse explorers and pirates) extended their territory as far as Dublin (Ireland) and Normandy (France). Their leader, Harald Fairhair, unified the country around the year 900, and King Olaf converted the Norwegians to Christianity. The Vikings were the first to cross the Atlantic Ocean, a feat accomplished with Erik the Red's voyages to Iceland and Greenland. Erik's son, Leif Erikson, landed on the coast of North America in the year 1001. Norway's long period of union with Denmark lasted from 1380 until 1814, when the Norwegians adopted their own constitution. Their short-lived independence ended as Norway was united with Sweden under one head of state until 1905. That year marked Norway's peaceful secession and installation of its own monarchy. Since Norway, long a subject people, had no royal family of its own, it chose Prince Carl of Denmark to become the new nation's first king, as Håkon VII.

Norway remained neutral during World War I (1914–18), but was invaded by Germany early in World War II (1939–45). Norwegian resistance to German occupation had severe consequences as the Nazis attempted to destroy the underground movement. The Norwegian merchant fleet played a vital role in aiding the Allies. Although it lost half its fleet, the country recovered quickly after the war.

Although Norway joined the European Free Trade Association (EFTA) in 1960, it rejected membership in the European Community (EC) in 1972, and decided against joining the new European Union in 1994.

2 ● LOCATION

Norway stretches across the north and west of the Scandinavian peninsula. It is a long country with bulges at the north and south, while its midsection is as narrow across as 3.9 miles (6.28 kilometers) at one point. It has an area of 125,051 square miles (323,882 square kilometers)—roughly the same size as the state of New Mexico. Norway is the longest country in Europe and one of the most mountainous: only one-fifth of its total area is less than 500 feet (150 meters) above sea level. Almost one-third of the country lies within the Arctic Circle. The sun shines almost round-the-clock at the height of summer in mid-June, but in winter there is very little sunlight in mid-December. Overseas territories claimed by Norway include the Svalbard islands and

Jan Mayen island (both in the Arctic Ocean), Peter I Island (off the coast of Antarctica) and Queen Maud Land (a wedge-shaped piece of Antarctica itself).

3 ● LANGUAGE

Norwegian is a Germanic language closely related to Swedish and Danish. There are actually two forms of Norwegian, both of which are considered official languages and can be understood by all Norwegians. *Bokmål*, the more common of the two, was developed from Danish during the nineteenth century, while *Nynorsk* grew out of nationalistic impulses at the same time. *Nynorsk* is a combination of rural dialects intended to be a distinctly Norwegian language, one not influenced by Danish. Today, *Bokmål* is mostly spoken by people living in cities and towns. Modern linguistic experts have proposed a third form of Norwegian, *Samnorsk,* that would simplify language use in Norway by combining elements of Bokmål and Nynorsk.

EXAMPLES OF BOKMÅL

English	Bokmål	Pronunciation
one	en	AYn
two	to	tOO
three	tre	trAY
four	fire	FEE-rer
five	fem	fEHmm
six	seks	sEHx
seven	syv	sEWv
eight	åtte	AH-teh
nine	ni	nEE
ten	ti	tEE
church	kirke	KHEER-ker
breakfast	frokost	FROO-kost

4 ● FOLKLORE

Norwegian mythology originated from the ancient religion of the region. The chief god, Odin, lived in a walled city called Valhalla and was escorted into battle by nine warrior maidens called the Valkyries. Norway has a strong tradition of storytelling, and its folklore is full of odd, sometimes grotesque, creatures. Probably the most famous creatures of Norwegian folklore are the trolls—large, powerful, grotesque beings. Some trolls are considered friendly, while others delight in causing harm to human beings. Trolls appear as mascots, in Norwegian place names, in folk art, and in many folktales.

Many Norwegian folktales portray a nearly senseless world; a world in which people never quite know what is going on.

"Silly Men and Cunning Wives" is one such tale:

One day two wives were fighting over who had the silliest husband. Both of them bragged that they could get their husbands to believe or do anything. They decided to put their husbands to the test.

One wife went home and waited for her husband, Master Northgrange, to come home from the woods. When he did, she put on quite a show, saying he looked like he was at death's door with an illness. The man said he felt fine, but his wife put on such a show of it that he began to feel ill. He took to bed and fell into a stupor, during which his wife laid him out for a funeral and then put him in a casket.

The other wife waited for her husband at the loom, pretending to spin the finest linen when actually none was there. When her husband, Master Southgrange, came home, he told her she was crazy to sit at a loom spinning nothing, but his wife laughed at him and said she was making the finest linen in Norway, so fine it could not even be seen. The man laughed at first, but because his wife worked so long and so hard producing a suit for him, he came to believe that the fabric was so fine it was simply invisible to him.

The next day Master Northgrange's wife let it be known that there would be a funeral for her husband. She told everyone that he had died during the night. Master Southgrange's wife told her husband of the tragedy and suggested he wear his new suit to the service. On their way, they attracted quite a lot of stares because Master South-

Norwegian Tourist Board

Norwegian Constitution Day Parade on May 17. At festivals, one may still see traditional costumes. Otherwise, Norwegians wear modern, Western-style clothes for casual, business, and formal wear.

grange was stark naked. Mistress Southgrange assured her husband they were stares of envy for his fine suit. When they got to the cemetery, Master Northgrange peered out of one of the holes his wife had drilled in the coffin and saw his friend walking with no clothes on and started laughing out loud. All the men carrying his coffin jumped in horror and dropped the box, spilling Master Northgrange onto the frozen green earth.

Afterward, the two men realized what their wives had done and they took their revenge. If anyone wants to know what

that revenge was, the tale says, he or she had better ask the woods trolls.

5 ● RELIGION

Norway's official religion is the Evangelical Lutheran Church of Norway. While 90 percent of the population are members, fewer than 20 percent are regular churchgoers. Norway also has small numbers of Roman Catholics, Greek Orthodox, Methodists, Baptists, Anglicans, Muslims, and Jews.

6 ● MAJOR HOLIDAYS

Constitution Day on May 17 is the Norwegian day of independence and commemorates the anniversary of the day in 1814 when Norway declared independence from Denmark. It is celebrated with parades and other gala events throughout the country, often with traditional folk costumes. Midsummer's Eve on June 23 is another major holiday. It marks the longest day of the year and is celebrated with bonfires along the country's lakes, rivers, and fjords (narrow inlets of the sea, bordered by steep cliffs). Celebrants continue eating, drinking, and dancing throughout the night. All Saints' Day is celebrated on November 1, but Christmas (December 25) is Norway's major winter holiday. On Christmas Eve (December 24), families celebrate with a traditional festive dinner that often includes pork and cabbage. Afterward they sing carols around the tree, which is decorated with white candles, and open the Christmas presents. Traditionally, the Norwegians perform a thorough housecleaning before Christmas, which actually extends until January 2, the end of the holiday season. Other religious holidays include Maundy Thursday, Good Friday, Easter, and Ascension Day (all in the spring).

7 ● RITES OF PASSAGE

Although Norwegians are not particularly religious, the overwhelming majority of parents have their children christened as infants. Norwegian children are permitted to play unsupervised, as the crime rate is very low and even the larger cities provide safe environments.

Most teenagers go through confirmation, the primary rite of passage for young men and women in Norway, at approximately age fifteen. One of the most important events in the school life of Norwegians is high school graduation, which is celebrated in a unique way. Graduates spend their final weeks of school wearing Russ gowns (gowns made of a coarse reddish brown cloth) and engaging in all sorts of public pranks, including parading down city streets and disrupting traffic and spray-painting mildly insulting rhymes about their teachers on sidewalks outside their schools. Military service is required for males starting at the age of nineteen.

8 ● RELATIONSHIPS

Norwegians are a hard-working and self-reliant people, with an independence fostered by their harsh climate with its long, dark winters. Emotionally reserved, they avoid direct confrontations in their relationships with other people. They are courteous and polite, and their social encounters are marked by repeated handshaking, by both men and women. Norwegians are also known for their hospitality, especially during the Christmas season. Guests in a Norwegian home do not touch their drinks until the host offers a toast using the word *skål* (pronounced "skawl").

EXAMPLES OF GREETINGS

English	Norwegian	Pronunciation
hello	hei	hAY
goodbye	adjo	AD-yurr

9 ● LIVING CONDITIONS

Norway has one of the highest standards of living in the world, enhanced by the discovery of petroleum and natural gas in the Norwegian section of the North Sea in the late 1960s. Norwegian houses are typically of stone or wood, with one or two stories. City-dwellers often join into a housing cooperative called a *borettslag* (BOOR-ehts-lahg), from which they rent apartments.

Norway's state-supported healthcare system covers most medical expenses for its residents. Average life expectancy in 1989 was seventy-six years, up from fifty-two years a century earlier. Like those in other industrialized nations, Norway's leading causes of death include cancer and heart disease. As the average life span of Norwegians has increased, a shortage of nursing and retirement homes has developed.

10 ● FAMILY LIFE

The typical marriage age for men is twenty-five to thirty, for women twenty to twenty-five. Norwegian families are getting smaller, and it is not unusual for women to decide not to have any children. The parent or parents of one spouse generally live with the family, often in a separate suite of rooms in the house or they may live in a separate apartment nearby. Husbands and wives generally share decision-making responsibilities. The divorce rate, while low, is rising, with incompatibility and alcoholism cited as the primary causes.

11 ● CLOTHING

Norwegians wear modern Western-style clothes for casual, business, and formal wear. At festivals, one may still see traditional costumes. Women's costumes include high-collared white blouses with embroidered or plaid bodices and ankle-length skirts, often in blue or red. This outfit may be completed by a hat of lace or other fine cloth. Men wear broad-brimmed hats, white shirts, colorful embroidered vests with dressy buttons, and tight, black knee-length breeches with white hose and silver-buckled shoes.

12 ● FOOD

Norwegians eat four meals a day, of which the main one is *middag* (MID-dahg), a hot meal usually eaten between 4:00 and 6:00 PM. A typical middag meal would be fish served with boiled potatoes and vegetables. The remaining meals are cold meals featuring the typical Scandinavian open-faced sandwich, called *smørbrød* (SMUR-brur) in Norway. These consist of ingredients such as cheese, jam, salmon spread, cucumber, boiled eggs, and sardines, served with bread and crackers. While fish is often served in mildly flavored forms such as fish loaf and fish balls, the more pungent smoked salmon (*røkelaks;* RUHR-kuh-lahks) and aged trout (*rakørret;* RAHK-uhr-ruht) are popular as well. Commonly eaten meats include mutton and meat balls. Lingonberry jam is a popular accompaniment to meals, and for dessert one may be served fresh berries, cream pudding (*rømmegrøt;* RUH-muh-gruhrt), or fruit soup. Potatoes have been a very important staple in the Norwegian diet since the 1800s, when the church urged people to plant them to help put an end to hunger during the long winters.

Coffee and aquavit, an alcoholic beverage, are the most commonly served beverages. Norwegians, like their Scandanavian neighbors, are some of the world's largest per capita consumers of coffee in the world. Norwegians generally drink it black.

Norwegians also are one of the world's largest consumers of chocolate. On average,

Recipe

Norwegian Christmas Bread

Ingredients

1 cup butter
¾ cup sugar
4 eggs, two of them separated
2 crushed cardamom seeds or 2 teaspoons ground cardamom
2 oz. yeast or 2 Tablespoons (packets) dry yeast
1 cup milk (bring to room temperature)
3½ to 4 cups all-purpose flour
⅔ cup candied citron
⅔ cup raisins

Directions

1. Cream butter and sugar.
2. Separate 2 eggs, saving the whites. Whip 2 more whole eggs with the 2 egg yolks. Add eggs and cardamom to butter and sugar mixture.
3. Dissolve yeast in milk.
4. Add about one-third of yeast mixture, slowly, to butter mixture.
5. Add about one-third of the flour. Repeat adding the yeast mixture, alternating with the flour.
6. Knead the dough for about 10 minutes on a floured surface. Add more flour if the dough is sticky.
7. Put the dough in a greased bowl, cover, and let it rise for about 3 hours.
8. Turn the dough back onto the floured surface and knead again, adding the finely chopped citron and raisins.
9. Place in a well-greased cake pan and let rise until twice the size (about 1 to 2 hours). Brush with egg whites and bake in a preheated oven at 350°F for 1 hour.

Norwegians consume 17.6 pounds (8 kilograms) of chocolate a year.

Norwegian Christmas bread is a staple of the holiday season. Cardamom seeds and candied citron may be difficult to find; try the local health food store. If they do not have any, they will probably be able to tell you where you can get some, or offer suggestions for replacements.

13 ● EDUCATION

Literacy (the ability to read and write) is nearly universal in Norway. School is required between the ages of seven and sixteen. Because of its concern with equality, Norway's national government develops a curriculum that is followed nationwide.

After the age of sixteen, students choose between vocational and college preparatory training. Higher education, which is free, is offered at four universities (Oslo, Trondheim, Bergen, and Tromsø) and a number of other institutions. About 1 percent of the population is enrolled in postsecondary schooling. Norway currently has a shortage of higher education facilities, especially vocational ones, which limits the number of students who may be admitted for postsecondary education.

14 ● CULTURAL HERITAGE

Norwegian literature begins with the Sagas and Eddas of the medieval Vikings, written in the language of Old Norse and found mainly in Icelandic texts. Norway's most illustrious writer during the period of Danish rule was the eighteenth-century playwright Ludvig Holberg, whose comedies are still performed in Norway and Denmark (and to whom the composer Edvard Grieg dedicated a suite of pieces). Norway's liberation from Danish rule in 1814 marked the beginning of the country's modern literary tradition. Its most famous author is the playwright Henrik Ibsen, whose works of realism and social criticism—including *A Doll's House, An Enemy of the People,* and *Peer Gynt*—are known and performed throughout the world. Other prominent nineteenth-century authors included Henrik Wergeland and Bjørnstjerne Bjørnson (a 1903 Nobel laureate). In the twentieth century, Knut Hamsun's novels explored social problems, and Sigrid Undset—who won the Nobel prize for literature in 1928—portrayed the Norwegian past in sweeping historical novels, the most famous being the trilogy *Kristin Lavransdatter.*

In the visual arts, the painter Edvard Munch—known worldwide for his famous painting *The Scream*—pioneered expressionism in Norway during the late nineteenth and early twentieth centuries, and Gustav Vigeland is known for his sculptures. Norway's most famous composer is Edvard Grieg, who during the nineteenth century incorporated elements of Norwegian folk music, culture, and history into his compositions.

15 ● EMPLOYMENT

Children under the age of fifteen are prohibited from working in Norway. Those under eighteen are not permitted to work at night or to work overtime. The government regulates other aspects of employment law as well. It requires four weeks of paid vacation each year, limits the number of hours employees can work in one week, and offers generous parental leave (with full pay) to new parents. Women are granted thirty-three weeks of maternity leave at full pay.

The economy of Norway provides most of its citizens with a comfortable, relatively wealthy lifestyle, regardless of career choice. Norwegians can also expect a lifetime of full social benefits paid for by the state.

Much of Norway's formerly agricultural employment has shifted to both small industries (paper, textiles, and food and beverage processing) and larger ones, such as shipbuilding, shipping, and North Sea oil development. Today only about 20 percent of the population is engaged in farming.

16 ● SPORTS

Skiing, once a means of transportation, is now the national sport. Children learn to ski at an early age. Downhill, cross-country, and slalom skiing are all popular. Other winter sports include iceskating and bandy, a game similar to hockey. Soccer (called "football") and tennis are popular summer sports.

17 ● RECREATION

Norwegians enjoy many outdoor activities such as hunting, fishing (including ice fishing), hiking, boating, and white-water rafting. Watching televised competitive skiing and speed skating events is a favorite pastime. Many people take skiing vacations in the mountains during Easter week. Summer vacations are often spent either in cabins in the mountains or in the area between the cities of Stavanger and Krageroe in the south. The fjords there are sheltered from the wind and sea, and vacationers enjoy swimming, sailing, relaxing on the sandy beaches, and viewing waterfalls.

18 ● CRAFTS AND HOBBIES

Norwegian craftspeople turn out knitted and woven goods, and wood products including utensils, bowls, and furniture. Another leading craft is the production of traditional Norwegian costumes. Folk dancing and singing are enjoying a revival and are practiced at festivals throughout the country.

19 ● SOCIAL PROBLEMS

Traditionally, heavy drinking and the resulting alcoholism have been Norway's most important social problem. Since the 1960s, drug use has been a significant problem as well. Drugs have not been legalized in Norway, and liquor and wine are only available through state-operated liquor stores.

20 ● BIBLIOGRAPHY

Bendure, Glenda, et al. *Scandinavian and Baltic Europe.* Hawthorn, Australia: Lonely Planet Publications, 1995.

Charbonneau, Claudette, and Patricia Slade Lander. *The Land and People of Norway.* New York: HarperCollins, 1992.

Gall, Timothy, and Susan Gall, eds. *Junior Worldmark Encyclopedia of the Nations.* Detroit: UXL, 1996.

Kagda, Sakina. *Norway.* New York: Marshall Cavendish, 1995.

Norway in Pictures. Minneapolis, Minn.: Lerner Publications Co., 1990.

Taylor-Wilkie, Doreen. *Norway.* Boston: Houghton-Mifflin, 1996.

Vanberg, Bent. *Of Norwegian Ways.* New York: Barnes & Noble, 1970.

WEB SITES:

Embassy of Norway, Washington, D.C. [Online] Available http://www.norway.org/, 1998.

Norway Online Information Service. [Online] Available http://www.hd.uib.no/norway.htm, 1998.

World Travel Guide. Norway. [Online] Available http://www.wtgonline.com/country/no/gen.html, 1998.

Sami

PRONUNCIATION: SAH-mee
ALTERNATE NAMES: Lapps; Samer
LOCATION: Norway; Sweden; Finland; Russia
POPULATION: About 50,000
LANGUAGE: Sami language in many dialects; also language of country in which they live
RELIGION: Lutheran Church

1 ● INTRODUCTION

While the Sami, or Lapps (as they were formerly called), are commonly thought of as the inhabitants of Lapland, they have never had a country of their own. They are the original inhabitants of northern Scandinavia and most of Finland. Their neighbors have called them Lapps, but they prefer to be called *Samer* or *Sami*, since Lapp means a patch of cloth for mending and was a name imposed on them by the people who settled on their lands. The Sami refer to their land as *Sapmi* or *Same.*

The Sami first appear in written history in the works of the Roman author Tacitus in about AD 98. Nearly 900 years later, a Norwegian chieftain visiting King Alfred the Great of England spoke of these reindeer

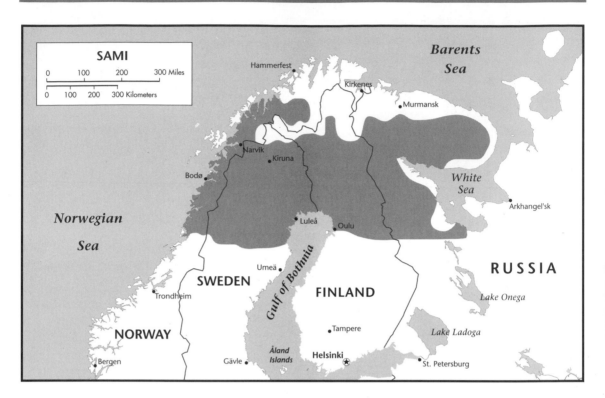

SAMI

herders, who were paying taxes to him in the form of furs, feathers, and whale bones. Over the centuries many armed nations—including the Karelians, Swedes, Danes, Finns, and Russians—demanded their loyalty and taxes. In some cases, the Sami had to pay taxes to two or three governments—as well as fines imposed by one country for paying taxes to another!

Today the Sami are citizens of the countries within whose borders they live, with full rights to education, social services, religious freedom, and participation in the political process. Norway, Sweden, and Finland all have Sami parliaments. At the same time, however, the Sami continue to preserve and defend their ethnic identity and traditional cultural values. Until the liberalization instituted by Soviet leader Mikhail

Gorbachev's government in the late 1980s, the Russian Sami had almost no contact with those in other areas. Sami living in Scandinavia formed the Nordic Sami Council in 1956 to promote cooperation between their populations in Norway, Sweden, and Finland. In 1973 the Nordic Sami Institute at Kautokeino, Norway, was founded to promote the study of the Sami language and culture. In 1989, a Sami College was established there as well. The universities of Tromsø in Norway, Umla in Sweden, and Oulu in Finland have Sami departments in which Sami topics are taught, both separately and as part of established disciplines.

2 ● LOCATION

The Sami live in tundra (arctic or subarctic treeless plain), taiga (subarctic forest), and coastal zones in the far north of Europe, spread out over four different countries: Norway, Sweden, Finland, and Russia's Kola peninsula. They live on coasts and islands warmed by the Gulf Stream, on plateaus dotted by lakes and streams, and on forested mountains. Sami territory lies at latitudes above 62 degrees north, and much of it is above the Arctic Circle, with dark, cold winters and warm, light summers. It is often called the "land of the midnight sun" because depending on the latitude, the sun may be visible for up to seventy days and nights straight in the summer. The far north sees almost three months of continuous daylight. Balancing this out, however, is an equally long period of darkness in the winter, which may last from October to March. Beginning in November, the sun disappears for weeks. Much of the Samis' land is at high altitudes, rising to over 6,000 feet (1,800 meters) above sea level. The highest point is Kebnekajse, at 6,960 feet (2,121 meters).

Traditionally, the Sami lived in a community of families called a *siida*, whose members cooperated in hunting, trapping, and fishing. Officially, the number of Sami is estimated at between 44,000 and 50,000 people. An estimated 30,000 to 35,000 live in Norway, 10,000 in Sweden, 3,000 to 4,000 in Finland, and 1,000 to 2,000 in Russia. However, some think the actual number is considerably higher. For many years, the Sami culture and way of life were criticized by their neighbors, causing many to conceal their true identity. Thus, it is difficult to know how many Sami there actually are (some estimates are as high as 200,000).

3 ●LANGUAGE

Sami is a Finno-Ugric language that is most closely related to Finnish, Estonian, Livonian, Votic, and several other little-known languages. While it varies from region to region, it does so based on the lifestyle of the Sami people rather than on the national boundaries of the lands in which they live. In fact, the present official definition of a Sami is primarily a linguistic one. Altogether there are fifty dialects, but these fall into three major groups (east, central, and south) which are unintelligible to one another, which is to say that speakers of one dialect sill not understand those of another dialect. Today almost all Sami also speak the language of their native country.

Sami is rich in words that describe reindeer, with words for different colors, sizes, antler spreads, and fur textures. Other words indicate how tame a reindeer is or how good it is at pulling sleds. There is actually a separate word describing a male reindeer in each year of his life. A poem by Nordic Council-prizewinning poet Nils-Aslak Valkeapää consists mainly of different Sami words for different kinds of reindeer. There are also hundreds of words that differentiate snow according to its age, depth, density, and hardness. For example, terms exist for powdery snow, snow that fell yesterday, and snow that is soft underneath with a hard crust on top.

The availability of schooling in the Sami language has become an important issue to those concerned with the preservation of the Sami culture and way of life. Nowadays Sami may be used as the language of instruction throughout primary and secondary school. Sami is taught and studied at the university level as well.

4 ● FOLKLORE

Traditionally, the Sami believed that specific spirits were associated with certain places and with the deceased. Many of their myths and legends concern the underworld. Others involve the Stallos, a race of troll-like giants who ate humans or sucked out their strength through an iron pipe. Many tales involve Sami outwitting the Stallos. Another kind of villian in Sami folklore is the *stallu,* a usually wicked person who can appear in various forms.

The Sami creation myth, directly related to their harsh environment, tells the story of a monstrous giant named Biegolmai, the Wind Man. In the beginning of time, Biegolmai created the Sapmi region by taking two huge shovels, one to whip up the wind and the other to drop such huge amounts of snow that no one could live there. One day, however, one of Biegolmai's shovels broke, the wind died down, and the Sami were able to enter Sapmi.

Some of the Sami epics trace Sami ancestry to the sun. In the mid-nineteenth century, a Sami minister, Anders Fjellner, recorded epic mythical poems in which the Daughter of the Sun favored the Sami and brought the reindeer to them. In a related myth, the Son of the Sun had three sons who became the ancestors of the Sami. At their deaths they became stars in the heavens, and can be seen today in the belt of the constellation Orion.

One of the most famous Sami folktales is the story of "The Pathfinder." In it, a Sami

village is attacked by a marauding tribe from the east called the Tjudes. The village fights as best it can, but the Tjudes vastly outnumber the Sami and soon kill all but one—a young boy. The Tjudes then force the young boy to lead them to the next village so they can attack and overtake it as well. The boy reluctantly agrees, leading the Tjudes by night through the mountains. At the top of one mountain, the Tjudes decide to wait until morning, fearing they will lose their way getting down the mountain. The Sami boy, however, urges them to follow him. He says he knows the mountain well and will lead them by torch. He suggests that they all tie themselves together by rope so none of them gets lost. The Tjudes agree, grateful that the Sami boy has become so loyal to them.

As they make their way down the mountain, however, the Sami boy leads them to a great cliff, stops at its edge and tosses his torch over the side, yelling, "Follow me!" The Tjudes, tied together, fall over the edge.

This story was made into a movie called *The Pathfinder.*

5 ● RELIGION

In the traditional Sami religion, both living beings and inanimate objects such as trees were thought to have souls. A priest or shaman, called a *noaidi,* acted as an intermediary between the spiritual and material worlds. He would consult with the dead while in a trance induced by beating on a magic drum and performing a special kind of chanting called *juoigan (yoik)* in Sami. Juoigan is the traditional Sami music.

Over the course of time, all of the Sami have converted to Christianity, in large part through the efforts of Lars Levi Laestadi-usin, a nineteenth-century evangelical Con-gregationalist. Today most Sami practice the dominant Lutheran religion of the Nor-dic countries in which they live.

6 ● MAJOR HOLIDAYS

Sami observe the major holidays of the Christian calendar. Every Easter (late March or early April), a big festival is held at Kau-tokeino in northern Norway, complete with typical Sami entertainments, including sled races and *yoik* singing. Many couples choose this setting for their weddings. Many Sami observe Finland's "little Christmas" (*Pikkujoulu*) early in December, marking the beginning of festivities that last through December 26. On Christmas Eve (December 24), special "midday trees" are adorned with candles, silver and gold ribbons, and other decorations. After readings from the Gospels, a festive meal is eaten, typically consisting of salmon, ham, vegetables, and rice pudding. Boxing Day on December 26 is marked by sled rides, lasso throwing, and other traditional games.

Secular holidays include the large spring celebrations held by the Sami every year, occasions on which they wear their best clothes and gather with friends to mark the end of winter.

7 ● RITES OF PASSAGE

The Sami held on to their traditional ways longer than most peoples in Europe and have yet to fully abandon traditional life for a modern way of life. Still, the dictates of today's world have forced them to follow rituals that would be easily recognized in the Western world. Most Sami, for instance, participate in the major Lutheran rituals even though they sometimes adapt them to their own use. The ritual of baptism and the way the Sami have both used and avoided it offer an interesting illustration of a tradi-tional culture struggling to maintain itself within the industrialized world.

The Scandanavian countries where the Sami live required surnames, and the Luthe-ran church applied pressure on the Sami to use traditional Christian names for their children. The Sami resisted for years, main-taining their tradition of no surnames and naming their children for recently deceased elders or infants. The Sami reluctantly cre-ated a system of surnames similar to the Scandanavian system of adding "son" *(sen)* or "daughter" *(dotter)* to the first name of a parent and began using traditional Scandan-avian names for baptism. Afterward, how-ever, when the family left the church, they would hold their own baptism ceremony in which the imposed name was "cleaned" away and a "stronger," more traditional name was given to the child.

Similar practices have been applied to other areas of traditional Sami life: a con-cession is made to modernism, while a con-nection is maintained to traditionalism.

8 ● RELATIONSHIPS

Sami society is traditionally open and egali-tarian, and the Sami are known for their courtesy and hospitality to outsiders. They willingly accept other Sami who may not be full-blooded. A person's attitude toward the treasured Sami language and traditions are considered more important than bloodlines.

A knowledge of the Sami language is considered one of the main ways of identifying someone as a Sami.

9 ● LIVING CONDITIONS

As a seminomadic people, the reindeer-herding Sami traditionally maintained permanent dwellings—sometimes more than one—and spent part of their time living in tents. The permanent homes were either frame buildings or sod huts. The Sami tent, called a *lavvo,* has a circular framework of poles leaning inward like the teepee or wigwam of Native Americans, and a floor of birch twigs covered with layers of reindeer fur. Both tents and huts are arranged around a central fire. Today most Sami, who are no longer reindeer herders, live in typical Scandinavian houses with central heating and running water. Family life typically centers on the kitchen.

The Sami receive the same level of health care as other citizens of the countries in which they live. Like their Scandinavian neighbors, they have a high rate of heart disease. However, Sami are often active and healthy into their eighties. They sometimes supplement Western-style medical care with home remedies or treatment derived from old beliefs in the curing power of the word of the shaman, or medicine man.

10 ● FAMILY LIFE

Traditionally, the Sami lived in a group of families called a *siida.* Today, the nuclear family is the basic social unit among the Sami, and families are close-knit with a great deal of attention paid to the children. The Sami language contains an unusually large number of words that refer to family

relationships. Traditionally, the males of the family were occupied with herding, hunting, and making boats, sleds, and tools, while the women cooked, made clothing and thread, and cured the meat. Each family had its own mark (and children had their own marks as well). Herding families use these marks to distinguish their reindeer from those of other families.

11 ● CLOTHING

Some, but not all, Sami still wear the group's brightly colored traditional clothing. It is most easily recognizable by the distinctive bands of bright red and yellow patterns against a deep blue background of wool or felt. These bands appear as decorations on men's tunics *(gaktis),* as borders on the women's skirts, and on the hats of both sexes. Men's hats vary by region; some are cone-shaped while others have four corners. Women and girls may drape fringed scarves around their shoulders. Warm reindeer-skin coats are worn by both sexes. The Sami wear moccasins of reindeer skin with turned-up toes, fastened with ribbons. However, they wear no socks. Instead, they stuff their moccasins with soft sedge grass to protect their feet against the cold and dampness.

Urban Sami dress in modern, Western-style clothing.

12 ● FOOD

Reindeer meat is a protein-rich dietary staple. Even the reindeer's blood is used, for sausages. Fish caught in the many lakes of the Sami's homelands are eaten boiled, grilled, dried, smoked, or salted. Wild berries are another mainstay of the Sami diet, especially the vitamin C–rich cloudberry. To help them stay warm and alert in their cold environment, the Sami drink coffee throughout the day. Supper is the main (and traditionally, the only hot) meal of the day.

13 ● EDUCATION

Traditionally, Sami children learned what they would need to know as adults by observing and helping their parents. Today, they generally attend the schools in the countries in which they live. There are several Sami high schools, where most of the subjects are taught in the Sami language. The universities of Tromsø in Norway, Umla in Sweden, and Oulu in Finland have Sami departments in which Sami topics are taught.

14 ● CULTURAL HERITAGE

The Sami have a rich tradition of storytelling. A Sami musical tradition that has recently been revived is the singing of the light-hearted, unaccompanied song called the *juoigan (yoik)*. It contains improvised words on almost any topic, but the musical element is the main focus. The yoik resembles the Native American practice of "melodizing" a feeling or mood. There are no collections of yoiks because they are so individualized and so private. A person's yoik is only shared within a close circle of friends and family. The yoik has been described by researchers as one of the most ancient musical traditions in Europe.

The Sami also invented their own musical instrument, a small reed pipe. There are also Sami theaters, publications, and arts and crafts organizations. In 1991 Nils-Aslak Valkeapää of Finland became the first Sami writer to win the Nordic Council prize for literature.

15 ● EMPLOYMENT

Young Sami often are faced with the decision of whether to remain working within their traditions or to adapt to modernism, which the governments of Scandinavia make available to them through schooling and programs of adaptation. For many years, there was intense government pressure for the Sami to abandon tradition and assimilate to Scandinavian life. In recent years, many Sami have rejected this pressure and there is now a considerable movement among the Sami to retain their cultural identity. A considerable number of young Sami who have been exposed to the modern, urban lifestyles of Scandinavia have rejected it for a more traditional lifestyle, although they still have modern conveniences unheard of in earlier generations. Still, it is more common to see a Sami driving a Volvo than to see one herding reindeer—a traditional occupation engaged in by only 10 percent of Sami.

Sami in Scandinavia have bright prospects for employment. While there is some discrimination, most Scandinavians are rigidly egalitarian, and virtually all occupations are open to the Sami.

16 ● SPORTS

The Samis' outdoor recreation is closely linked to the activities that provide their survival. They enjoy competing to see who can throw their reindeer lassos the farthest and with the greatest precision. Reindeer-drawn sled races are popular, especially at the Easter festivals in the heart of Sapmi.

17 ● RECREATION

Sami entertainment is provided both by expressive activities, including storytelling and *yoik* singing, and physical contests such as sled racing and lasso throwing.

A traditional board game, rarely played anymore, is *tablo* and involves one character playing the wolf or the fox and the other a hunter. The players maneuver their pieces around a board with the hunter trying to corner the predator before he or she "eats" all the hunter's pieces.

18 ● CRAFTS AND HOBBIES

The Sami produce beautiful crafts, carving a variety of objects—such as tools and utensils—from bone, wood, reindeer antlers, and silver, often with geometric motifs. They have also perfected a special kind of ribbon weaving. Their crafts are popular tourist purchases, although the Sami save many of their creations for their own use. Much of their artistic talent goes into the elaborate braided designs of their costumes.

19 ● SOCIAL PROBLEMS

The Sami homelands have been affected by the invasion of mining and logging companies, hydroelectric power projects, communication networks, and tourism, and threatened by pollution. A controversy that received particular attention was the building of the Alta hydroelectric dam in Norway, which flooded reindeer pastures important to the region's Sami herders. A group of Sami protesters traveled to the capital city of Oslo, where they set up *lavvos* (tents) in front of the Norwegian parliament and began a hunger strike. Their efforts were unsuccessful, but their actions drew worldwide attention.

Since 1968, the National Association of Norwegian Sami (NSR) has been working actively for Sami political rights, as well as improvements in cultural, social, and economic conditions.

The Sami were also affected by the 1986 nuclear accident at Chernobyl in Ukraine, which contaminated some of their grazing areas, making their reindeer potentially unsafe for them to market or eat themselves. Fish, berries, and drinking water in the affected areas were poisoned as well. Another problem for the Sami has been the increase of tourists from the south, who deplete important Sami resources, such as game birds, fish, and berries, without actually bringing much money into the community.

20 ● BIBLIOGRAPHY

Beach, Hugh. *A Year in Lapland.* Washington, D.C.: Smithsonian Institution, 1993.

Lander, Patricia Slade, and Claudette Charbonneau. *The Land and People of Finland.* New York: Lippincott, 1990.

Paine, Robert. *Herds of the Tundra: A Portrait of Saami Reindeer Pastoralism.* Washington, D.C.: Smithsonian Institution, 1994

Rajanen, Aini. *Of Finnish Ways.* Minneapolis, Minn.: Dillon Press, 1981.

Reynolds, Jan. *Far North.* New York: Harcourt Brace, 1992.

"Saami." *Encyclopedia of World Cultures (Europe).* Boston: G. K. Hall, 1992.

Vitebsky, Piers. *The Saami of Lapland.* New York: Thomson Learning, 1993.

WEB SITES

Introduction to the Sami People. [Online] Available http://www.itv.se/boreale/samieng.htm, 1998.

Samefolket. Sami Magazine. [Online] Available http://www.samefolket.se/, 1998.

Oman

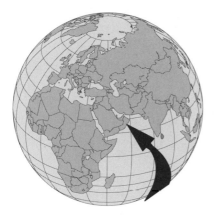

■ **OMANIS** 17

The people of Oman are called Omanis. On the northern coast, there are groups of Baluchi, Iranian, and African people. In Muscat and Matrah, there are Indians, Baluchis, and Pakistanis. Tribal groups are estimated to number over 200.

Omanis

PRONUNCIATION: oh-MAHN-eez
LOCATION: Oman
POPULATION: 1.5 million
LANGUAGE: Arabic; English
RELIGION: Islam (Ibadi sect)

1 ● INTRODUCTION

The present-day land of Oman was home to a fairly advanced civilization as far back as about 5000 BC. From 3000 BC until AD 1500, the Omanis were a prosperous, seafaring, export-oriented people. During the sixth to seventh centuries AD, Islam was brought to Oman by the Arabs.

During the 1500s, the Portuguese invaded and built forts in the coastal towns to control the Arabian (or Persian) Gulf trade route. The Portuguese occupied the area for about 100 years until the Omanis drove them out. Oman had trade agreements and dealings with other European nations during the 300 years that followed. For the most part, Oman has not been under foreign rule since the Portuguese were driven out in the 1600s.

During the early to mid-nineteenth century, Oman became an important commercial center for the Persian Gulf area, and relations with other countries were developed. In the 1860s, the invention of the steamship and the opening of the Suez Canal eliminated the demand for Omani sailing ships and the need to stop at Omani ports. Oman entered a time of economic hardship, which lasted until oil production began in 1970. Until 1970, Oman also had been kept completely isolated by a succession of rigidly fundamentalist rulers. In 1970, Sultan Said bin Tamir was forced into exile by his son, Qaboos, who then became sultan. Sultan Qaboos began the production of oil and used the profits to make much-needed improvements in the country. Sultan Qaboos has brought electricity and running water, free modern education and health

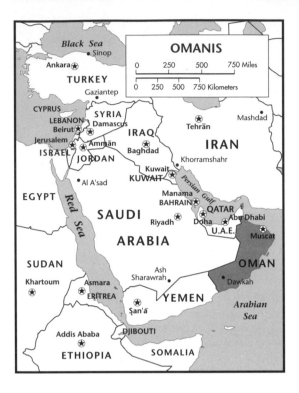

years still operates, carrying water from the mountains down into the dry plains below. Oman is known for its extreme heat and humidity. Summer temperatures can rise as high as 110°F (43°C) in the shade, and humidity reaches a drenching 96 percent.

3 ● LANGUAGE

Omanis speak Arabic. A few pockets of other languages exist as well. English is taught as a second language to all students beginning in primary school. Arabic, spoken by 100 million people worldwide, has many distinct dialects. Consequently, people living as few as 300 miles (about 500 kilometers) apart may not be able to understand one another. The written form of Arabic is the same for all literate Arabs (those able to read and write), regardless of how different their spoken dialects are. Arabic is written from right to left.

"Hello" in Arabic is *marhaba* or *ahlan,* to which one replies, *marhabtayn* or *ahlayn.* Other common greetings are *As-salam alaykum* (Peace be with you), with the reply of *Wa alaykum as-salam* (and to you peace). *Ma'assalama* means "Goodbye." "Thank you" is *Shukran,* and "You're welcome" is *Afwan.* "Yes" is *na'am* and "no" is *la'a.* The numbers one to ten in Arabic are *wahad, ithnayn, thalatha, arba'a, khamsa, sitta, saba'a, thamanya, tisa'a,* and *ashara.*

Arabs' names consist of their first name, their father's name, and their paternal grandfather's name. Women do not take their husband's name when they marry. They keep their father's family name as a sign of respect for their family of origin. First names usually indicate an Arab's religious affiliation. Muslims use names with

care, and great improvements in housing and roadways to Omanis.

The population of Oman is over two million. Approximately three-quarters are Omanis. The capital is Muscat, located on the northeast coast. All Omanis are Arabs.

2 ● LOCATION

Oman is located on the southeast corner of the Arabian Peninsula. The total area of Oman is slightly smaller than the state of Kansas. Its landscape includes a fertile coastal plain, mountains, and vast expanses of desert. Parts of Oman receive monsoon rains during the summer months. Rain also falls in the mountains. The rest of the country receives little or no rain, making water a very valuable commodity. An ancient water-management system dating back 2,500

AP/Wide World Photos

Omani nomads herd sheep, goats, and camels. Oman is the camel-breeding capital of the world.

Islamic religious significance, such as *Muhammad* and *Fatima,* while Christians often use Western names, as well as Arabic Christian names, such as *Elias* and *Butrus.*

4 ● FOLKLORE

Folktales include the legends of Sinbad the Sailor. There is also a legend that King Solomon of Israel flew to Oman on a magic carpet with his *jinn* (a spirit who can take on human or other animal form). He then built 10,000 channels for the ancient water-carrying system in ten days.

5 ● RELIGION

The original inhabitants of Oman were pantheists, worshiping various goddesses and gods. Many later converted to Christianity. When the Islamic revolution swept through in the seventh century AD, Omanis were among the first to adopt the new religion. All Omanis are Muslim, most belonging to the Ibadi sect. Ibadis are traditionalists who believe in maintaining the original purity of Islam as conceived by the Prophet Muhammad.

The Islamic religion has five so-called "pillars": (1) Muslims must pray five times a day; (2) Muslims must give alms, or *zakat,* to the poor; (3) Muslims must fast from dawn to dusk during the holy month of Ramadan; (4) Muslims must make the pilgrimage, or *hajj,* to Mecca (the spiritual center of Islam, located in Saudi Arabia); and (5) each Muslim must recite the *shahada,* which in English means, "I witness that there is no god but Allah and that Muhammad is the prophet of Allah." Arabs say all their prayers facing in the direction of Mecca.

Islam is a simple, straightforward faith with clear rules for correct living. It is a total way of life, inseparable from the rest of one's daily concerns. Therefore, there is no such thing as the "separation of church and state" in Islamic countries such as Oman.

6 ● MAJOR HOLIDAYS

The one secular holiday in Oman is National Day on November 18. Otherwise, all the holidays are Muslim ones. Muslim holidays follow the lunar calendar, so their dates on the standard Western (Gregorian) calendar move back by eleven days each Western year. The main Muslim holidays are *Eid al-Fitr,* a three-day festival at the end of Ramadan; *Eid al-Adha,* a three-day feast of sacrifice at the end of the month of pilgrimage to Mecca; the *First of Muharram,* or the Muslim New Year; *al-Mawlid An-Nabawi,* the prophet Muhammad's birthday; and *Eid al-Isra wa Al-Mi`raj,* a feast celebrating Muhammad's nocturnal visit to heaven. Friday is the Islamic day of rest, so most businesses and services are closed.

7 ● RITES OF PASSAGE

Omani boys are circumcised at either fifteen days or six years of age. In the past, circumcision was performed at the age of fifteen years in a ceremony involving both women and men.

Births are an occasion for celebration, particularly if the child is a boy. Weddings are perhaps the most elaborately celebrated occasions, with great feasts and dancing.

8 ● RELATIONSHIPS

Arab hospitality reigns in Oman. When talking, Arabs touch each other much more often, and stand much closer together, than Westerners do. People of the same sex will often hold hands while talking or walking. (In earlier days, members of the opposite sex, even married couples, never touched in public. This is changing today.) Arabs talk a great deal, talk loudly, repeat themselves often, and interrupt each other constantly. Conversations are highly emotional and full of gestures.

9 ● LIVING CONDITIONS

Before Sultan Qaboos took over in 1970, conditions in Oman were extremely primitive. There was no electricity or running water. Houses were built of either mud brick or woven and knotted palm fronds. There were almost no paved roads, and the only means of transportation were camels and donkeys. There were no newspapers and no television or radio stations. Since 1970, Sultan Qaboos has introduced electricity and running water to most of the country, built many new structures of cement block, constructed extensive paved roads, and modernized communications, health care, and education, all of which are provided free of charge. Most Omanis now own cars and trucks. The distance from the capital city of Muscat in the northeast to the city of Salalah at the other end of the country can now be crossed in one day. It used to take two weeks by camel caravan.

ARAMCO World

A nomadic man shops alongside town-dwellers in the market at Sanaw. Sanaw's busiest market day is Thursday, and other towns in the region schedule their markets for other days—a practice that allows merchants to travel from one market to another.

10 ● FAMILY LIFE

Omanis are a tribal people, and the family is the center of their life. Marriages are traditionally arranged by parents, with first cousins being the preferred match. The groom pays the bride a dowry (marriage gift of goods or money), or *mahr,* which becomes her property no matter what happens. Polygyny (more than one wife) is legal, but it is very rarely practiced. Divorce is rare. Girls can be betrothed (engaged) as young as eleven or twelve years of age.

An Omani woman's role is domestic, while the man's is public. Men take care of all business and public transactions, even doing most of the food shopping. Women take care of the home, doing all the cooking, cleaning, and child care. Women and children do most of the sheep, goat, and poultry herding. On farms, women do most of the work in the fields. Weaving and embroidery are also women's tasks. Although Oman is one of the most traditional Islamic countries, women are actually much less restricted in Oman than are women in other Arab nations. Omani women are the only women on the Arabian Peninsula who are allowed to vote.

11 ● CLOTHING

Omani men wear the traditional *dishdasha,* an ankle-length robe, usually white. Sometimes they wear a *bisht,* a kind of cloak, over their *dishdasha.* On their heads they wear a skullcap or a turban. Many Omani men carry a camel stick—a length of bamboo with a curved handle, like a cane. Almost all Omani men wear a curved dagger called a *khanjar* through their belt.

Women in Oman wear very colorful dresses over loose-fitting pants that are gathered tightly at the ankles. They wear scarves on their heads, and a lot of jewelry. In public, most Omani women wear a black ankle-length robe called an *abaya,* and many veil their faces.

All Omanis wear leather sandals on their feet.

12 ● FOOD

Staple foods in Oman consist of rice, dates, fruit, fish, and meat. Most meat is cooked in a *tanour,* a hole in the ground where a fire is built and then allowed to burn down to ashes. Meat is wrapped and cooked for twenty-four hours before eating. Omanis eat their meals on the floor or ground, the dishes spread on a cloth. Food and drink are always taken with the right hand. The main meal of the day is at noon; breakfast and supper are light meals. A favorite dessert is *halawa* (halvah), a sweet, flaky treat usually made of crushed sesame seeds and honey. Coffee is drunk strong and black, sometimes flavored with cardamom. *Bedu* (or Bedouin) nomads eat the locusts that swarm over farmers' crops.

13 ● EDUCATION

Before Sultan Qaboos took over in 1970, there were only three schools in Oman, with a total of 900 students, all boys. Today there are over 1,000 schools, with a total enrollment of 482,000 students, almost half girls. Girls and boys go to separate schools, but their education is similar. Education is free to all Omanis from the preschool through postgraduate levels. Children's education goes through primary, preparatory, and secondary stages. Some students attend college or technical training institutes after secondary school. The Sultan Qaboos University was opened for classes in September 1986. Sixty-five percent of its students are female. The literacy rate (ability to read and write) in 1995 was determined to be about 59 percent for Omanis over fifteen years of age. Hundreds of adult-education and literacy centers have been established to help eliminate illiteracy.

Recipe

Halvah Shortbread

Ingredients

½ cup butter, softened
½ cup tahini (sesame seed paste)
pinch of salt
1¼ cups brown sugar
2 cups unbleached pastry flour
½ cup toasted pecans or walnuts, chopped or ground
a few pecan or walnut halves

Directions

1. Preheat oven to 375°F.
2. Cream the butter with the tahini, using a food processor or electric mixer, or by hand. Add the salt and brown sugar, and blend until smooth.
3. Sprinkle in the flour, blending well. Mix in the chopped or ground nuts. The dough will be very stiff.
4. Lightly butter two 7-inch pie plates or shallow baking pans. Press the dough to evenly cover the bottom of the pie plates to a thickness of no more than 1 inch. Press a few nut halves into the surface to decorate.
5. Bake for 15 minutes. Check the shortbread frequently, and remove it from the oven as soon as the edges are golden-brown.
6. While it is still warm, cut each shortbread into 8 or 10 wedges in the pan (if you wait until it is cool to cut it, it will crumble).

Adapted from Moosewood Collective, *Sunday at the Moosewood Restaurant,* New York: Fireside Books, Simon & Schuster, 1990, pp. 84–85.

---

14 ● CULTURAL HERITAGE

The Ministry of National Heritage and Culture was established in 1976. It has restored many historic buildings, including forts, castles, and ancient houses. The Ministry has also built numerous historical museums, libraries, and cultural centers, and organized excavations of ancient remains. Excavations have uncovered pottery jars, beads, and arrowheads dating back to the third millennium BC.

Music is not encouraged by the Ibadi sect of Islam. Yet some folk music has developed in Oman. The Oman Center for Traditional Music was founded in August 1983 to collect and document Omani folk music. Folk music is played on traditional instruments such as drums, a trumpet made out of horn, a straight pipe, and the *rebaba,* a stringed instrument. *Sea chanteys* (sailors' songs) have been sung throughout the seafaring Omanis' history. In 1985, Sultan Qaboos established the Royal Oman Symphony Orchestra, as well as a music-training school that is attended by both sexes.

Visual arts in Oman are mostly confined to everyday objects, such as kitchen utensils, rugs, ceramic pots, and clothing.

15 ● EMPLOYMENT

In the fertile areas of Oman, most people are farmers. About 10 percent of Omanis are fishers in the Gulf of Oman and Arabian Sea. Boatbuilding is an ancient craft passed down from generation to generation. Traditionally, boats were built from palm fronds, and larger ones from wood. These traditional boats are still used, although recently many fishers have purchased aluminum boats. Sails and oars used to be the means of propulsion; most boats now have motors.

Omani nomads herd sheep, goats, and camels. Oman is the camel-breeding capital of the world.

Although most of Oman's revenue currently comes from oil, that industry employs only a few thousand Omanis. Roughly two-thirds of laborers in the work force are currently foreign workers.

16 ● SPORTS

Since 1970, Sultan Qaboos has increased the scope of sporting activities in the country. Sports complexes and sports clubs have been built throughout Oman. The traditional sport of camel racing is very popular, as is horse racing. Hockey was introduced into Oman from India in the nineteenth century and is very popular. Many Omanis enjoy target shooting, and some have won regional or international shooting competitions. Omani national teams have also competed in the Olympic games.

17 ● RECREATION

Omanis enjoy plays and concerts performed by the national Youth Theater, established in 1980. Boys have joined Boy Scout groups since 1948; girls have been able to be Girl Scouts since 1970. The National Organization for Scouts and Guides, established in 1975, aims to develop in youth a sense of service, self-reliance, responsibility, and public spirit. There are ten Scout camps in the country.

18 ● CRAFTS AND HOBBIES

All art in Oman is utilitarian (designed for usefulness rather than beauty) and can therefore be seen as folk art. Silver-, gold-, and coppersmithing are perhaps the most highly developed arts. Weaving, embroidery, and woodcarving also are highly intricate and require great skill. Pottery is also a well-developed utilitarian art.

19 ● SOCIAL PROBLEMS

Ecologically, Oman is a very clean country, with stiff fines for littering (or even for having a dirty car). However, there is a great deal of coastal pollution from oil tankers, from the mining of sand to build new roads, and from the dumping of wastes.

The once nearly extinct white oryx, an antelope, has been successfully reintroduced into the wild in Oman. However, several species of sea turtles continue to be endangered by the Omani taste for turtle soup. Groundwater reserves are being rapidly used up, and the dry climate of today cannot provide enough rain to refill them.

Politically, Oman has operated under a traditional sultanate structure, in which family members are given all the positions of authority and decision-making. This system is quickly becoming harmful to Oman's welfare. Many commoners are now much better educated and trained in the skills needed for government posts than members of the ruling family. Since the production of oil began in 1970, the ruling family has kept Oman's citizens quiet by giving them great benefits and financial gifts. In return, citizens have not questioned the way the government is run. But those days are quickly disappearing. Oman has very limited oil reserves and they are likely to run out soon. Government handouts will then have to be severely cut back. Sultan Qaboos is trying to develop non-oil industries, but he has had limited success so far.

20 ● BIBLIOGRAPHY

Dutton, Roderic. *An Arab Family.* Minneapolis, Minn.: Lerner Publications Co., 1985.

Hawley, Sir Donald. *Oman and Its Renaissance.* London: Stacey International, 1990.

Moss, Joyce, and George Wilson. *Peoples of the World: The Middle East and North Africa.* Detroit: Gale Research, 1992.

Zahlan, Rosemarie Said. *The Making of the Modern Gulf States: Kuwait, Bahrain, Qatar, the United Arab Emirates and Oman.* London: Unwin Hymen, 1989.

WEBSITES

ArabNet. Oman. [Online] Available http://www.arab.net/oman/oman_contents.html, 1998.

World Travel Guide. [Online] Available http://www.wtgonline.com / country / om/gen.html, 1998.

Pakistan

■ **PAKISTANIS** **25**
■ **BALUCHI** **35**
■ **BRAHUI** **41**
■ **PUNJABIS** **46**

The people of Pakistan are called Pakistanis. About two-thirds of the population are Punjabi, tracing their origin to the Punjab region of northwest India. Other major ethnic groups include the Sindhi (13 percent), Pashtun (8.5 percent), the Baluchi (2.5 percent). For more information on the Sindhi, see the article on India in Volume 4. For more information on the Pashtun, see the article on Afghanistan in Volume 1.

Pakistanis

PRONUNCIATION: pak-is-TAN-eez

LOCATION: Pakistan

POPULATION: 140.5 million

LANGUAGE: Urdu (official national language); English; Punjabi (60 percent); Sindhi (13 percent); Pushto (8 percent); Baluchi (2 percent)

RELIGION: Islam (majority); Hinduism; Christianity; Buddhism; Baha'i; Parsi (Zoroastrianism)

1 ● INTRODUCTION

Pakistanis are citizens of the Islamic Republic of Pakistan *(Islam-i Jamhuriya-e Pakistan)*. The nation of Pakistan came into existence in 1947. Before that time, the region formed part of the British Indian Empire.

Pakistan's history dates back nearly 5,000 years to one of the world's first urban (city-based) civilizations, which grew up along the Indus River. Pakistan was settled by peoples of varied ethnic and cultural backgrounds. In the Urdu language, the name *Pakistan* translates as "Land of the Pure."

At the beginning of the eleventh century, rulers from Afghanistan mounted military campaigns over the mountain passes into the region that is India and Pakistan today. For over 650 years, a Muslim government based in Delhi ruled much of the area that makes up modern Pakistan. Toward the end of the sixteenth century, one emperor, Akbar, made Lahore the capital of his

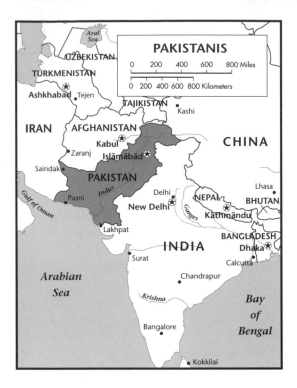

307,304 square miles (796,095 square kilometers). Pakistan occupies the territories of Jammu and Kashmir, which officially belong to India. In size, Pakistan is slightly larger than the state of Texas. Its southern border is formed by a 650-mile (1,046-kilometer) stretch of coastline along the Arabian Sea. From there, the country extends northward for 1,000 miles (1,600 kilometers) to the mountains that lie along its northern border with China. To the west, Pakistan shares borders with Iran and Afghanistan. India lies to the east, and in the northeast is the disputed territory of Kashmir.

Pakistan's western boundary was established by the British as part of their Indian Empire. The eastern boundary was set in the mid-twentieth century. When the British were preparing to give up control of their Indian Empire, Muslims living there were concerned that they would be a minority in a Hindu-controlled independent country. They demanded their own country. When the British left India, the Muslim majority areas in the north—one in the west and the other in the east—were separated to form Pakistan.

Pakistan was then made up of two "wings" separated by 1,000 miles (1,600 kilometers) of land belonging to India. East Pakistan, even though it had a Muslim majority, was culturally different from the West Pakistan. Eventually, civil war erupted. East Pakistan broke away (with Indian help) and became the independent nation of Bangladesh in 1971.

The boundary between India and West Pakistan divided the region of the Punjab in two. In 1947 when the boundary was set,

empire. Lahore is a major city in modern Pakistan.

Britain took over the plains of the Punjab in 1849. Over the next hundred years, the British colonial government in India gained control over virtually all the lands and peoples that were to make up Pakistan.

The modern state of Pakistan was created in 1947, when the British colonial possessions were divided between Pakistan and India. Pakistan's capital city is Islamabad. The traditional conflict with India has led to several military confrontations, with wars fought in 1947, 1965, and 1971.

2 ● LOCATION

Pakistan lies in the northwest part of the Indian subcontinent. It has an area of many people moved to live closer to people who were like them—Sikhs and Hindus moved into India, and a Muslims moved into Pakistan. This process was not peaceful, and an estimated 1 million people died in the process.

In the territory known as Jammu and Kashmir (usually called simply "Kashmir"), there have been tensions. In 1947, Kashmir had more Muslims in its population. But the ruler was Hindu, and he was reluctant to join either Pakistan or India. From 1947–49, there was armed conflict. A ceasefire was negotiated by the United Nations in 1949, but Kashmir remains divided, with Pakistani and Indian troops facing each other across the ceasefire line.

The 140.5 million people of Pakistan encompass a range of distinct ethnic groups. Baluchis are found in the southwest, and Sindhis, in the south. The Punjabis of the northern plains of the Indus River make up the largest, and most politically influential, group in the country. In the northwest, Pashtun (also called Pakhtun or Pathan) are the main group. Tribal areas are administered by the federal government rather than by provincial governments. The ethnic mix of Pakistan is further modified by the *muhajirs* (Muslims from India who crossed into Pakistan in 1947, along with their descendants), who represent perhaps 10 percent of Pakistan's population. During the Soviet occupation of Afghanistan (1979–88), there were an estimated 3 million Afghani refugees (mainly Pashtuns) in northwestern Pakistan.

Pakistan is roughly divided into three geographic regions: the Indus plains, the northern mountains, and the hills and plateaus that extend from the Khyber Pass to Baluchistan. The Indus plains, and especially the northern region of the Punjab, form the heart of the country. In spite of the dry climate (Karachi receives about 8 inches, or 20 centimeters, of rain a year) and maximum temperatures that may hover above 104°F (40°C) for months at a time, the plains support the largest part of Pakistan's population. Agriculture depends heavily on irrigation from the waters of the Indus River system.

The northern mountain zone has some of the most rugged land found anywhere in the world. Nearly all the region lies above 7,800 feet (approximately 2,400 meters). The Karakoram Mountains contain some of the highest peaks in the world. More than fifty peaks are over 21,000 feet (6,500 meters) in elevation. The area is difficult to cross, especially in the winter months. It is sparsely populated with tribespeople who display a fierce sense of independence.

3 ●LANGUAGE

Over twenty languages are spoken in Pakistan. Punjabi is spoken by almost 60 percent of the population. Other languages include Sindhi (13 percent); Pushto or Pashtu, the language of the Pathans (8 percent); and Baluchi (2 percent). Kashmiri is the language of the disputed areas of the former Jammu and Kashmir State.

Balti, spoken in the extreme Northeast, belongs to the Sino-Tibetan, rather than the Indo-European, language family.

The origins of the Burushaski language (spoken in the Hunza region) are still unknown.

Brahui, spoken by some 2.5 million people in Baluchistan Province, is of interest. Unlike most languages of Pakistan, it belongs to the Dravidian language family. It is linguistically related to the languages of southern India.

With this great variety, and because of the role of language in cultural identity, Urdu has been adopted as Pakistan's national language. However, it has been adopted only by the intellectuals and the educated, wealthy classes of the cities, so it cannot be viewed as "national." Only about 10 percent of the population speaks Urdu. Urdu is written in Persian-Arabic script. Urdu and English—the latter a legacy of the colonial era—are official languages in which government and business are conducted.

4 ● FOLKLORE

Given that the Pakistani identity was created by a political decision in 1947, it is not surprising that the peoples of Pakistan tend to identify more with their own communities than with their nation. In other words, one is a Punjabi, Baluchi, Sindhi, or Pashtun before one is a Pakistani. Individual people respect the folk traditions and folk heroes of their own community. However, Muhammad Ali Jinnah (1875–1948) has reached the status of a national hero for many Pakistanis. It was Jinnah, Pakistan's first leader, who demanded a separate Muslim country in India. He is responsible for the existence of Pakistan and is known as the Great Leader, the *Quaid-e-Azam*.

5 ● RELIGION

The majority of Pakistanis are Muslims (followers of Islam). Religious minorities, accounting for just over 3 percent of the population, include Hindus, Christians, Buddhists, and Baha'is (who are of Iranian descent). There is a small Parsi (Zoroastrian) community, concentrated in Karachi.

Within the Muslim community, the Sunnis sect forms the majority. About 25 percent of Muslims are Shi'ah (or Shi'ite), who are often at odds with the Sunni majority. The Ahmadiyas, a modern Islamic sect, have beliefs that are so different that many other Muslims don't consider them Muslim. There are over 2 million Ahmadiyas, and they face discrimination from other Pakistanis.

6 ● MAJOR HOLIDAYS

The two great religious festivals celebrated by the Pakistanis are *Eid-al-Fitr*, celebrating the end of the fast of *Ramadan*, and *Bakr-Eid,* the feast of sacrifice. Ramadan, the month of fasting, is observed by all Muslims. *Muharram* is a major day of remembrance among the Shi'ahs. The *Urs* festivals, commemorating dates of the deaths of Sufi saints, are important festivals celebrated at the saints' shrines. (Sufis are members of another of the Muslim sects.) The Muslim religious holidays follow the lunar calendar, so they fall on different days on the Western calendar each year.

In addition to religious holidays, Pakistanis observe certain national holidays. These include Independence Day (August 14), Pakistan Day (March 23), Defence of Pakistan Day (September 6), and the birth-

Pakistan has 121,000 miles (195,000 kilometers) of roads, although only a little more than half are paved. State-run bus services and private minibuses are available to the public.

date and deathdate of M. A. Jinnah, the *Quaid-e-Azam* (December 25 and September 11, respectively).

7 ● RITES OF PASSAGE .

Pakistanis follow the rites of passage associated with the Islamic faith. Newborns are sanctified by prayer and undergo head-shaving and naming ceremonies. All males undergo the ritual of circumcision *(sunnat).* Among some Muslims, a ceremony known as *Bismillah* marks the beginning of a child's education in religious matters.

Ceremonies associated with death and burial combine practices from the *shari'ah,* (Islamic law), with local customs and tradi-tions. The body is ritually bathed and wrapped in a white shroud in preparation for burial. The body is brought out of the house, and the face of the deceased person is shown to relatives and neighbors. Mourn-ers, led by a priest, say prayers over the body, which is then taken in procession to the graveyard.

8 ● RELATIONSHIPS

Traditional Pakistanis use the formal greet-ing of Muslims the world over, *Salaam alai-kum* (Peace be with you). The correct reply to this is the sentence, *Wa alaikum as Salaam* (And also unto you). Less formally, men shake hands and friends embrace each

Cory Langley

Men all over Pakistan wear salwar, *loose baggy trousers, and* kurta, *a long shirtlike tunic. A variety of head coverings, from turbans to caps, complete the outfit. The man in the center of the first row in this photograph is the American photographer responsible for this picture.*

other. Pathans embrace twice, once from the left side and once from the right. Men are addressed as *Sahib* ("Mister" or "Sir"); when used with a name, the word *Sahib* comes last (as in "Johnson *Sahib*"). The equivalent form of address for a woman is *Begum. Khan,* although a name, is also a title of respect.

9 ● LIVING CONDITIONS

In spite of the improvements in the nation's health standards since independence, many Pakistanis continue to face major health hazards. Leading causes of death include malaria, childhood diseases (measles, diphtheria, whooping cough), typhoid, gastrointestinal (digestive-system) problems, and respiratory infections (in the breathing apparatus). Bad sewage disposal, lack of safe drinking water, and malnutrition (lack of enough food or the right kind of food) contribute to health problems. Infant mortality rates (the proportion of babies who die very young) are high. Fertility rates are also high; the average woman has six babies. The natural increase of population is 3 percent per year, the highest rate in southern Asia.

Although the majority of the population lives in rural villages, many Pakistanis live in cities. Karachi has over 5 million people and Lahore has over 3 million people. Islamabad was built specifically to be Pakistan's capital. The prosperous upper-class city people live in large, air-conditioned houses with the latest modern conveniences. Rural house types, construction materials, and furnishings vary according to region.

Pakistan has 121,000 miles (195,000 kilometers) of roads, although only 54 percent of them are paved. State-run bus services and private minibuses are available to the public. The train still remains the most common means of long-distance travel for Pakistanis. Pakistan also has a state-run airline that operates scheduled domestic and international flights.

10 ● FAMILY LIFE

Social relations among Pakistanis are very much influenced by caste (inherited social status and job categories). (This is true even though the religion of the majority, Islam, rejects the caste system.) The caste system does not have the religious aspects of the true Hindu caste system of India, but it does define the job roles of specific groups in the villages. It is also important for selecting a marriage partner.

Pakistanis follow the general customs of Islam in marriage *(nikah),* but details vary according to community and region. Parents take great care in arranging marriages for their children. Pakistani society is patrilocal (the daughter-in-law enters the household of her husband's family). The role of women in traditional Pakistani society is clearly defined: to bear sons, to manage the house-hold, and to see to the needs of the men of the family. However, behind the scenes, women have influence in family matters.

11 ● CLOTHING

The standard clothing of men all over Pakistan is the *salwar,* loose baggy trousers, and *kurta,* a long shirtlike tunic. This is worn with a variety of head coverings, from turbans to caps. On formal occasions, the *kurta* is replaced by an *achkan* or *serwani*, a long coat that buttons up to the neck.

The Jinnah cap, favored by Muslim Indian politician M. A. Jinnah (1876–1948), is popular among politicians, government officials, and other groups in the cities and towns of Pakistan.

Women commonly wear the *salwar*, *kamiz*, and *dupatta* (scarf), or the sari. Orthodox Muslim women cover themselves from head to foot in the tent-like *burqa,* the long garment that covers them from head to toe.

12 ● FOOD

It is difficult to identify food that is specifically Pakistani because the region shares food traditions with its neighbor, India. The main difference between Pakistani and Indian food is that Pakistani food tends to be less spicy. Pakistani dishes are often made with yogurt, which reduces the effect of the hot spices used in cooking.

Wheat is the staple food for most of the people. It is eaten in the form of flat, unleavened bread called *chapatis* or *roti,* together with spiced lentils *(dal)* and vegetables in season. Sweetened tea, buttermilk, or *lassi,* a drink made from yogurt, rounds

Recipe

CARROT HALWA
(Carrot Dessert)

Ingredients

1½ pounds carrots
2 cups milk
¼ cup butter
¾ cup jaggary (dark brown sugar may be substituted)
2 cardamon pods, peeled, and seeds cracked
1 Tablespoon rose water
slivered, toasted, blanched almonds

Directions

1. Grate carrots in blender with milk.
2. Cook mixture for 1½ hours until all moisture has evaporated.
3. Add butter, jaggary, and cracked cardamon seeds and mix well. Cook mixture for ten minutes; mixture should be dry.
4. Just before serving, drizzle mixture with rose water. Garnish with almonds. This dessert may served hot or cold.

Adapted from Castle, Coralie and Margaret Gin. *Peasant Cooking of Many Lands*. San Fransisco, Calif.: 101 Productions, 1972, p. 45.

RAITHA
(Yogurt and Vegetable Salad)

Ingredients

1 cup yogurt
3–4 cups mixed vegetables, such as raw spinach and cucumber, cooked potatoes or eggplant
½ cup chopped onions
1 dried red chili pepper, crushed, or ¼ teaspoon cayenne pepper
2 Tablespoons minced fresh mint leaves
½ teaspoon each cumin powder and salt
¼ teaspoon black pepper

Directions

1. Combine all ingredients in large bowl.
2. Mix well. Serves 6-8.

Adapted from Castle, Coralie, and Margaret Gin. *Peasant Cooking of Many Lands*. San Fransisco, Calif.: 101 Productions, 1972, p. 45.

out the meal. Those who can afford to buy it eat meat or poultry, although in rural areas these are usually festival foods. Goat meat is a favorite. Pakistanis will not eat pork, because Muslims regard it as unclean.

The *Mughal* style of cooking was developed in the Muslim courts of India. It uses a blend of herbs and spices, rather than chilis and peppers, and offers a selection of meats and poultry served in sauces, *tandoori* dishes baked in a clay oven, breads such as *nan,* and rice dishes.

13 ● EDUCATION

Despite the expansion of educational facilities since independence, only 35 percent of Pakistanis over fifteen years of age were literate (could read and write) as of 1993 (47.3 percent for males and 22.3 percent for females). The variation in literacy between city and rural populations is also great.

Attendance at school remains low in rural areas because many children must work in the fields, and the dropout rate is high. Over two-thirds of adults have no formal schooling. Less than 2 percent of the population attends universities.

14 ● CULTURAL HERITAGE

Buddhism has left its mark on Pakistan. The ancient kingdom of Gandhara, in northern Pakistan, was a major center of Buddhist learning and arts from the first to fifth centuries AD. With influences from the West, Buddhists developed a tradition of Gandhara art that combined motifs from Persia, Greece, and Rome with Buddhist forms. The Indian-Islamic style of architecture, the many shrines of the *pirs* (Sufi saints), and the mosques such as the Badshahi Mosque in Lahore indicate the influence of Islam.

The poetry and music of the Sufis are widely known. The singing of *qawwalis,* religious songs, is extremely popular, and some *qawwali* singers enjoy the kind of fame pop stars have in the West. There is a rich tradition of poetry in Urdu and other regional languages.

15 ● EMPLOYMENT

Pakistan is mainly an agricultural nation, with 68 percent of its people living in rural areas. Pakistan's rapid population growth has increased the demand for food and slowed industrial expansion. There is a surplus of laborers. This has given rise to unique businesses, such as the world's largest ship-breaking operation. It is located on the beaches of the Arabian Sea coast, and the sometimes dangerous work of tearing

apart old boats and ships is done almost entirely by hand. Many Pakistanis work in the oil-exporting countries of the Middle East, where workers are in demand. They earn much higher incomes than they could in Pakistan. This is an important source of foreign currency (money) for the country.

16 ● SPORTS

Sports and games enjoyed by children in rural areas include hide-and-seek, marbles, kite flying, *gulli-danda* (a stick game played by boys), and *kabaddi,* a wrestling game. For men, cockfighting, partridge fighting, and pigeon flying (and betting on the outcome) are favorite pastimes. Polo, played more informally than in the West, is popular in northern areas.

Pakistanis also play modern sports. The entire country is addicted to cricket, a leftover from British colonial days. In recent years, the Pakistani national (Test) cricket team has regularly defeated England's team. The Pakistani national field hockey team is also one of the best in the world, a frequent winner of the Olympic gold medal. Games such as soccer, tennis, badminton, and table tennis are also played. Pakistanis have regularly won the world championship in squash, a court game similar to racquetball.

17 ● RECREATION

Radio and television are available in Pakistan, although these forms of communication are controlled by the government. Television shows are broadcast only during certain hours, and the programming is not always interesting. It includes quiz programs, dramas highlighting the country's social problems, soap operas, and reruns of

Cory Langley

Poverty, illiteracy (inability to read and write), unemployment, economic inflation, and a widening gap between rich and poor are among the problems Pakistan faced in the 1990s.

old sitcoms from the West. Films in Urdu and in English are popular. Many well-to-do households have VCRs, and rented videos are available in the bazaars (markets).

Movie theaters abound in Pakistani cities and towns, showing films in Punjabi and Urdu. The films, starring well-known actors and actresses, tend to be melodramas, with much action, singing, and dancing, and with predictable plots. Music from films is popular and can be heard on the radio, in buses, and in the bazaars at all hours of the day.

18 ● CRAFTS AND HOBBIES

Every region in Pakistan specializes in its own local arts and crafts. These include rugs and carpets, embroidered and appliquéd bedspreads and table linens, colorful fabrics, mirror work, leather goods, copper and brass articles, onyx ornaments, woodwork, inlaid furniture, lacquerware, and gold and silver jewelry.

19 ● SOCIAL PROBLEMS

Pakistanis face many of the social and economic problems typical of developing nations. Poverty, illiteracy (inability to read and write), unemployment, economic inflation, and a widening gap between rich and poor are only a few of the country's ills. These problems have been intensified by wars with India, high spending on the military, and the continuing conflict in Kashmir. The frequency with which the Pakistani Army has overthrown democratically elected governments has added to political instability in the country. India and Pakistan both conducted nuclear tests in 1998, heightening political tension.

There has been some enthusiasm for the creation of an independent Pashtu-speaking state (Pakhtunistan) on Pakistan's northwest frontier.

In recent years, the presence of 3 million Afghan war refugees has been an added economic and social burden on the country.

Punjabis are viewed as having too much power and influence, and conflict between *muhajirs* and Sindhis has led to unrest in the south, especially in the city of Karachi.

The government's policy of Islamization (increasing the role of Islam in the country), combined with the outspoken fundamentalism of many religious leaders, has created conflict between segments of the Muslim community.

20 ● BIBLIOGRAPHY

Blood, Peter R., ed. *Pakistan, a Country Study.* 6th ed. Washington, D.C.: Federal Research Division, Library of Congress, 1995.

Castle, Coralie and Margaret Gin. *Peasant Cooking of Many Lands.* San Fransisco, Calif.: 101 Productions, 1972.

Eglar, Zekiye. *A Punjabi Village in Pakistan.* New York: Columbia University Press, 1960

National Institute of Folk Heritage. *Folk Heritage of Pakistan.* Islamabad, Pakistan: National Institute of Folk Heritage, 1977.

Quddus, Syed Abdul. *The Cultural Patterns of Pakistan.* Lahore, Pakistan: Ferozsons, 1989.

WEBSITES

Embassy of Pakistan, Washington, DC. [Online] Available http://www.pakistan-embassy.com, 1998.

Interknowledge Corp. [Online] Available http://www.interknowledge.com/pakistan/, 1998.

World Travel Guide, Pakistan. [Online] Available http://www.wtgonline.com/country/pk/gen.html, 1998.

Baluchi

PRONUNCIATION: bal-OOCH-i
ALTERNATE NAMES: Baloch; Balochi
LOCATION: Pakistan (Province of Baluchistan); Iran; Afghanistan; Turkmenistan; Oman; East African coast
POPULATION: 7.5–11 million
LANGUAGE: Baluchi
RELIGION: Islam (mostly Sunni Muslim; also the Zikri sect)

1 ● INTRODUCTION

The Baluchi (also Baloch, or Balochi) are a seminomadic people (they travel with their herds on a seasonal basis but also have a home area where they grow some food crops). They live in the southern mountains and coastal regions of South Asia's western borderlands. Their traditional homeland is divided among Pakistan, Iran, and Afghanistan.

The Baluchi believe they are descendants of Amir Hamza, an uncle of the Prophet Muhammad. They settled in their present homeland sometime between the fifth and seventh centuries AD. Persians, Arabs, Hindus, and others have laid claim to parts of Baluchistan, the traditional Baluchi homeland, at various times. Conflict within tribes and rivalries between tribes were frequent throughout the region. The reason was often

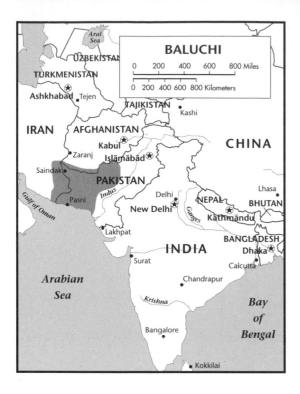

BALUCHI

0   200   400   600   800 Miles

0 200 400 600 800 Kilometers

competition for land, money, and resources. In the eighteenth century, almost all of the Baluchi tribes were loosely united.

In 1843, the frontier of British India bordered Baluchistan. By the early twentieth century, the British had control over much of the region. The British Province of Baluchistan passed to Pakistan when that country came into being in 1947. Pakistan also inherited the problems of the region. Opposition to the central government led to brutal battles with the Pakistani military in the mid-1970s. The military bombed villages and civilians in an effort to subdue the Baluchi rebels. Today, the Baluchi see themselves as a neglected minority in a country whose government is controlled by non-Baluchi ethnic groups such as the Punjabis.

2 ● LOCATION

The Baluchi population today is estimated at 7.5 million. In addition, there are many more people who are Baluchi in culture but have adopted the language of their neighbors. The Baluchi could total over 11 million in number.

The traditional homeland of the Baluchi extends west from the borders of the Punjab and the Sind (a province of Pakistan in the valley of the Indus River), across a small section of Afghanistan, to the areas of the Iranian Plateau southeast of Kirman. The southern boundary is defined by the coast of the Arabian Sea and the Gulf of Oman.

The Province of Baluchistan, in which some 6 million people (80 percent of the total Baluchi population) live lies within Pakistan. Just over 1 million Baluchi live within the borders of Iran, and there are 300,000 more in Afghanistan.

3 ● LANGUAGE

The Baluchi language is an Indo-Iranian language of the Indo-European family. Modern Baluchi shows borrowings from Persian, Arabic, Sindhi, and other languages. No written form of the language existed before the early nineteenth century. Persian was used for official purposes until that time.

4 ● FOLKLORE

The Baluchi respect bravery and courage. Many tribal heroes are honored in folk songs and ballads.

Doda, for example, is remembered for defending the principle of *ahot,* or protection. Legend tells of a wealthy widow, Sammi, who sought protection in the village of Doda Gorgez. One day, Beebagr, a relative of Sammi's deceased husband, carried off some of Sammi's cows. Even though Doda had just been married, he pursued the thieves because he was honor-bound to safeguard the property, as well as the life, of the widow. Doda was killed in the battle that followed. In keeping with Baluchi tradition, Doda's death was eventually avenged by his brother Balach.

5 ● RELIGION

The Baluchi are Muslim, mostly Sunni, but also including members of the Zikri sect. Zikris (pronounced "ZIG-ris" in Baluchi) are estimated to number over 750,000. They live mostly in southern Pakistan. They are followers of a fifteenth-century *mahdi,* an Islamic messiah, called Nur Pak (Pure Light).

The Baluchi do not support the idea of a religious nation that underlies national policies put in place by Pakistani governments in the 1990s.

6 ● MAJOR HOLIDAYS

The Baluchi observe the festivals of *Eid al-Fitr,* which marks the end of *Ramadan,* and *Eid al-Adha,* the Feast of Sacrifice that falls at the end of the Islamic year. On these occasions, people put on clean clothes and begin the day with prayer. The rest of the holiday is spent in gambling, horseracing, and general merrymaking.

Eid al-Adha is celebrated with the sacrifice of goats and sheep. The meat is distributed among relatives, friends, and the poor. Alms (donations) are given to beggars. The tenth day of the month of *Muharram* is observed by visits to the graves of relatives, followed by prayers and the giving of alms to the poor. In general, the Baluchi pay less attention to celebrating festivals than do other Muslim peoples in South Asia.

7 ● RITES OF PASSAGE

The birth of a child is greeted with rejoicing, music, and singing. Food and sweets are prepared and given out. The birth of a boy is cause for greater celebration, and some groups barely recognize the arrival of a girl. Names common among the Baluchi include *Lalla, Bijjar, Kannar,* and *Jihand.*

Other ceremonies mark occasions such as the circumcision of boys, the time when a child begins to walk, and the first wearing of trousers. This last event, occurring around the age of fifteeen, was traditionally an important stage in a boy's life. It marked his becoming an adult and the time when he took up arms and joined his people in warfare.

8 ● RELATIONSHIPS

When Baluchi greet each other, they normally shake hands. However, if an ordinary tribesperson meets a religious leader, the tribesperson reverently touches the leader's feet. A meeting usually begins with inquiries after health *(durahi)* and then goes on to an exchange of news *(hal).* It is considered the height of rudeness not to ask for news from the person one is meeting.

The Baluchi are guided in their daily lives and social relations by a code of conduct known as *Baluchmayar,* or "the

Cory Langley

Nomadic people use pack animals, such as camels, to carry all their belongings, including their tent, when they move from place to place.

Baluchi way." A Baluchi is expected to be generous in hospitality to guests, offer refuge to people who seek protection, and be honest in dealings with others. A Baluchi man must be merciful to women and refrain from killing a man who has found sanctuary in the shrine of a *pir* (Sufi saint). He is also expected to defend his honor *(izzat)* and the honor of the women in his family, and his other relatives.

9 ● LIVING CONDITIONS

Baluchi nomads live in tents *(gidam)* made of palm matting stretched on poles. A coarse goat-hair carpet forms the floor of the tent. There are permanent settlements to live in during the summer months. More recently, houses have been built of sun-dried brick. They are scattered along narrow, winding village lanes. Both old and newer houses have an open courtyard in front, enclosed by a low mud wall or palm fence.

10 ● FAMILY LIFE

Baluchi women are seen as inferior to men and are expected to be obedient to their husbands. However, Baluchi women are less restrained than women among other Muslim peoples in South Asia. Traditionally, the custom of *purdah* (seclusion of women) was not followed. But some upper-class families have now taken up the custom.

In addition to household chores, women share in tending the family's herds. The gathering of wild plants, water, and firewood is designated as women's work.

Baluchi have strong prohibitions against marrying outside the Baluchi community. Marriages are arranged, and it is common for first cousins to marry. Divorce occurs for reasons such as the inability to have children, but it is considered a matter of great disgrace. A widow returns to her father's home on the death of a husband, and she is allowed to remarry if it is acceptable to her family. Inheritance of property goes from father to son.

11 ● CLOTHING

Traditional clothing for the Baluchi man is a long, loose shirt *(jamag* or *kurta)* that reaches below the knees, worn with baggy trousers *(salwar),* and a turban *(pag).* The turban is a long cloth wound around a turban cap on the head. Leather shoes or palm-leaf sandals are worn. A shawl or wrap *(chaddar)* provides extra warmth in winter but can also be used as a towel, sash, or headcloth; it can be used to carry things.

Women wear a long shift *(pashk)* reaching to the ankles, with a wrap used to cover the head, shoulders, and upper body. The wearing of trousers under the shift has been restricted to women of high status. Bright colors are usually avoided, but scarlet is popular among girls of marriageable age. Widows wear black. Women wear an assortment of jewelry, including rings (nose rings, earrings, rings on fingers and toes), necklaces, bracelets, and hair ornaments. Jewelry is made of gold or silver, depending on what a person can afford.

12 ● FOOD

The Baluchi have two meals a day, in the morning and evening. The food for the whole family is cooked together, but men and women eat separately. The most important grain is wheat, but millet and rice are also eaten. Grains are ground into flour and made into unleavened bread (flat bread, without any ingredients to make it rise), which is baked in mud ovens.

Meat is an important part of the Baluchi diet. *Sajji* is a favorite dish that is often served to honored guests. A sheep is killed, skinned, and carved into joints. The meat is sprinkled with salt. The pieces of meat are spitted on green twigs, which are stuck into the ground in front of a blazing log. Once cooked, this dish is eaten with a knife, although Baluchi usually eat with their hands.

Milk is drunk and also made into fresh cheese, buttermilk, and butter. In summer, a sherbet *(lassi)* is made with milk, molasses, and sugar. Dates and wild fruits and vegetables also form an important part of the Baluchi diet.

13 ● EDUCATION

Baluchi have little opportunity for formal education. Only an estimated 10 percent to 15 percent of Baluchi children attend school, mainly in the more settled areas of the country. For this reason, illiteracy (the inability to read and write) among the Baluchi is high.

14 ● CULTURAL HERITAGE

The Baluchi have a rich tradition of story-telling. Poets and storytellers are traditionally held in high respect. The oral tradition conveys the theme of *Baluchmayar,* the Baluchi code of honor. Among the more popular of these poems recount the legendary exploits of Mir Chakur, a sixteenth-century Baluchi warrior and chieftain of the Rind tribe.

Music plays a role in all ceremonies except death rituals. Dancing accompanies many events, such as weddings and other festivals. Men's dances reflect the warrior traditions of the Baluchi. The drum, the lute, and the shepherd's flute are the most common instruments for accompanying the singing and dancing.

15 ● EMPLOYMENT

The traditional economy of the Baluchi combines cereal (grain) farming and the seminomadic herding of sheep, goats, and cattle. Some Baluchi communities along the coast make a living from fishing. Baluchi think of formal trade and business as unworthy occupations.

16 ● SPORTS

Popular games include *chauk,* a type of checkers played with wooden pieces on a cloth divided into squares. Moves are directed by six or seven cowrie shells, thrown onto the ground like dice.

Ji, a game of tag, is played by village boys and young men. Games such as wrestling and horse racing are useful in developing the skills that young men will need for warfare. Shooting and hunting are favorite pastimes among the wealthier people. Card games and gambling are also popular among some groups.

17 ● RECREATION

Baluchi living in Karachi and other towns of southern Pakistan enjoy all the recreational facilities available to the city resident. Those who follow a traditional, seminomadic way of life in the remote Baluchi heartland rely on festivals, music, dancing, and folk culture for their entertainment.

18 ● CRAFTS AND HOBBIES

The Baluchi are not known for their folk art or crafts. However, the women are skilled at embroidery and decorate their clothes with elaborate geometric and abstract designs. They make felt from sheep's wool, and also weave rugs for their own use and for sale.

19 ● SOCIAL PROBLEMS

The Baluchi do not live well in modern Pakistan. They are viewed as virtual "savages" by the ruling majority in the country. It is little wonder that the Baluchi do not have a very strong sense of identity with Pakistani nationalism.

This situation is not helped by the government. It has failed to promote economic development in Baluchistan, one of the most underdeveloped areas of the country.

Even in major cities such as Karachi, Baluchi children are at a disadvantage. Although they speak Baluchi at home, at school they have to struggle with Urdu, Sindhi, English (the language of business and university education), and Arabic or Persian. Few Baluchi advance beyond high school or low-status jobs.

20 ● BIBLIOGRAPHY

Bray, Denys. *Ethnographic Survey of Baluchistan.* Bombay, India: The Times Press, 1913.

Janmahmad. *The Baloch Cultural Heritage.* Karachi, Pakistan: Royal Book Company, 1982.

Pehrson, Robert N. *The Social Organization of the Marri Baluch.* Chicago: Aldine Publishing Company, 1966.

WEBSITES

Embassy of Pakistan, Washington, D.C. [Online] Available http://www.pakistan-embassy.com/, 1998.

Interknowledge Corp. [Online] Available http://www.interknowledge.com/pakistan/, 1998.

World Travel Guide, Pakistan. [Online] Available http://www.wtgonline.com/country/pk/gen.html, 1998.

Brahui

PRONUNCIATION: brah-HOO-ee
ALTERNATE NAMES: Brohi
LOCATION: Pakistan (Baluchistan Province); a small number live in southern Afghanistan and Iran
POPULATION: 861,000 to over 1.5 million
LANGUAGE: Brahui; Sindhi
RELIGION: Islam (Sunni Muslim)

1 ● INTRODUCTION

The tribes known as the Brahui (also Brohi) live in the rugged hills of Pakistan's western borderland. Various explanations of the name *Brahui* have been suggested. The most likely one is that it is a variation of *Barohi,* meaning "mountain dweller" or "highlander."

During the seventeenth century, the Brahui rose to prominence in Kalat, in Baluchistan, a province of modern Pakistan. For the next 300 years there was an unbroken line of Brahui rulers. The British eventually acquired control over the strategically located Kalat, although the state remained independent until it was incorporated into Pakistan in 1948.

2 ● LOCATION

Estimates of the Brahui population vary from 861,000 to over 1.5 million. Most of this number is concentrated in Pakistan's Baluchistan Province around the town of Kalat. Brahui-speakers are also found in southern Afghanistan and Iran.

The Brahui homeland lies on the Kalat Plateau, where elevations vary between 7,000–8,000 feet (2,100–2,400 meters). The region is extremely arid (dry), with annual rainfall averaging less than eight inches (twenty centimeters). Strong northwesterly winds prevail through the area, bringing dust from the Iranian deserts and scorching temperatures in summer, and bitter cold in winter. The plateau consists of extensive areas of barren rock, or hills with a thin cover of drought-resistant vegetation.

3 ● LANGUAGE

The Brahui language is related to the languages spoken in South India. This language similarilty to people living almost 1,000 miles (1,600 kilometers) away has long puzzled South Asian linguists (people who study language). There is no Brahui script. Many Brahui-speakers are bilingual, speaking Baluchi or other local languages.

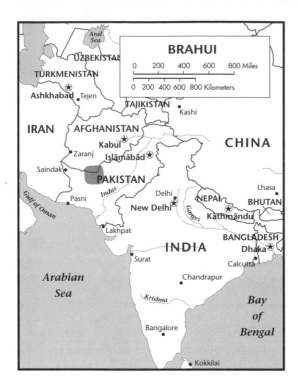

BRAHUI

| 0 | 200 | 400 | 600 | 800 Miles |

| 0 | 200 | 400 | 600 | 800 Kilometers |

4 ● FOLKLORE

A Brahui story tells of Mulla Mansur, an orphan who got a job in the house of a *qadi* (a Muslim religious leader). The qadi was an insensitive man. Even though Mansur had served him loyally for seven long years, he beat him over a trifling mistake. Mansur left the qadi and took to traveling the world. He met an old shepherd, fell in love with his daughter, and married her. When Mansur and his wife returned to his home, the beauty of his wife caused such a stir that everyone from the qadi to the king desired to possess her. However, Mansur's wife was steadfast in her fidelity to her husband. When the qadi continued to make advances and tried to seduce her, she exposed him publicly. All the people joined in condemning the qadi, and the king banished him

from the Brahui lands. This tale presents the Brahui view of the qualities and strength of character desirable in a wife, as well an element of scepticism toward religious leaders who preach purity to the world but practice otherwise.

5 ● RELIGION

The Brahui are Muslim, belonging mostly to the Sunni sect of Islam. They follow Islamic religious beliefs and practices as set out in the *Qu'ran* (Koran), though many of their social customs are Indian in origin. Communal worship focuses on the mosque, and *mullahs* (Muslim priests) see to the spiritual and ritual needs of the people. Reverence for saints *(pirs)* is also deeply entrenched in Brahui culture. Every family has its particular saint, and women often keep in their houses some earth *(khwarda)* from the saint's shrine to be used in time of need. The Brahui believe in sorcery and possession by *jinn* or evil spirits. A mullah or *sayyed* (holy man) is often called in to read from the Qu'ran or provide charms and amulets to exorcise these spirits. Should this fail, a sheikh, who is known for his power over jinn may cast them out by dancing.

6 ● MAJOR HOLIDAYS

The Brahui observe the usual holy days of the Muslim calendar. The holiest of all is the eve of the tenth day of the month of Muharram, which is known as *Imamak*. Women prepare special dishes of meat and rice during the day. The family gathers near sunset in the presence of a *mullah* (Muslim priest), who reads from the Qu'ran and recites prayers for the dead over the food. Dishes of food are then sent to relatives and neighbors, who reciprocate with their own offerings. The following morning is an occasion for the head of the house to visit the graveyard to pray at the graves of his dead relatives.

7 ● RITES OF PASSAGE

The birth of a son is of utmost importance for a Brahui. A daughter is seen as little more than a gift to one's neighbor. When a son is born, the father announces it to the community by firing gunshots in the air. Various rituals are followed to protect the mother and child from the attention of witches and *jinn* (evil spirits). Sheep are killed (two for a son and one for a daughter) and a feast held for relatives, friends, and neighbors. The child is then named, sometimes after a worthy ancestor. The head-shaving ritual *(sar-kuti)* is performed by the time the child is two years old, often at the shrine of a favored saint. A male child may undergo circumcision *(sunnat)* within six months, though the cost associated with the celebrations cause many to postpone it until as late as the age of ten or twelve.

No particular ceremonies accompany the male reaching puberty. An unusual rite is reported to be followed when a girl begins to menstruate for the first time. At sunset, the mother arranges three stones in a triangular pattern on the ground and has her daughter leap over them three times. It is thought that this will ensure that the girl's periods during the rest of her life will last no more than three days. If a girl were not married as a child, she would be soon after puberty.

At death, word is sent to relatives and friends, who gather for the funeral. A shroud is sent for from outside the house, and when the *mullah* (Muslim priest) arrives, the body is carried to a place of washing. It is washed by the mullah and near kinsmen (or the mullah's wife and female relatives, in the case of a woman), then wrapped in the shroud. The body is taken in procession to the graveyard, with the mourners reciting the *kalima,* the profession of faith. At the graveside, the mullah offers the prayer for the dead, and the body is given its burial. Other rituals include the singing of dirges *(moda),* and a death feast *(varagh).* Another feast is held on the first anniversary of the death.

8 ● RELATIONSHIPS

On meeting, the Brahui stop, shake hands, and embrace each other. The encounter continues with inquiries after each other's health and then proceeds to an exchange of news *(hal)* concerning family, friends, cattle, and other matters of interest. Brahui are known for their hospitality to their guests.

9 ● LIVING CONDITIONS

Brahui settlements essentially reflect the economic activities of their inhabitants. Pastoral nomadism was the traditional occupation of many Brahui: nomadic herders lived in tents and temporary camps, migrating with their herds in search of pasture. Pastoralism has declined in importance in recent years. Many Brahui have adopted a way of life based on a seasonal migration to differing elevations. Villages in the highlands suitable for cultivation are occupied for nine-month growing season. During the winter months, these Brahui drive their herds to the lowlands where they live in tent camps.

10 ● FAMILY LIFE

The Brahui are organized into tribes, each of which has a hereditary chief *(sadar)*. The tribes are loosely structured units based on patrilineal descent (tracing descent through the father) and political allegiance. This clan system allows for Baluchi and Pathan groups to be incorporated into the Brahui tribal units. Some of the largest Brahui tribes are the Mengals, Zahris, and Muhammad Hosanis.

The favored marriage among the Brahui is with the father's brother's daughter. Marriages are arranged, although the wishes of the couple are taken into consideration. In the past, child marriage was common, though this practice is now banned under Pakistani law. The betrothal and marriage ceremonies are important events in the life of both family and tribe. Disputes within tribes are usually settled at the time of marriages. A bride price *(lab)* is paid by the groom's family. Although Muslim law allows polygyny (multiple wives), economic realities mean most Brahui marriages are monogamous. Family structure tends to reflect economic systems. The nuclear family predominates among nomadic Brahui, while extended families are common among village inhabitants. Divorce, though simple, is rare. In the past, adultery was punishable by death, although such practices are forbidden by Pakistani law. Widow remarriage is accepted.

11 ● CLOTHING

A young boy is given his first trousers at about three years of age, and thereafter wears clothes similar to those of adult males—the *kurti* (long shirt), worn over the *salwar,* the loose, baggy trousers found throughout the area. For men, a turban *(pag)* completes the outfit.

Women wear a long shift over trousers, although among Brahui nomads women wear skirts rather than trousers. Among the Brahui of the Jhalawan region, women's shifts are typically black in color. Women's clothes are embroidered with various patterns and designs in colored thread. Women's ornaments include finger rings *(challav),* nose rings *(vat),* and earrings *(panara).* Brahui settled in the Sind region tend to dress like the Sindhi population.

12 ● FOOD

The settled Brahui cultivate wheat and millet, which are ground into flour and baked into unleavened breads. Rice is also eaten, but usually only on special occasions. Mutton and goat are important in the diet of the Brahui. The more-affluent farmers in lowland areas may raise cattle. As is common throughout South Asia, food is eaten with one's hands, and often from a communal platter. Milk is drunk and also made into curds, *ghi* (clarified butter), buttermilk, and butter. Dates, wild fruits, and vegetables are also part of the Brahui diet. Tea is drunk at meals and is also taken as part of various social ceremonies.

13 ● EDUCATION

Levels of literacy (the ability to read and write) among the Brahui are extremely low. The 1972 census for the Kalat Division of Baluchistan Province recorded an overall literacy rate of only 6 percent in the population over ten years of age. The Brahui live in areas of Pakistan where there is no access to formal schooling, and even where schools do exist, attendance is low. In settled areas such as the Sind region where Brahui children are more likely to attend school, they are taught in the local language rather than in Brahui.

14 ● CULTURAL HERITAGE

The Brahuis have an oral tradition of folk songs and heroic poems. These are sung by a class of professional minstrels and musicians called Dombs, who are attached to every Brahui community. Musical instruments include the *rabab* (an Afghan stringed instrument plucked with a piece of wood), the *siroz* (a stringed instrument played with a bow), and the *punzik* (a reed instrument). These have replaced the *dambura* (a three-stringed instrument played with the fingers) which is found in the more isolated areas. Dancing is an important feature at events such as weddings and funerals.

15 ● EMPLOYMENT

Historically, the Brahui were pastoral nomads, migrating with their herds of sheep, goats, and cattle from the upland plateaus to the low-lying plains. Today, however, many Brahui have abandoned their pastoral activities in favor of transhumant (seasonal migration between lower and higher elevations) or settled agriculture. In the Kacchi lowlands, river and canal irrigation support cultivation, but settlements in other areas of the Brahui region depend on *qanat* irrigation, a system of tunnels dug between shafts to carry water.

16 ● SPORTS

Horse-racing and target-shooting were traditional sports popular among the more affluent sections of the Brahui community.

17 ● RECREATION

In the past, the Brahui had to depend on their own resources for entertainment and recreation. They found this in their family celebrations, their traditions of folk song and dance, and in the festivities accompanying religious observances. This is still true for nomadic Brahui today. Those settled in Karachi or villages on the plains have access to more modern forms of recreation.

18 ● CRAFTS AND HOBBIES

Brahui women embroider their garments with colorful designs. Tents and rugs are made from sheep's wool or goats' hair.

19 ● SOCIAL PROBLEMS

The Brahui tribes inhabit some of the harshest, most-isolated, and least-productive environments in Pakistan. This is reflected in the relative inefficiency of traditional economic systems and the generally low standards of living of the community. Belated government efforts to bring development to the region have done little for the welfare of the Brahui, who are essentially nomadic and rural in character. The Brahui are one of the many tribal minorities in a country dominated by ethnic elites such as the Punjabis and Sindhis. The lack of a written literature (what there is dates only from the 1960s) has hindered the development of a tribal consciousness, and matters are made worse by the declining numbers of people speaking Brahui. The Brahui appear to be rapidly assimilating with the surrounding Baluchi populations.

20 ● BIBLIOGRAPHY

Bray, Denys. *The Life-History of a Brahui.* Karachi, Pakistan: Royal Book Company, 1977 [1913].

Rooman, Anwar. *The Brahuis of Quetta-Kalat Region.* Memoir No. 3. Karachi, Pakistan: Pakistan Historical Society, 1960.

Swidler, Nina. "Brahui." In *Muslim Peoples: A World Ethnographic Survey,* edited by Richard Weekes. Westport, Conn.: Greenwood Press, 1984.

WEBSITES

Embassy of Pakistan, Washington, D.C. [Online] Available http://www.pakistan-embassy.com/, 1998.

Interknowledge Corp. [Online] Available http://www.interknowledge.com/pakistan/, 1998.

World Travel Guide, Pakistan. [Online] Available http://www.wtgonline.com/country/pk/gen.html, 1998.

Punjabis

PRONUNCIATION: puhn-JAHB-eez
LOCATION: Pakistan (Punjab province); India (Punjab state)
LANGUAGE: Punjabi
RELIGION: Hinduism; Islam; Buddhism; Sikhism; Christianity

1 ● INTRODUCTION

Punjabis derive their name from a geographical, historical, and cultural region located in the northwest of the Indian subcontinent. *Punjab* comes from the Persian words *panj* (five) and *ab* (river) and means "Land of the Five Rivers." It was the name used for the lands to the east of the Indus River that are drained by its five tributaries (the Jhelum, Chenab, Ravi, Beas, and Sutlej). Culturally, the Punjab extends beyond this area to include parts of the North West Frontier Province of Pakistan, the foothills of the Himalayas, and the northern fringes of the Thar (Great Indian) Desert in Rajasthan.

The Punjab is an ancient center of culture in the Indian subcontinent. It lay within the bounds of the Harappan civilization, the sophisticated urban (city-based) culture that flowered in the Indus Valley during the third millennium BC. Harappa, one of the two great cities of this civilization, was located on the Ravi River in what is now Pakistan's Punjab Province. The Punjab has also been one of the great crossroads of southern Asian history. Nomadic tribes speaking Indo-European languages descended from the mountain passes in the northwest to settle on the plains of the Punjab around 1700 BC. After then, Persians, Greeks, Huns, Turks, and Afghans were among the many peoples that entered the Indian subcontinent through the northwestern passes and left their mark on the region. Punjabis, who are basically of Aryan, or Indo-European ancestry, are the modern descendants of the mixture of peoples that passed through the region.

At times in the past, the Punjab and its population have enjoyed a special political identity as well as a cultural identity. During the sixteenth and seventeenth centuries AD, the region was administered as a province of the Mogul Empire. As recently as the nineteenth century, much of the area was united under the Sikh nation of Ranjit Singh. Britain administered the Punjab as a province of its Indian Empire. However, in the redrawing of political boundaries in 1947, the Punjab was divided between India and Pakistan. In spite of their common cultural heritage, Punjabis are now either Indians or Pakistanis by nationality.

2 ● LOCATION

Punjabis number about 88 million people. About 68 million live in the Pakistan Punjab, and just over 20 million live in the Indian state of Punjab. Punjab Province in Pakistan includes just about all of the Punjab (West Punjab) that was assigned to Pakistan in 1947. The Indian Punjab State (East Punjab) extended from the international border with Pakistan to Delhi. In 1966, however, agitation for a Punjabi-speaking state led to the creation of the present Punjab State. The location of India's Punjab State along the border with Pakistan and only some 25 miles (40 kilometers) from the city of Lahore, gives it great military significance.

The Punjab is an agricultural region. Punjabis, whether in India or in Pakistan, share the agrarian (farming) social structure based on *caste* that is found throughout southern Asia. The *Jats*, who are mainly landowners *(zamindars)* and cultivators, are the largest caste in the Punjab. Other agricultural castes include Rajputs, Arains, Awans, and Gujars. Among the lower-ranked service and artisan castes are the Lohars, Tarkhans, and Chamars.

The homeland of the Punjabis lies on the plains of the upper Indus Valley, covering an area of roughly 104,200 square miles (270,000 square kilometers). It stretches from the Salt Ranges in the north to the fringes of the Thar Desert in the southeast.

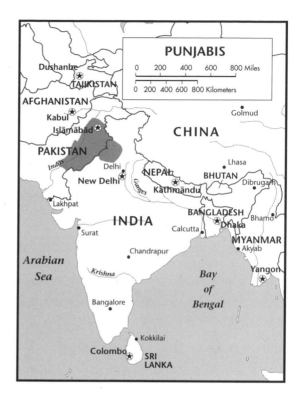

The western margins lie along the base of Pakistan's Sulaiman Range. The Shiwaliks, the outer foothills of the Himalayas, define the Punjab's eastern boundary. The region is a vast plain, drained by the Indus River and its tributaries. In the northeast, the plain lies at just under 1,000 feet (about 300 meters) above sea level, but it declines to under 250 feet (75 meters) in elevation along the Indus River in the south. The hills bordering the plain are higher than 4,000 feet (1,200 meters) in the Shiwaliks and about 5,000 feet (1,500 meters) in the Salt Range.

The Punjab has a subtropical climate, with hot summers and cool winters. The average temperature for June is 93°F (34°C), with daily maximums often rising much higher. The mean maximum temperature for

Lahore in June is 115°F (46°C). Dust storms are common in the hot weather. The average January temperature is 55°F (13°C), although minimums drop close to freezing and hard frosts are common. Rainfall varies from about 49 inches (125 centimeters) in the hills in the northeast to no more than 8 inches (20 centimeters) in the dry southwest. Rain falls mainly in the summer months. However, weather systems from the northwest bring valuable amounts of rain in the winter.

3 ● LANGUAGE

Punjabi is the name of the language, as well as the people, of the Punjab region. In Pakistan, Punjabi is written using the Persian-Arabic script, which was introduced to the region during the Muslim conquests. Punjabis in India use a different script. Punjabi is spoken by two-thirds of the population of Pakistan. In India, Punjabi is the mother tongue of just under 3 percent of the population. Punjabi was raised to the status of one of India's official languages in 1966.

4 ● FOLKLORE

Punjabis have a rich mythology and folklore that includes folktales, songs, ballads, epics, and romances. Much of the folk tradition is oral, passed on through the generations by traditional peasant singers, mystics, and wandering gypsies. Many folk tales are sung to the accompaniment of music. There are songs for birth and marriage, love songs, songs of war, and songs glorifying legendary heroes of the past. The *Mahiya* is a romantic song of the Punjab. *Sehra Bandi* is a marriage song, and *Mehndi* songs are sung when henna (a red dye) is being applied to the bride and groom in preparation for marriage.

Heera Ranjha and *Mirza Sahiban* are folk romances known in every Punjab household. Wandering Sufi (Islamic mysticism) clergymen are well known in the Punjab for their poetry and music. They contributed a verse form that became special in Punjabi literature. The mixture of Hindu, Sikh, and Muslim themes in Punjabi folklore mirrors the presence of these religious traditions in the region.

5 ● RELIGION

The religious variety of the Punjabis reflects the Punjab's long and varied history. Early Hinduism took shape in the Punjab, Buddhism flowered in the region, and followers of Islam held political power in the area for nearly six centuries. Sikhism had its origins in the Punjab, where Sikh states survived until the middle of the twentieth century. The British annexed the Punjab in the nineteenth century and introduced Christianity to the region. Thus Hinduism, Islam, Buddhism, Sikhism, and Christianity are all represented among the Punjabi peoples.

When India and Pakistan were separated in 1947, Hindus and Sikhs fled Pakistan for India, while Muslims sought a home in Pakistan. Armed conflict at that time among Hindus, Sikhs, and Muslims left as many as one million people dead. Today, Punjab Province in Pakistan is 97 percent Muslim and 2 percent Christian, with small numbers of Hindus and other groups. Sikhs account for 61 percent of the people in India's Punjab State, while 37 percent are Hindu, and 1 percent each are Muslim and Christian.

Small numbers of Buddhists, Jains, and other groups are also present.

6 ● MAJOR HOLIDAYS

Festivals are events shared by the entire community, no matter what their religion. Many are seasonal or agricultural festivals. Thus *Basant*, when the mustard fields are yellow, marks the end of the cold weather; Punjabis celebrate by wearing yellow clothes, going kite-flying, and feasting. *Holi* is the great spring festival of India and a time for much gaiety and for visiting friends and relatives. *Vaisakh (Baisakh)*, in April, marks the beginning of the Hindu New Year and also is of special importance for Sikhs, since it commemorates the founding of the Sikh Khalsa. *Tij* marks the beginning of the rainy season and is a time when girls set up swings, wear new clothes, and sing special songs for the occasion. *Dasahara, Diwali*, and other festivals of the Hindu calendar are celebrated with much enthusiasm. The Sikhs have *gurpurbs*, holidays associated with the lives of the gurus (holy men), while Muslims commemorate the festivals of *Muharram, Eid al-Fitr*, and *Bakr-Id*.

7 ● RITES OF PASSAGE

Punjabi rites of passage follow the customs of the community to which a person belongs. Among Muslims, the *mullah* or priest will visit a house within three days of the birth of a boy to recite holy words, including the Call to Prayer, in the baby's ear. The child is named in consultation with the mullah. Males undergo circumcision (*sunnat*) at any time before age twelve.

Sikh birth rituals are simpler. The child is taken to the temple for offerings, prayers, and the naming ceremony. The *Adi Granth*, the sacred book of the Sikhs, is opened at random, and the parents choose a name that begins with the first letter of the first word on the left-hand page. An important ceremony for the Sikhs is the baptism, or initiation into the Sikh religion. This usually takes place in the late teens.

For Hindus, it is important that a child be born at an auspicious (lucky) time. A Brahman priest is consulted. If he judges the time of birth to be unfavorable, special ceremonies are held to prevent any harmful effects. In the past, a mother had to stay away from other people for forty days after giving birth, but this custom is disappearing. The ritual shaving of the child's head is usually performed during the first five years of the child's life.

At death, Muslims wrap the body in white cloth before taking it to the mosque. White is the color of mourning throughout southern Asia. At the mosque, the mullah reads the holy words over the body, which is then buried in the graveyard. Sometimes a stone slab is placed on the grave, and each of the mourners places a handful of earth on the grave. This symbolizes breaking ties with the person who died. The mullah prays for the dead for three days. Hindus and Sikhs cremate their dead. On the fourth day after cremation, Hindus collect the ashes and charred remains of bones from the funeral pyre and place them in the sacred Ganges River, at the city of Haridwar if possible. Sikhs usually place the ashes at Kiratpur Sahib, on the River Sutlej.

8 ● RELATIONSHIPS

Forms of address and greetings vary according to the situation and social context. In rural areas, a man is usually referred to as *Bhaiji* or *Bhai Sahib* (Brother) and a woman, as *Bibiji* (Mistress) or *Bhainji* (Sister). Sikhs are addressed as *Sardar* (Mr.) or *Sardarni* (Mrs.). When they meet, Sikhs put their hands together in front of them, with their palms touching, and say, *Sat Sri Akal* (God is Truth). Hindus accompany the same gesture with the word *Namaste* (Greetings). The common Muslim greeting is *Salaam* (Peace or Greetings) or *Salaam Alaikum* (Peace be with you).

9 ● LIVING CONDITIONS

Punjabi villages are compact settlements, with houses clustered around a mosque, temple, or *gurdwara* (Sikh temple). The houses on the outside edge of the village are built to look like a walled settlement with few openings. The main entrance to a village is through an arched gateway called a *darwaza* (door or gate), which is also a meeting place for the village. Houses are built close together, often sharing walls. Rooms are built around a central courtyard where animals are tethered and farming implements are stored. Most villages are made up of people in the variety of roles needed in a farming economy—landowners, cultivators, artisans, and service castes.

Households usually have comfortable furniture, ceiling fans for the hot summers, and conveniences such as telephones, radios, televisions, and even refrigerators. Many farmers have tractors. Scooters and motorcycles are common, and the wealthier families have cars and jeeps. Punjabis have one of the highest standards of living in Pakistan. However, some areas lack the transportation infrastructure and some other developments seen in the rest of the province.

10 ● FAMILY LIFE

Caste or *jati*, is the most important social grouping among Punjabis. It defines social relations, possible marriage partners, and often jobs as well. Castes exist even among Muslims and Sikhs, whose religions condemn the caste system. Castes are divided into numerous *gots*, or clans. One cannot marry within the gots of one's four grandparents.

Among Muslims, castes are known as *qaums* or *zats*, but at the village level it is the *biradari*, or patrilineage (descent from the father's side), that is the more significant social unit. All men who can trace their descent back to a common male ancestor belong to the same biradari, and all members of the biradari are regarded as family. Members of a biradari often act united in village business and disputes, for they share a sense of collective honor and identity.

The family is the basic unit of Punjabi society. The joint family is most common; sons and their wives and children, plus any unmarried adults, live in the household of their parents. The men oversee the agricultural or business activities of the family. Women, directed by the mother-in-law or senior wife, see to the running of the household, the preparation of foods, and the care and raising of children. Among peasant farmers, women as well as men do the agricultural work. Both men and women in the

Cory Langley

Both women and men among the peasant classes do agricultural or other manual labor for hire.

laboring castes work for hire, as agricultural workers or at other manual labor.

Women are expected to marry and have children as their main role in Punjabi society. Marriages are arranged by the parents of the boy and girl, and each community follows its own marriage rituals and customs. Among Muslims, for example, the best match is thought to be marriage between first cousins. The Muslim marriage ceremony is called the *Nikah*. The girl is given a dowry, which she keeps as her property.

Hindu Punjabis seek marriage partners within their own caste but outside the specific clans that are closed to them (the clans of one's grandparents). The dowry is an important factor in negotiations for a Hindu marriage. Hindu rituals include the traditional journey of the *barat* (wedding party) to the bride's house, the draping of garlands of flowers on the bride and groom, and the ritual walk around the sacred fire.

Sikhs, on the other hand, do not give or take dowries, and they solemnize their marriages before the *Granth*, their sacred book. In all communities, however, residence is patrilocal—the new wife moves into the home of her husband's family.

Different Punjabi communities have different customs regarding divorce and remarriage. Although Islam makes provisions for a man to divorce his wife, in rural society divorce is strongly opposed, and there are strong social pressures against it. Muslims do not approve of widows who remarry. Sikhs do not permit divorce, but do allow widows to remarry. Widow remarriage is not common among Hindus, but the Jats permit a widow to marry the younger brother of her husband. Divorce is not customary among Hindus, but there are ways in which marriages can be brought to an end informally.

11 ● CLOTHING

The standard clothing for men in the rural Punjab is the *kurta, tahmat,* or *pyjama,* and turban. The *kurta* is a long shirt or tunic that hangs down to the thighs. The *tahmat* is a long piece of cloth that is wrapped around the waist and legs like a kilt. The *pyjama,* from which the English word "pajamas" is derived, is a pair of loose-fitting trousers. Turbans are worn in various styles in different areas and by different groups. Among farmers, the turban is a relatively short piece of cloth, about three feet (one meter) in length, and is wrapped loosely around the head. The formal Punjabi turban, worn by men of social standing, is much longer, with one end starched and sticking up like a fan. The Sikhs favor the peaked turban. Locally made leather shoes complete the outfit. During the winter a sweater, woolen jacket, or blanket is added. Men wear rings, and sometimes, earrings.

Women wear the *salwar* (baggy pants drawn in at the ankles) and *kamiz* (tunic), along with the *dupatta* (scarf). Sometimes a *ghaghra,* a long skirt dating back to Mogul times, replaces the *salwar.* Ornaments decorate the hair, rings or jewels are worn in the nose, and earrings, necklaces, and bangles are popular.

In cities and towns, traditional clothes are giving way to modern styles. Men wear jackets, suits, and ties. Women wear *saris* (a long cloth wrapped around the body and draped over the shoulder), dresses, skirts, and even jeans.

12 ● FOOD

The basic diet of Punjabis consists of cereals (wheat, corn, or millet), vegetables, legumes (such as lentils), and milk products. Goat meat is eaten, but mainly on special occasions, such as weddings. A typical meal consists of flat bread *(roti)* made from wheat, a cup of lentils or other legumes *(dal),* and buttermilk or hot tea. In winter, the bread is made of corn, and vegetables such as mustard greens *(sag)* may be added.

Dal and sag are prepared in a similar way. Sliced or chopped garlic and onion are fried in butter, along with chili peppers, cloves, black pepper, and ginger. The vegetables or legumes are added and the food is cooked, sometimes for several hours, until it is tender.

No utensils are used; food is eaten with the fingers. People use only the right hand, taking a piece of roti to scoop up the lentils or the vegetable. A recipe for roti accompanies this article.

Tea is drunk in generous quantities at all times of the day. It is made with half water and half milk and sweetened with three or four teaspoonfuls of sugar. Fish, chicken, and eggs are rarely eaten.

Recipe

ROTI

Ingredients

4 cups flour
4 teaspoons baking powder
1 teaspoon salt
1½ cups water

Directions

1. Combine flour, baking powder, and salt in a large bowl.
2. Add water ¼ cup at a time, mixing well after each addition. A soft dough will form.
3. Knead well for 10 minutes on a clean surface that has been lightly dusted with flour.
4. Form dough into a large ball. Cover with a clean, dampened dishcloth and allow dough to rest for 30 minutes.
5. Divide dough into quarters, and shape each quarter into a ball.
6. Roll ball into a flat circle, about ½ inch thick.
7. Place dough circles, one at a time, into a frying pan. Cook over medium heat until dough begins to brown slighty and puffs up.
8. Turn to cook other side until browned.
9. Repeat with remaining dough circles.

Serve with salad, soup, or dip. Break off pieces of roti to scoop up food, and eat.

13 ● EDUCATION

Punjabis have made great strides in education in recent years, although there is still room for improvement. According to 1981 census returns from Pakistan, some 45 percent of the population under ten years of age attended school, but less than 20 percent completed high school and only 2.8 percent earned general university degrees. The literacy rate (the proportion of people who can read and write) in the population over ten years of age in the Pakistan Punjab was 27 percent. However, this varied from 55 percent among men in the cities and towns to only 9.4 percent among rural women. Comparative 1981 figures for the Indian Punjab are 41 percent overall—61 percent for city men, and 28 percent for rural women. The overall literacy rate in the Indian Punjab jumped to 59 percent in 1991.

Both Indian and Pakistani Punjabs have a tradition of education, with many institutions of higher learning. The University of the Punjab and the University of Engineering and Technology are located in Lahore, Pakistan. Among the institutions of higher learning in the Indian Punjab are Punjab University in Chandigarh, Punjabi University in Patiala, and Guru Nanak University in Amritsar.

14 ● CULTURAL HERITAGE

Alhough Punjabis never developed any classical traditions of dance, they are known for several forms of folk dance. These are usually performed at religious fairs and festivals or at harvest time. The most famous is the *Bhangra*, which is performed to celebrate a marriage, the birth of a son, or a similar event. Young men of the village, dressed in brightly colored clothes, gather in a circle around a drummer who beats out the rhythm of the dance. Moving around the drummer, slowly at first, then faster as the tempo of the drum quickens, they dance and sing with great abandon. The *Giddha* is a dance for women and girls. *Jhumar, Sammi, Luddi*, and the sword dance are all popular folk dances of the Punjab.

In addition to the music associated with folk culture (songs, epics, and dances), Punjabis share in the traditions of Sikh sacred music and Sufi mysticism. The religious compositions of the Sikh gurus combine aspects of classical Indian music with popular Punjabi folk tunes. The contributions of wandering Muslim mystics, along with the sacred songs of the Hindus and Sikhs, became part of the Punjabi regional musical tradition. More formal Muslim music forms, such as the *qawwali* and *ghazal*, continue to be popular in the region today.

The folk epics and romances, Sikh sacred literature, and poetic compositions of the Sufis (Islamic mystics) are all part of a literary tradition that continues today. Modern Punjabi literature has its beginnings in the mid-nineteenth century, with writers such as Charan Singh and Vir Singh. Noted modern writers include Amrita Pritam, Khushwant Singh, Harcharan Singh, and I. C. Nanda.

15 ● EMPLOYMENT

Most Punjabis are farmers. With its development as a center of modern commercial agriculture, the Punjab (both Indian and Pakistani) is one of the most important agricultural regions of southern Asia. The Punjabi also have a proud military tradition that extends back several centuries and continues in modern times. Between the two world wars (between 1918 and 1939), Sikhs made up 20 percent of the British Indian Army, although they accounted for only 2 percent of the Indian population. This tradition of military service continues today, with Sikhs making up an unusually high proportion of the Indian armed forces. In Pakistan, too, Punjabis—especially Jats and Rajputs—have a distinguished tradition of military service.

16 ● SPORTS

Among games popular with children are hide-and-seek, kite flying, and Indian cricket *(gulli-danda),* a stick-game played by boys. *Kabaddi,* a team wrestling game, is played by boys and men. Wrestling, partridge fighting, cock fighting, pigeon flying, and gambling are favorite pastimes of Punjabi men.

Modern sports such as soccer, cricket, and field hockey are widely played and watched. Punjab State in India has a government department that organizes and promotes sports and athletics, and the National Institute of Sports is located at Patiala. Punjabis are well represented in Indian national sports teams. In Pakistan, too, Punjabis have a strong presence on the country's national sports teams.

17 ● RECREATION

In the past, Punjabis found much of their entertainment and recreation in their traditional sports and games, in religious fairs and festivals, and in their rich tradition of folklore and folk culture. They had their songs, romantic epics, folk dances, and castes of traveling entertainers. This has changed in recent times with the increasing popularity of radio, television, and movies. Soundtrack music is popular, and the Indian Punjab even has a small film industry pro-

Cory Langley

The standard clothing for men in the Punjab includes the turban. Turbans are worn in various styles in different areas and by different groups.

ducing feature films in the Punjabi language.

18 ● CRAFTS AND HOBBIES

Modern folk arts in the Punjab represent traditions that may extend back several thousand years. Village potters make clay toys that look very similar to figurines recovered from archaeological sites. Peasant women follow a tradition of painting intricate designs on the mud walls of their houses for festival days. The Punjab is noted for its elaborate embroidery work. Local crafts include woodwork, metalwork, and basketry.

19 ● SOCIAL PROBLEMS

In spite of overall prosperity, problems exist among the Punjabis, ranging from alcoholism in rural areas to unemployment in the cities. Illiteracy (the inability to read and write) is still high in villages, especially among women. Punjabis who have migrated from rural areas to cities are cut off from the ties and support system of their families and their village communities. If they do find work, it tends to be in low-level office jobs.

In the 1980s and 1990s, the Punjab has experienced conflict between Sikh extremists and the central government.

20 ● BIBLIOGRAPHY

Ahmad, Sagir. *Class and Power in a Punjabi Village.* New York: Monthly Review Press, 1977.

Aryan, K. C. *The Cultural Heritage of Punjab: 3000 BC to 1947 AD.* New Delhi, India: Rekha Prakashan, 1983.

Bajwa, Ranjeet Singh. *Semiotics of Birth Ceremonies in Punjab.* New Delhi, India: Bahri Publications, 1991.

Fox, Richard Gabriel. *Lions of the Punjab: Culture in the Making.* Berkeley: University of California Press, 1985.

Singh, Mohinder. *History and Culture of Panjab.* New Delhi, India: Atlantic Publishers and Distributors, 1988.

WEBSITES

Embassy of Pakistan, Washington, D.C. [Online] Available http://www.pakistan-embassy.com/, 1998.

Interknowledge Corp. [Online] Available http://www.interknowledge.com/pakistan/, 1998.

World Travel Guide, Pakistan. [Online] Available http://www.wtgonline.com/country/pk/gen.html, 1998.

Panama

■ **PANAMANIANS** 57
■ **CUNAS** 64

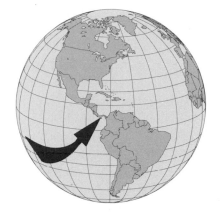

The people of Panama arc called Panamanians. About 70 percent of the population is mestizo (mixed white and Amerindian or native) or mulatto (mixed white and black); 14 percent are black; a little more than 10 percent are white (mostly Europeans); and 5 to 8 percent are Amerindian (native people).

Panamanians

PRONUNCIATION: pah-nuh-MAY-nee-uhns
LOCATION: Panama
POPULATION: 2.6 million
LANGUAGE: Spanish; English; native Indian languages
RELIGION: Roman Catholicism; Protestantism; Islam; small numbers of Jews, Hindus, and Baha'is

1 ● INTRODUCTION

Panama first made an impact on world history in 1513 when Spanish explorer Vasco Nuñez de Balboa crossed the isthmus (narrow strip of land) of Panama and discovered the Pacific Ocean. Geography made Panama strategically valuable to the Spanish Empire, particularly for shipping gold and silver from Peru. Panama declared its independence from Spain in 1821 and became part of Colombia.

The discovery of gold in California in 1848 changed Panama forever. Hundreds of thousands of fortune seekers from Europe and the eastern United States travelled through Panama. For them, the isthmus crossing was the fastest route to the gold fields. A rail line was built to speed them on their way. In the 1880s the French tried, but failed, to build a canal across the isthmus. When Colombia refused to allow the United States to take over the project, Panama declared its independence from Colombia, with U.S. backing, in 1903. The Panama Canal was completed in 1914. The United States was granted "in perpetuity" (continuously) a 5-mile (8-kilometer) strip on either side of the canal.

Before long, Panamanians were demanding a revision of the treaty that, in effect, cut their nation in two. A settlement was finally reached in 1977. The United States agreed to return the Canal Zone to Panama in 1979.

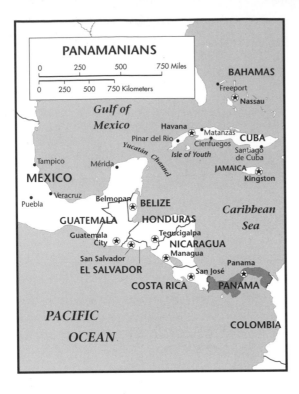

It was also agreed that the canal itself would be returned to Panama at the beginning of the year 2000.

Relations between Panama and the United States plummeted again in 1988. Panama's dictator, General Manuel Antonio Noriega, was charged in U.S. courts with drug traficking. In December 1989, 23,000 U.S. troops landed in Panama City, seizing Noriega and installing a new government.

2 ● LOCATION

Panama is a little smaller than the state of South Carolina. It occupies the narrowest part of the American mainland separating the Atlantic and Pacific oceans. Heavily forested mountain ranges form the spine of the

country. The Panama Canal runs through a gap in these mountains. There are also more than 1,600 islands off the shores of the mainland. The climate is tropical except at mountain elevations, and rainfall is heavy.

Panama has a varied racial composition. More than two-thirds of its people are *mestizo* (of mixed blood), including Indian, European, and African ancestry. A smaller number are white or black. The blacks are descendants of migrants from the British West Indies who helped construct the railway and canal, and who worked on banana plantations. The Indian population is mostly Guaymí, Cuna, and Chocó. There are also significant numbers of Chinese, Asian Indians (from India), and Arabs.

3 ● LANGUAGE

Spanish is the official and almost universally spoken language. Panamanian Spanish is spoken very rapidly in a distinctive accent. It includes a great deal of slang and many distinctive words. English is the first language of some of the Blacks who are descended from West Indians. It is widely spoken and understood in the world of business. It is also the required second language in schools. The Indian groups still speak their own languages, as do immigrants from many parts of the world.

4 ● FOLKLORE

Many peasants believe that on All Souls' Day (November 2), those who died during the previous year are summoned before God and the Devil for judgment. There are two types of *curanderos* (folk healers). One is the herbal-medicine practitioner, who also may cure by praying and making the sign of

Cory Langley

Panama City boasts modern high-rise apartment buildings.

the cross over the patient. The other is the *hechicero* (sorcerer), who uses secret potions. The witch *(bruja)* is an evil old woman possessed by the Devil. Witches can change themselves into animals, especially deer, but only some witches can fly. To avoid harm from witches, one should turn a piece of clothing inside out. Also to be feared are black dogs and black cats and the *chivato,* an evil animal spirit.

There are numerous other spirits, including *duendos* (fairies). A red shirt on a newborn wards off evil, as does a necklace of the teeth of jaguars or crocodiles. Infants gain protection by being bathed in water in which certain leaves and plants have been

steeped. Panamanian folklore is perhaps best expressed in the nation's many festivals, during which folk dramas and dances are performed.

5 ● RELIGION

More than 80 percent of Panamanians are Roman Catholic. Protestants and Muslims (followers of Islam) account for about another 5 percent each. Some religious practice is a required for complete integration into Panama society. As elsewhere in Latin America, women are the mainstay of the church. In addition to churches and mosques, Panama City has a Jewish synagogue and Hindu and Baha'i temples.

6 ● MAJOR HOLIDAYS

Carnival is celebrated on the four days before Ash Wednesday (in February). In Panama City, the festivities include music, dancing, costumes, and a big Mardi Gras parade. Carnival comes to an end at dawn on Ash Wednesday with a mock ceremony called the "Burial of the Sardine." Holy Week (late March or early April) also is marked by costumed dances and drama, and by Good Friday processions.

Portobelo's Festival of the Black Christ, on October 21, draws pilgrims to a life-size statue said to have miraculous powers. Similar is the pilgrimage to the shrine of Jesus of Nazareth in Atalaya on the first Sunday of Lent. Each town has a yearly fiesta in honor of its patron saint.

The chief secular holidays are November 3 and 28, which commemorate Panama's independence from Colombia and Spain, respectively. Mother's Day, which falls on the day of the Immaculate Conception (December 8) in the church calendar, is also a national holiday, reverently observed.

7 ● RITES OF PASSAGE

Baptism is absolutely necessary for Panama's Catholics. It is believed that fairies, witches, or the Devil can carry away a child who is not baptized. First Communion is generally observed only by the middle and upper classes. A country boy receives his first machete (swordlike knife) at the age of seven or eight. This is an early symbol of *machismo,* the spirit of male assertiveness common to Hispanic America.

The street is the playground for lower-class urban youth, who also may join a

Cory Langley

A girl's fifteenth birthday is an important event. In families that can afford it, the daughter is honored with a debut party introducing her to society, featuring a reception and dance.

padilla (gang). Girls are more closely supervised. A girl's fifteenth birthday is an important event. In well-off families it is marked by a debut with a reception and dance.

8 ● RELATIONSHIPS

Like other Hispanic Americans, Panamanians greet friends and relatives more demonstratively than is the custom in the United States. Common among men is the *abrazo* (embrace), particularly if they have not seen each other for some time. Acquaintances will shake hands both on meeting and departing. Women often embrace and kiss on one or both cheeks. People are likely to stand closer to one another in conversation than is common in North America.

9 ● LIVING CONDITIONS

The basic peasant dwelling in Panama is the *rancho* or *quincha*. It is a hut supported by poles, with walls of palm fronds, cane, clay, or boards. The thatched roof is of palm fronds or grass. Neighbors gather to help build these houses. Houses in town are often of cement block, with a tile roof. The urban poor usually live in overcrowded, decaying two-story frame houses with tin roofs. Migrants from rural areas often settle in squatter communities (on lands or in housing to which they have no rights and for which they pay no rent) on the urban outskirts. There are high-rise apartment buildings in Panama City.

Panama, Costa Rica, and Belize are more prosperous than the other Central American countries. In the early 1990s, 80 percent or more of the people had access to health care services, safe water, and adequate sanitation.

10 ● FAMILY LIFE

The nuclear family of parents and children is central in Panama. The average household has three children. Wider kinship relations are essential, however. The extended family provides economic support in a society where the larger community cannot be counted on for help. Married children may visit their parents every day, and grandparents, uncles and aunts, and cousins routinely gather together on Sundays, holidays, and birthdays. Godparents are additional support for families. They are expected to take a lifelong interest in their godchild's welfare, as well as to provide gifts on special occasions.

Church and civil marriage are both legal. Formal marriage is not the rule outside the middle and upper classes. Most new couples merely take up residence in a new home. Well over half of Panama's children are born from unstable, short-term unions. There is little social disapproval of illegitimacy. Many households are headed by a woman. In contrast to men, women are expected to be gentle, long-suffering, forgiving and, above all, devoted to their children.

11 ● CLOTHING

Peasant clothing has traditionally consisted of simple cotton garments, homemade sandals, and handwoven straw hats. More recently rural folk have begun to adopt urban dress, much like the summertime clothing in North America.

By contrast, there is a wealth of costume displayed at the nation's many fiestas. The spectacular *pollera,* the national costume for women, is perhaps the most beautiful traditional apparel in Latin America. It consists of an embroidered two-piece dress with an off-the-shoulder neckline, handmade lace and petticoats, gold chains around the neck, flowers and jewelry in the hair, and satin slippers. The far simpler and more rustic men's *montuno* is of Indian origin. It is made of unbleached muslin embroidered in bright colors, and consists of a long fringed shirt, short trousers, sandals, and a true Panama hat: braided, not woven.

Cory Langley

Most important to Panama's economy are government services, commerce, and agriculture. Many Panamanians, like the men pictured above, find work in the food processing industry.

12 ● FOOD

Unlike other Central American countries (except Belize), rice is at least as important as corn in Panama. A basic breakfast is *guacho,* rice mixed with red beans. Meat, yams, yucca, and other ingredients can be added for a more filling meal. Cornmeal is used for tortillas, tamales, and empanadas (like tamales but fried). *Lechona* (suckling pig) is wedding fare. *Carima–ola* is yucca root fried and wrapped around seasoned ground meat. Panama's bountiful seafood catch yields many dishes. Roasted iguana, tapir, and monkey are treats in the remote forested areas.

13 ● EDUCATION

Panama's literacy rate (percentage of adults who are able to read and write) approached 90 percent in 1990. Public education is free between the ages of six and fifteen, and six years of primary school are required. Most children attend primary school, and about half go on to secondary school. School attendance is higher than in most other Central American countries. Panama has three universities.

14 ● CULTURAL HERITAGE

Panama has two traditional song forms, both of Spanish origin: the *copla,* sung by women, and the *mejorana,* sung by men and accompanied by the small native guitar of the same name. The *saloma* is a male song style with yodeling and falsetto. Blacks sing calypso, and the Cuna and Chocó have their own songs which are sung to the accompaniment of flutes. Panama has a national symphonic orchestra and a national school of music.

The most popular folk dance, the *tamborito,* is of African origin. Drums furnish the rhythmic background, while female voices sing to the melody. Couples dance one at a time within a circular area. Panama has a rich variety of folk dances.

Costumed folk dramas are performed at festivals. In *Los Montezumas,* the confrontation of the Spanish and Aztecs in Mexico is acted out. *Los Grandiablos,* a dance-drama, portrays Lucifer and his band of devils in battle with the Archangel Michael for the possession of a soul.

Important Panamanian poets have included Dário Herrera (1870–1914) and Ricardo Miró (1888–1940). Panamanian painters have included Roberto Lewis (1874–1949) and Humberto Ivaldi (1909–47). Among composers have been Narciso Garay (1876–1953), Roque Cordero, and Gonzalo Brenes.

15 ● EMPLOYMENT

Most important to Panama's economy are government services, commerce, and agriculture. Traditional subsistence farmers (who grow their own food but have little or no surplus for marketing) are being displaced by cattle ranchers. Other peasants find seasonal work on banana, sugar, and coffee plantations. Most factory jobs are in food processing. Panama has become one of the major international banking centers in the Americas. The Colón Free Zone is the world's second-most important duty-free trading zone (Hong Kong ranks first).

16 ● SPORTS

Baseball is Panama's most popular sport. A number of Panamanians have played in the North American major leagues. Panama-born Rod Carew (b.1945) is in baseball's Hall of Fame. There have also been several Panamanian boxing champions, including Roberto Durán (b.1951). Swimming, fishing, hunting, and horseback riding are popular. Panama City has horse racing.

Bullfighting in Panama is merely teasing, in which participants annoy the beast while avoiding danger. It is performed at festivals. Cockfights, accompanied by betting, are popular throughout the country. Cuna and Guaymí Indians hold pole-tossing contests. Children play a game like marbles with cashew seeds.

17 ● RECREATION

For rural people, festivals are still the high points of the year. These include agricultural fairs, in which a queen is crowned, judges pick prize-winning animals, and carnival rides draw youngsters. Traditional forms of live entertainment, however, are giving way to the lure of discos, movies, and television. By law, all foreign-language movies must be subtitled in Spanish. Panama City has many nightclubs and more than twenty gambling casinos.

18 ● CRAFTS AND HOBBIES

Handicraft articles include baskets, straw hats, net and saddle bags, hammocks, straw mats, gourds, woodcarvings, and masks. Most pottery is dark red and dull-finished. *Molas* are colorful handstitched appliqué. Georgina Linares is known for her paintings on leather.

19 ● SOCIAL PROBLEMS

There is a serious street-crime problem in urban slums. Domestic violence against women is widespread. According to official 1994 statistics, one-fifth of all families do not have enough money for a minimum diet, and a further one-fourth cannot meet their basic needs. The nation's forests are being reduced at an alarming rate, and soil erosion is a serious problem.

20 ● BIBLIOGRAPHY

Adams, Richard N. *Cultural Surveys of Panama, Nicaragua, Guatemala, El Salvador, Honduras.* Detroit: B. Ethridge, 1976.

Biesanz, Richard, and Mavis Biesanz. *The People of Panama.* New York: Columbia University Press, 1955.

Cheville, Lila R., and Richard A. Cheville. *Festivals and Dances of Panama.* Privately printed in Panama, 1977.

WEBSITES

World Travel Guide. Panama. [Online] Available http://www.wtgonline.com/country/pa/gen.html, 1998.

Cunas

PRONUNCIATION: KOO-nas
ALTERNATE NAMES: Cuna-Cueva
LOCATION: San Blas Islands (or Mulatas Archipelago), along the Gulf of Darien from Panama to the Colombian border
LANGUAGE: Cuna (Chibchan group of languages)
RELIGION: Indigenous spirit-based beliefs

1 ● INTRODUCTION

The Cuna Indians are the original inhabitants of what is now Panama. Like other Amerindian peoples, they are believed to be descended from Central Asians who migrated across the Bering Strait (separating Siberia and Alaska) some 20,000 years ago and moved southward. The Spanish began exploring the Panamanian coastline early in the sixteenth century AD. They intended to establish a colony (settlement of Spanish people). Three Spanish explorers, including Christopher Columbus (on his fourth voyage to America), came in the first decade of the 1500s. All failed to establish a colony, in part because the native Amerindians were hostile to foreign takeover. Eventually Martín Fernández de Enciso succeeded in founding the settlement of Santa María.

Panama was part of Colombia until it became an independent nation in 1903. The Cunas live in an area that includes part of Panama and part of Colombia.

2 ● LOCATION

The Cuna Indians inhabit thirty or forty islands in an archipelago (group or chain) of some 400 islands strung along the Gulf of

Darien from Panama to the Colombian border. Some Cunas also live on Colombia's Pacific coast near the Panamanian border. The archipelago is sometimes referred to as the San Blas Islands or the Mulatas Archipelago. Its inhabitants also farm along the shores of the Panamanian coastline proper, which is very close to the islands. The hinterland (back country) is jungle and has very few roads. The relative isolation of the Cuna settlements has helped them preserve their traditional way of life.

3 ●LANGUAGE

The language of the Cunas belongs to the Chibchan group of languages. The original inhabitants of the great plateaus of the Andean highlands in central Colombia were known as Chibchas. They are now extinct, but their descendants mixed with the Spanish and now form a significant part of the *mestizo* (mixed) population of Colombia.

Names are sacred, and naming ceremonies take place when girls and boys become teenagers. These ceremonies have an unusual feature: there is a special chanting of all available names. The parents of a child listen closely, and when they hear a name they like they interrupt the ceremony and the choice of the name is made immediately.

Many Cunas also have Spanish names. Because the United States has been prominent in the Panama Canal Zone, some have also taken English names.

4 ●FOLKLORE

Since the time of the Spanish explorers, the Cuna have had a small population (estimated to be less than 1 percent of the total

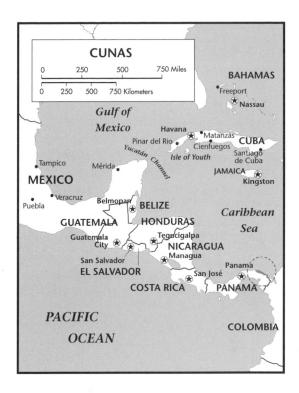

population) of albinos (people with no pigmentation, causing them to have white skin, white hair, and pink or blue eyes), most of whom lived on one island. They were somewhat of an outcast group in the Cuna society, and many folktales grew up around them. Here is a Cuna legend reflecting the historic Cuna practice of Sun worship, which is no longer carried out today:

The Cunas, descendants of the Sun, lived in the fertile Darien region since the beginning of time. They were blessed by the gods with a beautiful homeland, including magical lakes, rushing rivers, rich jungles filled with strange and beautiful animals and plants, and mountains where gold was stored.

Once upon a time, the Sun wanted to reward the tribe's shaman (holy man), called the *nele,* for his wisdom, goodness, and generosity. Appearing before the nele one afternoon at the hour of the sacrifice, the Sun offered to grant him anything he desired. Although the shaman's humility at first prevented him from making a request, the Sun repeated his offer. The shaman was old and did not have long to live. He resolved to ask for something that would benefit the entire tribe after he was gone.

He asked the Sun to send his own son to the Cunas, to serve as their leader. Although this was a difficult request, the Sun agreed. After three days two beautiful blond children–a boy and a girl–appeared in the sky at dawn, surrounded by golden light, and came down to earth. The people were overjoyed and gave thanks to the Sun for this miraculous event. The children were raised in a golden palace with huge gardens. When grown, they were married in a festive ceremony.

Eventually, however, they were unfaithful, both to each other and to their divine origins. As punishment, the Sun turned them from divine beings into mere mortals, condemned to suffer like other human beings. However, from their first union came the albinos. With their blue eyes and nearly white hair, they are still considered children of the Sun. It is said that they cannot bear the light of day. The rest of the Cunas, believed to be descended from the later unions of the two original children of the Sun, still consider themselves to be descendents of a god.

Although the albinos comprise a small percentage of the Cuna population, their existence caused early explorers to label the Cuna the "white Indians."

5 ● RELIGION

The Cunas have a close connection with nature and see themselves as a part of it. Every living thing has a spirit counterpart–animals, men, bodies of water, rocks, trees, and plants. The Cuna believe that what is taken from nature must be replaced in some way.

Becoming a shaman is regarded as an important vocation. Shamans may be men or women. They perform three types of functions: curing illness in individuals, believed to be caused in most cases by the loss of one's soul; curing villages of epidemic illness; and establishing a good relationship with spirits, leading to the ability to predict the future. The shaman who serves the latter function is typically born into the role but also receives training, usually requiring a period of jungle isolation.

6 ● MAJOR HOLIDAYS

Most Cunas are Panamanian or Colombian citizens. Many continue to resist assimilation (incorporation into the surrounding culture) and do not celebrate their respective country's major national holidays. However, some Cunas have allowed and even encouraged their young people to receive a Western-style education. After education, most return to the islands. These Cunas speak Spanish, and in a few cases some have even learned English. While living among non-Cuna people, Cunas take part in the celebration of national holidays. These include in the jungle on the mainland. The husband or wife chants a song of praise and lamentation (mourning).

8 ● RELATIONSHIPS

The Cunas respect the different positions that family members hold, and greet each other accordingly. Greetings are different when the Cunas are working or are engaged in trade. On these occasions, the men are in the background and the women are the dominant partners. They can be very forward and even fierce. When entertaining visitors, the men again stay in the background and the women play a more forthright role.

Modern Cuna women appear to have no difficulty in being assertive. The Cuna culture is matrilineal (tracing descent through the maternal line). Traditionally, women have held a powerful position in their culture.

9 ● LIVING CONDITIONS

Cuna houses are quite long and have enough room for extended family (relatives other than mother, father, and children). The thatched roofs are made out of palm fronds, and the walls out of bamboo or cane. The houses of some villages are very close together.

The Cuna are excellent sailors. They use canoes known as *cayucas* made from a single, hollowed-out tree trunk. The canoes are often fitted out with sails and are well suited for navigating the waters of the Darien between the Panamanian coast and the islands. In the forests beyond the coast, the men go hunting on foot.

Cory Langley

A Cuna woman and her child.

Independence Day, celebrated in both Panama (November 5) and Colombia (July 20).

7 ● RITES OF PASSAGE

The Cunas are fond of their children. Although respect for elders is expected, they are not harsh in the upbringing of young children. Parents decide on a husband for their daughter when she is young. As she approaches adulthood, parents cut their daughter's hair, and there is a special celebration in honor of this occasion.

When a person dies, he or she is wrapped in a hammock and buried in a lonely place

10 ● FAMILY LIFE

Many aspects of Cuna family life indicate a matriarchal society in which women play a leading role. Among the Cunas, women own almost everything. A man cannot trade or sell any article without first seeking his wife's permission. On the other hand, it is her right to sell the perfumed berry beads she has made into necklaces, or garments she has made. She does not have to get permission from anyone.

Women give birth in a special hut set aside for this purpose and which men are not permitted to enter. If a girl is born, there is a joyous response on the father's part. He is then allowed to leave the matrilineal household of his wife's family and set up his home independently with his wife and daughter. If a son is born, the father has to remain in his father-in-law's home. A father is not permitted full authority over his sons in the beginning. The father-in-law has that privilege and duty, until he considers that the young father has learned his parenting skills adequately.

The Cunas keep dogs as pets.

11 ● CLOTHING

The Cunas are famous for their techniques in preparing layer upon layer of cloth, cutting out patterns, and sewing pieces on top of each other. The patterns are geometric and include vivid colors such as red, yellow, and black. Cunas prepare blouses for women using this technique; these are widely admired in both Colombia and Panama. Women wear long, narrow skirts that are tightly wrapped. They use ankle bands as well as arm bands of many beaded strands. They also wear striking earrings that are large, thin gold disks, rather like flaming suns. The men wear dark trousers, bright shirts, and straw hats. In many areas, Cunas wear these traditional articles of handcrafted clothing and jewelry in addition to a Western-style wardrobe.

12 ● FOOD

The Cunas grow yams, corn, and sugarcane in jungle clearings along the coastline. Their diet also includes a variety of fruits such as plantains, bananas, and mangoes. They also drink *chicha,* a fermented drink prepared from sugarcane mixed with plantains, corn, and water. In Cuna family homes there are big jars where the chicha is stored. A refreshing drink, called *coco de agua,* is provided by the green coconut.

The Cunas also eat fish and a species of iguana. They stew sea turtle and eat rice boiled in coconut milk. Their traditional hunting weapons were spears and blow guns.

13 ● EDUCATION

The men teach their sons hunting and fishing skills, as well as how to sew their own simple garments. The women teach their daughters how to prepare and cook food, and basic farming skills. They also teach them the elaborate sewing techniques to make the decorations, known as *molas,* that adorn their beautiful blouses.

Some Cuna men have received a Western-style education on the Panamanian mainland. Generally, the Cunas expect young men who have been educated to return to their island and mainland settlements.

EPD Photos

Molas are created by Cuna women by sewing several layers of fabric together and then cutting and stitching geometric patterns, allowing the colorful fabric layers to show through. Cuna women use molas to adorn their blouses. Outside the Cuna culture, people—especially tourists—value molas like this one as works of art.

14 ● CULTURAL HERITAGE

Music and dance are important for the Cuna. They preserve their strong cultural identity by passing down to their children accounts of their background, history, and values through stories, myths, and legends.

15 ● EMPLOYMENT

Work is divided in very specific ways among the Cunas. The men hunt and fish and also make their own clothes. The women make their own distinctive clothes, cook, weave, sew, and make hammocks. The women also work as sailors and traders.

Cuna women sail in their canoes to meet tourist and trading boats to sell their goods. They are accompanied by men who do not participate in the actual trading.

The coconut palm is important in this region. It was once used as a form of currency (money). For the modern Cuna, it provides fibers for making clothing, brooms, threads for sewing and weaving, lamp wicks, rope, and hammocks. It provides sweet coconut water for drinking and coconut milk for cooking. The coconut palm is also a source of fuel, and dishes are made from coconut shells.

16 ● SPORTS

Cunas are skillful sailors and fishers, but do not consider these activities sports in the Western sense. They engage in these activities for their livelihood.

17 ● RECREATION

Important occasions are celebrated with feasts. It is considered appropriate to mark these occasions with generous amounts of food and drink.

18 ● CRAFTS AND HOBBIES

The Cunas are noted for their skills with textiles. They dye fabric in a variety of bright colors, sew several layers together, and then cut and stitch geometric designs. Each cut allows the colorful fabric from the layer below to show through. Black or deep red are often used as the top fabric layer to accentuate the strong designs. The fabric ornaments, known as *molas*, adorn the blouses of the Cuna women. The molas are prized outside the Cuna community in Panama and neighboring Colombia. Molas have found their way into exhibitions of Amerindian art. Molas may also be framed and hung as works of art, or used to make cushions, but this is not the way the Cuna women use them. These practices are generally found outside the Cuna communities. The Cunas also make beaded necklaces and woodcarvings.

19 ● SOCIAL PROBLEMS

The Cunas have tried to defend their way of life for centuries, and have strongly resisted assimilation. In the 1920s, the Panamanian government decided that the Cunas were too autonomous (independent). They sent a troop of officers to police the islands of San Blas and the surrounding coastal area in the Gulf of Darien. The police officers were all killed by the Cunas.

Since that disastrous interaction, a more peaceful climate of coexistence has generally prevailed. There is now a Panamanian governor for the archipelago. The governor's residence is in El Porvenir, a small, clean, whitewashed town on the mainland. A few markets have been established there, where the Cuna women sell their wares to visitors. Visitors may only come to El Porvenir for the day.

On the Pacific coast of the Colombian mainland near the Panamanian border where some Cunas live, there are real worries that development may threaten the way of life of the Cunas there.

20 ● BIBLIOGRAPHY

Cobb, Charles E. Jr. "Panama: Ever at the Crossroads." *National Geographic Magazine* (April 1986).

Marden, Luis. "The Land that Links the Americas." *National Geographic Magazine* (November 1941).

WEBSITES

Mining Company. Molas. [Online] Available http://quilting.miningco.com/library/weekly/aa072297.htm, 1997.

World Travel Guide. [Online] Available http://www.wtgonline.com/country/pa/gen.html, 1998.

Papua New Guinea

■ **MELANESIANS** **71**
■ **IATMUL** **79**
■ **MELPA** **84**
■ **MOTU** **89**

The people of Papua New Guinea are called Melanesians. They are usually classified by language group. Of the non-native population, the largest group is Australian, followed by others of European and Chinese origin.

Melanesians

PRONUNCIATION: mel-uh-NEE-zhuns
ALTERNATE NAMES: Papuans
LOCATION: Papua New Guinea, Indonesia (Irian Jaya), Vanuatu (the former New Hebrides), New Caledonia, the Solomon Islands, and some smaller neighboring islands
POPULATION: Unknown
LANGUAGE: English; Tok Pisin, Hiri Motu (Papua New Guinea); Bislama (Vanuatu); Solomon Islands Pidgin English (Solomon Islands); Bahasa Indonesia (Irian Jaya); other native languages
RELIGION: Christianity; some native religions

1 ● INTRODUCTION

Melanesia is not a country, but instead a "culture area." Culture area is a term used by anthropologists to refer to a geographical region where people share many of the same traits. These traits include family structure, marriage rules, organization of society, and ways of gaining survival needs or making a living. Melanesia itself is part of a larger culture area called Oceania that includes Melanesia, Polynesia, Micronesia, and Australia. The native inhabitants of Melanesia, called Melanesians, are characteristically dark-skinned with frizzy hair. They are sometimes referred to as "Papuans," from the Malay word *papua* meaning "frizzy haired."

2 ● LOCATION

Melanesia includes the islands of New Guinea, Vanuatu (the former New Hebrides), New Caledonia, the Solomon Islands, and some smaller neighboring islands. The island of New Guinea is divided politically down the middle. The western half of the island is a province of

Cory Langley

The native inhabitants of Melanesia, called Melanesians, are characteristically dark-skinned with frizzy hair. They are sometimes referred to as "Papuans," from the Malay word papua *meaning "frizzy haired."*

Indonesia called Irian Jaya. The eastern half is the independent nation of Papua New Guinea. New Caledonia is under the administration of France, and Vanuatu became an independent nation in 1980. The Solomon Islands are divided between Papua New Guinea and the independent country of the Solomon Islands (formerly a British Protectorate).

All of Melanesia lies within the tropics of Cancer and Capricorn and is south of the equator. Melanesians migrate locally to other nearby islands or to Australia. A small percentage leave the region entirely and take up residence in the United States, Canada, or Europe.

3 ● LANGUAGE

In many of the island nations that comprise Melanesia, there is more than one official national language. For instance, Papua New Guinea has three official languages: English, Tok Pisin (an English-based pidgin language), and Hiri Motu (an Austronesian-based pidgin language). Tok Pisin has a history based in colonialism and forced plantation labor during the 1800s in the South Pacific. The language derives from a kind of nautical English that was spread throughout the Pacific by sailors. It has similarities to English as well as to the Austronesian languages spoken by the plantation laborers. A sample sentence in Tok Pisin might look like this: *Bai mi kaikai wanpela kaukau,* meaning "I will eat a yam."

Within the region of Melanesia, the island of New Guinea alone has more than one thousand different languages. Some of these languages have as few as fifty speakers, while others, such as Enga, have a few hundred thousand. Many of the these languages have never been documented or described.

4 ● FOLKLORE

None of the cultures of Melanesia ever developed a native writing system. Consequently, oral history (historical information passed on through stories) is important to them. In the Sepik River region of Papua New Guinea, the origin myth of many groups tells of a crocodile who split in two. His upper jaw became the heavens and his lower jaw became the earth. For many of these groups, there was also an original pair of humans that sprang from the mud and are responsible for populating the Earth. In this origin myth, however, the original pair are brothers.

5 ● RELIGION

Christianity has spread throughout Melanesia. Missionaries are very active in this region. Native religions are still practiced by many groups, although in modified form. In many societies in the Sepik River region of Papua New Guinea, the original belief systems included aspects of headhunting and cannibalism. Both practices have been illegal in the region since the late 1920s. Most groups believe in a variety of spirits that inhabit the forests, mountains, and swamps. They also believe that the ghosts of

their ancestors inhabit the same plane of reality that they do. In fact, in the highlands of Papua New Guinea, when Melanesians saw the first Europeans, they believed them to be the ghosts of their dead ancestors returning to the community. Some groups jokingly refer to white tourists in the same way.

6 ● MAJOR HOLIDAYS

Independence Day is a major holiday for the independent Melanesian nations of Papua New Guinea and Vanuatu. For those that belong to the British Commonwealth, British holidays such as the Queen's birthday are celebrated in urban areas. Banks and schools are closed for those holidays, but in areas where there are no banks or schools, these holidays have little meaning.

7 ● RITES OF PASSAGE

Puberty is an especially important rite in all Melanesian societies. However, these societies differ in regard to which sex undergoes initiation rites. In the Sepik River region, males used to undergo extreme and elaborate initiation rites. These involved extensive scarification (scarring) as well as brutal treatment by older males. Scarification has all but disappeared in the Sepik region, except for the few males who can afford this expensive process. In some societies, males at puberty were expected to kill someone and take their first head. This process was halted by colonial administrators in the 1920s, soon after the first European contacts in the region. Girls generally had less harsh puberty rites. With the onset of menstruation, they often underwent a brief period of seclusion. Funerals were also important rites of passage in traditional

Cynthia Bassett

This large ceremonial men's house is a national mounument in Papua New Guinea.

Melanesian societies. They involved much feasting and display of emotion.

8 ● RELATIONSHIPS

Urban and rural Melanesians greet and take leave of each other in extremely different ways. In parts of the highlands of Papua New Guinea, males used to greet each other by rubbing each other's groin region. In most of these cultures, the Western handshake has replaced this traditional form of greeting. Special ceremonial greetings took place when one group went to trade with another.

Many groups require that marriages occur between persons who come from dif- ferent villages. Special courtship rituals still take place between men and women in these instances. Among the Chimbu of Papua New Guinea, men use their singing ability to woo women. They also decorate their bodies in elaborate ways to look beautiful for the women they are trying to court. Marriages, however, have to be negotiated between the families. They usually involve the payment of a "bride price" to the bride's father by the prospective son-in-law.

9 ● LIVING CONDITIONS

Melanesia is a tropical region and its inhabitants experience the hardships of life in an environment where rain, heat, and mosqui-

Cynthia Bassett

Except for a few people in very isolated areas, most Melanesian men wear Western-style shorts or long trousers and shirts. However, some men still decorate themselves for the annual sing sing, *a competition among tribes that includes feasting and boasting.*

toes are ever-present. Malaria is endemic (native) to the region and most local inhabitants of the low-lying areas suffer from this debilitating disease. Healing is a long process in the tropics and, as a result, infection is a serious problem. Most of Melanesia, though, is a relatively healthy region of the world.

10 ● FAMILY LIFE

In many Melanesian societies, there is a great deal of antagonism (hostility or opposition) between men and women. It is common in many villages to have separate men's and women's houses. In the Sepik River region, men's ceremonial houses are off-limits to all women and to uninitiated (non-adult) males. Men would traditionally spend most of their time in this large house where matters of ceremonial importance were often planned. Men would also often take their meals here. There were no real family meals in traditional societies along the Sepik. Food for the day was often placed in a woven basket that was suspended from the house rafters. People simply ate when they got hungry.

Women are the primary caregivers to children and the primary food producers.

Cynthia Bassett

This woman in traditional dress processes sago palm, an important part of the daily diet.

Women play important roles in ceremonial and political life in many Melanesian societies.

Households vary in size. In some very small societies, everyone in the group lives in one house. Antagonism between the sexes is not as dramatic among these groups as it is among larger groups. In all societies, however, the domestic space is divided between males and females.

11 ●CLOTHING

Traditional clothing in Melanesia was minimal by Western European standards. In the highland societies of New Guinea, men went naked except for a penis sheath made from the gourd of a vine. Nowadays, men only dress this way in a few remote societies. For the most part they wear Western-style shorts or long trousers and shirts. In these societies, women wear skirts made from handmade fiber. Traditionally, an important part of personal adornment in these societies was body decoration, including elaborate painting and the use of various headgear, wigs, and other items. The most extensive adornment took place when exchanges between groups were to occur.

Cory Langley

Many parts of Melanesia do not have access to formal, European-style education. However, schools are part of urban life for Melanesians and have reached some remote areas.

These exchanges were times of feasting and boasting, and individual beauty was an important aspect of these events. Some individuals at these events still adorn themselves in this manner.

In many parts of Melanesia the all-purpose *laplap* has become the standard unisex item of clothing. Laplap refers to a piece of cloth, usually store-bought, that is wrapped around the waist or up under the armpits to cover the body, somewhat like a sarong. In the lower altitude areas, women still prefer not to wear any covering on their upper body. However, when tourists are in the village, Melanesian women may adjust the laplap to cover their breasts.

12 ● FOOD

The sago palm is an important foodstuff in parts of the lowland areas of Melanesia. The pith (core tissue) of the palm is processed into a starch that can be made into pancakes or dumplings. A sago pancake has the appearance of a freshly cooked, soft tortilla. In the higher elevations, yams are the staple diet, with pork eaten on ceremonial occasions.

13 ● EDUCATION

Many parts of Melanesia do not have access to formal, European-style education. Education focuses on traditional ways of life and the values of the society. Schools are part of urban life for Melanesians and have reached some remote areas. Education in schools revolves around literacy (establishing reading and writing skills) in the national language(s). They also prepare Melanesians for urban life, such as civil service (governmental administration) careers. In Papua New Guinea, the educational system is based on the Australian model, where formal, required education ends at grade ten. Grades eleven and twelve are only for students who wish to pursue a university education. Literacy in Tok Pisin is growing among the urban population in particular, while literacy in English is lower. Children who attend school have at least basic skills in written English.

14 ● CULTURAL HERITAGE

There are a number of musical traditions within Melanesia. In the Solomon Islands, there is a tradition of panpipe orchestras. Drums are nearly universal in the musical traditions of Melanesia. Melanesian drums are usually hand-held, hourglass-shaped, and single-headed. The Tok Pisin word for this type of drum is *kundu*. In many highland societies of Papua New Guinea, large groups of men play drums together at ceremonial gatherings called *sing sing*.

Dance is another important part of ritual life. Both men and women dance; however, in many societies there are separate men's and women's dances.

Written literature is a recent development in Melanesia. Many pieces of written literature are the transcriptions of folklore and oral history.

15 ● EMPLOYMENT

Wage labor was introduced to Melanesia by European colonists. Prior to this, work was often cooperative and it continues to be for village-based projects. Individuals have certain responsibilities to their relatives and in-laws. These typically include working for them on cooperative projects such as house-building. In some societies, a son-in-law has to work in his father-in-law's gardens for a fixed period of time after his marriage. Anthropologists call this practice "bride service."

16 ● SPORTS

Soccer, rugby, and cricket are important sports in Melanesia. Some societies have changed these sports in unique ways or adapted them to meet local conditions. In a well-known case in the Trobriand Islands off the coast of Papua New Guinea, cricket is played by local rules that do not allow for a winner. In many remote villages of the various islands in the region, the inhabitants have no knowledge of these sports.

17 ● RECREATION

Electricity does not reach many Melanesian homes, so television is a luxury of the urban dwellers. There is one television station in Papua New Guinea called *Em TV* in Tok Pisin, one of the national languages of the country. *Em* in Tok Pisin means "it, he, or she," so the station's name means something close to "It's TV." Australian, American, and locally produced shows are aired during a limited viewing schedule. Cable and satellite service are available to the wealthy residents of the islands.

Traditional recreation involves storytelling and performances of music, dance, and song. No recreational event is complete without chewing betel nuts, which are a stimulant and a favorite of most Melanesians.

18 ● CRAFTS AND HOBBIES

Art in most Melanesian societies is utilitarian (designed for usefulness rather than beauty). In the Sepik River region, there is an extremely well developed tradition of artistic expression involving sculpture and painting. Every item is elaborately decorated with important animals and birds, as well as geometric and abstract designs. Masks, once an important aspect of ritual performances, have now become important items of tourist art. Every year, several thousand tourists visit this area of New Guinea to purchase the art and artifacts of these people. It is not an industry that creates any wealthy Papuans, however.

19 ● SOCIAL PROBLEMS

Like every other group of people, Melanesians are dealing with the modern world. Alcoholism is becoming a more serious problem in parts of Melanesia where males have money and time on their hands. AIDS poses a serious health threat in Papua New Guinea, especially in urban areas. Condoms have only recently become available. The social phenomenon of "rascals" in parts of Papua New Guinea is a cause for concern for locals and visitors alike. Rascals are unemployed, disadvantaged youths who rob people as well as businesses, often assaulting their victims. Guns are rarely used in these robberies since they are difficult to come by and ammunition is illegal by Papua New Guinea law.

20 ● BIBLIOGRAPHY

Codrington, Robert Henry. *The Melanesians: Studies in Their Anthropology and Folklore.* New Haven, Conn.: HRAF Press, 1957.

Holdsworth, David. *Festivals and Celebrations in Papua New Guinea.* Bathurst, Australia: Robert Brown & Associates, 1982.

Ryan, P., ed. *The Encyclopedia of Papua New Guinea.* Melbourne: Melbourne University Press, 1972.

Spriggs, Matthew. *The Island Melanesians.* Oxford: Blackwell, 1997.

WEBSITES

Interknowledge Corp. [Online] Available http://www.interknowledge.com/papua-newguinea/, 1998.

World Travel Guide. Papua New Guinea. [Online] Available http://www.wtgonline.com/country/pg/gen.html, 1998.

Iatmul

PRONUNCIATION: YAHT-mool
ALTERNATE NAMES: Nyara
LOCATION: Papua New Guinea
POPULATION: Approximately 10,000
LANGUAGE: Iatmul; Nyara; Tok Pisin; some English
RELIGION: Traditional Iatmul; Christianity

1 ● INTRODUCTION

The art of Iatmul people is the most well represented of all the indigenous peoples of Papua New Guinea. However, few people have much knowledge or understanding of the complex culture that produced these appealing sculptures, carvings, and masks. The Iatmul were cannibals and headhunters in the times before contact with European missionaries in the 1930s. The violence in traditional Iatmul society was necessary for males to gain status. However, after the arrival of the Europeans, Iatmuls who practiced cannibalism and headhunting were labeled as murderers. After some of the men were publicly executed, these violent practices ended.

2 ● LOCATION

The total Iatmul population is about 10,000 people. The homeland of the Iatmul is along the middle course of the Sepik River in the country of Papua New Guinea. The Sepik is a river that changes with the seasons. During the rainy season that lasts for around five months, the river may rise dramatically and flood the surrounding lowlands. Iatmul villages become a cluster of houses perched on stilts situated within a body of muddy water. All movement has to be done by canoe during this time.

The Iatmul's location in the middle reaches of the vast river has been advantageous to them. Prior to the arrival of Europeans, they were able to serve as brokers in the extensive trade networks of the Sepik River Basin. The location still serves them well, as they are able to attract large numbers of tourists to their villages due to the relative accessibility of the area.

A large number of Iatmul have left the Sepik region and now live in other parts of Papua New Guinea. Emigration from Iatmul villages may be as high as 50 percent.

3 ● LANGUAGE

The Iatmul language is classified by linguists as a Papuan, or non-Austronesian, language that belongs to the Ndu language family. The Papuan languages are spoken throughout the island of New Guinea and on a few smaller neighboring islands in Indonesia. There is very little information on the Iatmul language. The Iatmul refer to their language by the word *nyara*. The language has two dialects. Iatmul children and many adults are also fluent in Tok Pisin (an English-based pidgin language), one of the national languages of Papua New Guinea.

4 ● FOLKLORE

Iatmul mythology states that they originated from a hole in the mud in the present-day territory of the neighboring Sawos people. Some groups tell stories of a great flood. The survivors floated down the river (the Sepik) on rafts or pieces of grass-covered ground that became lodged in the river. The piece of land that this created became the

site of the first men's house for the Iatmul ancestors. The present-day men's houses are supposed to be representations of the original piece of earth that was became the Iatmul world. Other myths tell of the formation of the heavens and earth from the great ancestral crocodile that split in two, with his upper jaw becoming the heavens and his lower jaw becoming the earthly realms.

5 ● RELIGION

Traditional religious beliefs of the Iatmul people centered on the spirits of the rivers, forests, and swamps. There was also a concern for the ghosts of the dead and the harm they could do to the living. Many myths explain the natural and supernatural world for the Iatmul clans. Important in these myths are the people and places where events took place in the mythological past. Different clans (groups of people with common descent) have secret knowledge of the names of the characters and events in their particular collection of myths. Clans would try to learn the secret names of other clans; to do so was to gain power over that group.

Missionaries have been active among the Iatmul since the 1930s. There are many converts to Christianity along the Sepik River. Some missionaries went as far as to burn the men's house and the artifacts and art that it contained. An enormous amount of cultural information was lost in the process.

6 ● MAJOR HOLIDAYS

Christian holidays are celebrated by converted Iatmul. Holidays like Christmas (December 25) and Easter (late March or early April) do not have the degree of commercial emphasis found in the United States. National holidays of the country are recognized, but since there are no banks or post offices in the area, these holidays have little meaning.

7 ● RITES OF PASSAGE

Male initiation was a common practice among the Iatmul. It involved extensive ceremonial activities that ended with the scarification (ritual scarring) of the upper back and chest of the young initiate. The patterns that are made are said to resemble the skin of the crocodile, the most important animal in Iatmul folklore and mythology. Very few men still undergo this practice, not because of the pain involved, but because of the expense. It costs a few hundred dollars and several pigs to hire someone to do the scarification.

The Iatmul also celebrated important events in the lives of males and females. For example, the Iatmul would celebrate the first time a girl made a *sago* (starch made from palm trees) pancake or the first time a boy carved a canoe. These celebrations were called *naven*. Naven ceremonies have all but disappeared from Iatmul culture today.

8 ● RELATIONSHIPS

Traditional greetings between men of different villages who traded with each other consisted of formal ceremonial dialogues where men had well-defined roles. The style of interaction between adult Iatmul men is often described as being aggressive. Tourists are often perplexed because Iatmul men put on a very fierce face instead of a smile when they pose for pictures. Iatmul women were in charge of the trade that took place with the Sawos and Chambri, two neighboring groups. Iatmul women exchanged fish for the *sago* (starch) produced by women from these neighboring groups. While men were aggressive, combative, and quick to anger, Iatmul women maintained harmony within the community and relations with outside communities. The Iatmul have been exposed to Western culture since the 1930s, and as a result they have adopted some of its aspects. Greetings are Westernized and consist of the use of stock phrases and handshakes.

9 ● LIVING CONDITIONS

Iatmul villages vary in size from 300 to 1,000 people. Villages traditionally centered on a men's house, which was the architectural centerpiece of the village. These buildings were massive structures elaborately decorated with carvings and paintings. They also housed the majority of religious items including drums, flutes, and sacred sculptures. At the present time, most men's houses are warehouses for the storage of artifacts that are sold to tourists and art collectors. They also serve as meeting places for adult men.

Electricity and running water are not available in Iatmul villages. Without plumbing, dishes are washed in the Sepik River, as are clothes. The Iatmul also rely on the Sepik to bathe. When the river is swollen but not flooded, bathing is a challenge. A person will walk upstream, get in the river, and then wash while the current carries them to the place where they started. Getting out of the river and staying clean are also a challenge, since the banks of the river are mounds of knee-deep mud.

10 ● FAMILY LIFE

Women play important roles in Iatmul daily life. Women are responsible for catching fish to trade with neighboring villages to obtain the *sago* flour to make pancakes. Women are also the primary caregivers.

In traditional Iatmul society, marriage partners were determined by strict rules. Acceptable marriage partners for a man included his father's mother's brother's son's daughter (a second cousin), his father's sister's daughter (a first cousin), or a woman that he would get in exchange for a sister he would give to another man. Anthropologists refer to this last type of marriage as "sister exchange."

A married couple takes up residence in the husband's father's house. The house will also be occupied by the father's other sons and their families. Each nuclear family has its own space within the large house. Each family also has its own hearth for cooking. Husbands often sleep in the men's house.

11 ● CLOTHING

Most Iatmul men dress in Western-style clothes consisting of athletic shorts and a T-shirt. Shoes are rarely worn. Women's dress is more varied and depends on what type of activity they are engaged in and who is around at the time. It ranges from Western-style dresses to the use of the wrap-around *laplap* (a sarong-like cloth) to cover the body from the waist down. Children tend to dress like adults, but small children go naked.

12 ● FOOD

The Iatmul diet consists primarily of fish and the edible palm tree called *sago*. Iatmul houses do not have tables; everyone sits on the floor. The midday meal is likely to be the only meal that the family eats together. At other times of day, people eat whenever they get hungry. The food for the day is stored in a woven basket that hangs from a carved and decorated hook near each person's sleeping area. Dried fish and sago pancakes are placed in the basket in the morning. Fruit and greens are sometimes collected from the forest. Canned curry from Indonesia and Malaysia has now become popular, as well as rice and tinned fish. These products are expensive and sometimes difficult to come by.

13 ● EDUCATION

Traditional education is still important to the Iatmul. Boys and girls are trained to become competent adults able to perform the tasks that men and women do to keep the village functioning. Western school is an option for children whose parents want to send them. However, very few communities have their own school and typically children have to travel to other villages if they wish to attend.

14 ● CULTURAL HERITAGE

Music is an important part of Iatmul ceremonial life. Today, ritual music is still performed at festivals and during special ceremonies.

Men play sacred flutes during initiation rituals, which are carried out less often today than in the past. The sacred bamboo flutes are stored in the rafters of houses or in the men's house itself. The sound produced is supposed to be the voices of the ancestral spirits. Women and children were traditionally forbidden to see the flutes.

The sacred flutes are also played after the death of an important man in the village. A pair of flutists plays during the night under the house of the deceased. During the day, the female relatives perform a kind of ritual lament that had a definite musical quality.

15 ● EMPLOYMENT

Work was traditionally divided along lines of sex and age. Adult women were responsible for fishing and gardening. Women also prepared the fish they caught, preserving a great deal of it by smoking it. Men were responsible for hunting, building, and performing most religious rituals. Girls and young boys would help their mothers with her chores. However, boys who had passed through initiation would not consider performing women's work. During initiation, boys would learn aspects of male work and ceremonial life. In the present, these patterns have remained the same with the exception that very few boys undergo initiation. Men often seek wage labor outside the village. Some men rent their canoes and conduct tours along the Sepik River.

16 ● SPORTS

For the Iatmul who still live along the Sepik River, sports are relatively unimportant. Boys make slingshots to shoot hard, dried mud balls at birds and other living targets. Men who have moved to towns and cities are more likely to follow rugby and soccer teams.

17 ● RECREATION

In an area without access to electricity, television, videos, and movies are virtually unknown. People who live in towns and cities with electricity go to movies, and some houses have television. Traditional entertainment consisted of storytelling, ritual performances, and music.

18 ● CRAFTS AND HOBBIES

Artistic expression in traditional Iatmul society was completely utilitarian (designed for usefulness rather than beauty). Every item of daily use was decorated with carving or painting. Tourism has changed art production and appreciation in Iatmul society. Producing art for tourists is an important money-making endeavor for the present-day Iatmul. Masks and sculpture are the most sought-after items in the tourist art market.

In men's houses in Iatmul villages, there was an important ceremonial item referred to as a "debating stool." This was a free-standing sculpture with an oversized, stylized human head supported by a small body. On the back of the sculpture was a ledge that looked somewhat like a stool. The stool was used in debates that were held to settle disputes that might otherwise have ended in bloodshed. Debaters from each clan would beat a bunch of specially chosen leaves while they made their points. These stools are now produced for outsiders. While a debating stool purchased from an Iatmul on the Sepik River might cost around $100, a stool purchased from a dealer in Australia would cost around $1,500. Iatmul art has become a very profitable business for dealers in foreign countries.

19 ● SOCIAL PROBLEMS

Cultural change and emigration are major problems for the Iatmul today. Young people are the most likely to emigrate, and as a result, they do not learn about their culture. They move to cities and towns and begin using Tok Pisin as their primary language. Tourism has brought major changes to the Iatmul traditional way of life. Wage earning has become important. Western items such as tennis shoes and toothpaste are becoming important items for the modern Iatmul.

20 ● BIBLIOGRAPHY

Bateson, Gregory. *Naven.* 2d ed. Stanford, Calif.: Stanford University Press, 1954.

Lutkehaus, Nancy, et al., ed. *Sepik Heritage: Tradition and Change in Papua New Guinea.* Durham, N.C.: Carolina University Press, 1990.

WEBSITES

Interknowledge Corp. [Online] Available http://www.interknowledge.com/papua-newguinea/, 1998.

World Travel Guide. Papua New Guinea. [Online] Available http://www.wtgonline.com/country/pg/gen.html, 1998.

Melpa

PRONUNCIATION: MEL-pah
ALTERNATE NAMES: Medlpa; Hageners
LOCATION: Papua New Guinea
POPULATION: 60,000
LANGUAGE: Melpa; Tok Pisin
RELIGION: Christianity; native Melpa religion

1 ● INTRODUCTION

The Melpa (also spelled Medlpa) are some of the first Papuans that tourists and visitors to the island of New Guinea see when they step off planes arriving in Mount Hagen. (The Melpa are often called "Hageners.") The Melpa frequent the airport, offering modern "stone axes," colorful string bags, and other artifacts for sale. Some of them also provide taxi and bus service to the local hotels and guest houses.

The Melpa are a highland group. Until 1933 (when Europeans arrived in the highlands) New Guinea had been unknown to the outside world. Conversely, the highlanders had never before seen people who lived beyond their mountain valleys and plains. The first contact between these two groups was recorded on film. It provides a fascinating record of this monumental time of discovery for both groups.

2 ● LOCATION

The Melpa live in the Western Highlands Province of the independent Pacific nation of Papua New Guinea. They are highlands-dwelling people who occupy the areas north and south of the town of Mount Hagen. There are about 60,000 Melpa in total. The climate in the area is relatively mild, especially by tropical standards. The temperature rarely exceeds 86°F (36°C) in the summer months and rarely falls below freezing in winter. Rainfall is heaviest between October and March, with a dry period from April until September. Mosquitoes are nonexistent in this region of Papua New Guinea and therefore, malaria is not a problem.

3 ● LANGUAGE

The Melpa speak a Papuan language belonging to the East New Guinea Highlands stock. Melpa has over 60,000 speakers, and a portion of that population speaks Tok Pisin (an English-based pidgin language) as a second language. Tok Pisin is one of the official languages of Papua New Guinea. Melpa is not under threat from Tok Pisin, as are some other languages in the country. Most Melpa children still grow up speaking Melpa as their first language.

4 ● FOLKLORE

Myths relating the origins of the clans (group of people with common descent) were and still are told within Melpa society. Sacred objects or living beings associated with these myths and clans are called *mi*. Extended speeches and epic stories are performed to tell the deeds of clan heroes and ancestors.

5 ● RELIGION

Ghosts of dead family and clan members are the focal point of non-Christian religious practice among the Melpa. Pig sacrifices are made to keep these ghosts happy. These sacrifices are made when illness occurs within the village or before any dangerous task begins. The Melpa have religious experts who are responsible for curing the sick and act as intermediaries (go-betweens) between the human world and the spirit world. Women are not allowed to be curers but can be possessed by spirits and can also foretell the future.

Christianity has existed in the Melpa region ever since the founding of Mount Hagen as an administrative, trade, and missionary center in the 1930s. A number of the Melpa are now practicing Christians and attend the local churches on a regular basis.

6 ● MAJOR HOLIDAYS

The Mount Hagen Show is an important local holiday for Hageners. Groups from all over the highlands region attend to perform traditional songs, music, and dance wearing ceremonial clothing. Body decoration reaches it height for this event. National holidays such as Independence Day (September 16) are recognized by the Melpa who live and work in Mount Hagen, but not by rural Melpa.

The most important and well known ceremonial event in traditional Melpa society was an exchange process known as the *moka*. An individual male gave an gift to another male, who then gave a gift, plus something more, to that individual. Exchange partnerships would continue through the adult lives of men. Before the introduction of European goods into the highlands, the major items of exchange in the moka were pigs, both living and cooked, and pearlshell necklaces. Nowadays, cash, machetes (large knives), and even four-wheel-drive vehicles are exchanged in moka ceremonies. The goal of the exchange is to gain status and prestige in the eyes of the larger society by giving more than one received. Men who are accomplished at achieving this goal are known as "big-men" in the community and arc viewed as leaders. True big-men are able to arrange large-scale, multiple moka exchanges involving many pairs of exchange partners. Anthropologists refer to this type of exchange as "redistribution." The goal is not to gather goods or wealth for personal use, but instead to redistribute (share) items among the community.

7 ● RITES OF PASSAGE

The Melpa people do not socially recognize or celebrate a girl's first menstruation, as most other highland groups from Papua New Guinea do. However, like other groups in the area, the Melpa do segregate males and females due to the fear of pollution of males by females, especially through menstrual blood.

In the past, the Melpa had elaborate initiation rites for males. Through contact with the outside world, these have been greatly reduced.

8 ● RELATIONSHIPS

In some parts of the highlands, villages are separated by valleys and mountain ridges. Especially in the more rural Melpa region, villages may be widely separated from each other. In these areas, greetings are accomplished long distance via yodeling. Requests, directions, commands, and challenges are often yodeled back and forth by men across a ravine or a ridge, completely out of visual range of each other.

Inheritance is based on patrilineal principles: sons inherit from their fathers. The most important item for inheritance is land. Parcels of a father's land are given to his sons at the time that the sons are married. When daughters are married, their fathers may grant them gardening rights to parcels of land.

9 ● LIVING CONDITIONS

There are two types of traditional Melpa houses: men's and women's. Men's houses are round with cone-shaped roofs. This is where men live and where preteenage boys live once they have been separated from their mothers (around the age of eight). Women and their unmarried daughters live in the rectangular-shaped women's house. The women's house also contains pig stalls to keep the pigs from wandering off at night or being stolen. A village consists of at least one men's house and one women's house. Members of a clan traditionally resided in the same area, which was linked by paths to nearby gardening areas. Missionaries encouraged the building of family homes where a husband, a wife, and their children would sleep together. Some Melpa have adopted this new form of residence while others have chosen not to.

10 ● FAMILY LIFE

Marriage involves the exchange of valuables by both families. The majority of the goods are given by the groom's family to the bride's family. They constitute what anthropologists refer to as "bride wealth" or "bride price." Traditionally, the groom's family and kinfolk would provide a number of pigs and shells to the father of the bride in compensation for the loss of his daughter. Nowadays, cash payments are included in the transaction. The bride's family provides the new couple with a number of breeding pigs. The negotiation of a bride price is a significant part of the marriage transaction and can cause a potential marriage to be canceled.

The Melpa trace their genealogies through the male line. Clans are created through common descent from a shared male ancestor. Individuals choose their spouses from clans outside their own. After marriage, the couple moves into the groom's father's village. Later, they will build a new women's house for the bride near the groom's men's house. Divorce consists of repayment of part of the bride price, especially if the woman is seen to have been at fault.

11 ● CLOTHING

The Melpa who live or work in Mount Hagen wear Western-style clothing. Men usually wear shorts, T-shirts, shoes if they own them, and a knitted cap, and they carry a string bag. Women wear A-line dresses often made of a floral print fabric. They also carry string bags, but much larger than those of the men. Women also wear shoes if they own them; however, men are more likely than women to own shoes. The concept of owning a wardrobe of clothing does not exist for the majority of Melpa. Most people own only one change of clothing. It is still possible to see Melpa dressed in traditional clothing, including the wig made from human hair that adult Melpa men wear on important occasions. In some cases, Melpa from rural villages will travel by plane to visit other highland communities. During these travels, the rural Melpa may dress in their traditional clothing and carry the tools of traditional life, such as stone axes and digging sticks. The airport at Mount Hagen is truly a meeting place of the jet age and the stone age.

12 ● FOOD

Like other Highland cultures in Papua New Guinea, the Melpa's traditional staple foods were sweet potatoes and pork. Sweet potatoes are still an important staple. Western-style foodstuffs have gained in importance now that they are available in trade stores and since eating this type of food increases a person's status in the eyes of the community.

13 ● EDUCATION

Traditional education consisted of socializing young boys and girls to become competent members of adult Melpa society. Although this is still true today, public and parochial schools (church-run, private schools) are also open to Hageners. In the highlands region, Western-style education has been integrated with traditional ways of life to produce individuals who seem to exist in two very different worlds at the same time.

14 ● CULTURAL HERITAGE

Vocal music is especially important in Melpa society. Courtship songs are common in many highland cultures in New Guinea. Men woo their mates by composing and performing songs that have double-entendre lyrics (words with two sets of meanings, one often sexual in nature). When men go to sing to women in other villages, they paint and decorate themselves very elaborately.

15 ● EMPLOYMENT

The traditional division of labor was between the sexes. Men were responsible for creating gardens and building fences to keep out the pigs. Women tended the pigs, planted the staple crop of sweet potatoes and other foodstuffs such as greens and taro (a starch), and weeded and harvested the garden plot.

Modern Melpa work in a variety of jobs in the town of Mount Hagen. Driving taxis and buses, porting baggage at the airport, and working in shops are among the types of employment that the Hageners pursue.

16 ● SPORTS

As in other parts of Papua New Guinea, rugby is an important sport in the area around Mount Hagen. Mount Hagen is the venue (location) for many rugby games involving Hageners and other Papuans from throughout the island.

17 ● RECREATION

Town-dwelling Melpa have access to electricity and many of them enjoy watching television. There are very few locally produced television shows in the country. Most programs are bought from Australian broadcasting, which in turn purchases shows from the United States. Therefore, Hageners are exposed to American society in the form of situation comedies.

18 ● CRAFTS AND HOBBIES

Body decoration is the major art form in the Hagen region. *Moka* (exchanges) and ceremonial events have historically been important times for elaborate decoration to take place. Body paint is produced from local dyes mixed with pig fat. Traditional materials such as feathers and shells are used to decorate elaborate headdresses. Today, traditional headdresses are decorated with modern items, such as labels of various products and the tops of tin cans. The American product Liquid Paper (white correction fluid) has also become a favorite substitute for traditional white paint. The intensity of whiteness is cited as the reason for the switch.

19 ● SOCIAL PROBLEMS

Revenge was the basis for many violent actions taken by the Melpa in the time before pacification (when they were forced by European missionaries to become more peaceful). Revenge murders often pitted the male members of one clan against those of another. This mentality has not completely disappeared from the Melpa. Hundreds of men wearing full war dress can occasionally be seen running along the Highlands Highway toward a neighboring village. Their intent is to exact revenge for a death or wrongdoing that took place in the past. Events like these alarm tourists and government officials. As a result, warnings are sometimes issued regarding travel in the region.

20 ● BIBLIOGRAPHY

Strathern, Andrew. *The Rope of Moka: Big-Men and Ceremonial Exchange in Mount Hagen, New Guinea.* Cambridge: Cambridge University Press, 1971.

WEBSITES
Interknowledge Corp. [Online] Available http://www.interknowledge.com/papua-newguinea/, 1998.
World Travel Guide. Papua New Guinea. [Online] Available http://www.wtgonline.com/country/pg/gen.html, 1998.

Motu

PRONUNCIATION: MOH-too
LOCATION: Southern coast of Papua New Guinea
LANGUAGE: Motu (Hiri Motu); Tok Pisin; English
RELIGION: Christianity

1 ● INTRODUCTION

The Motu are a group who live on the southern coast of Papua New Guinea. They occupy a stretch of coastline that was the first area of permanent European settlement on the island of New Guinea. The Motu are well chronicled because of their elaborate annual trading expeditions to distant parts of the Gulf of Papua. The Motu men built large sailing boats called *lagatoi,* which were multihulled rafts built out of large logs that were lashed together. These rafts were propelled by crab-claw-shaped sails made of coconut fiber. A crew of thirty men was needed to sail one of these vessels. Although the annual *hiri* (trade) expeditions are no longer undertaken by the Motu, annual ceremonies and events commemorate the tradition.

2 ● LOCATION

The Motu homeland is in the Central Province of Papua New Guinea. Papua New Guinea has been an independent nation since 1975. It occupies the eastern half of the island of New Guinea, the third-largest island in the world. The capital of Papua New Guinea is Port Moresby, a city that divides the traditional Motu territory in half. The first European accounts of the Motu record the same fourteen villages that are still occupied by the Motu today. The Motu coastline has two distinct seasons: a hot, dry period from April to November; and a wet, humid period from November to March. Some Motu have left their villages and moved to small settlements on the outskirts of Port Moresby. Others live in the city itself in modern homes with running water and electricity.

3 ● LANGUAGE

The language of the Motu is related to the other Austronesian languages of New Guinea and the South Pacific region. Austronesian languages are in the minority in Papua New Guinea, and speakers of these languages are usually only found in coastal regions. (The Papuan languages are the majority languages of this island nation.) During their annual trading expeditions, the Motu used a special form of their language referred to now as "Hiri Motu." Some Motu also speak Tok Pisin (an English-based pidgin language) and English.

4 ● FOLKLORE

The existing body of folklore and mythology of the Motu is being lost at a rapid rate due to urbanization and, in some cases, education. In many cases, children no longer have the opportunity to learn the traditional stories of the past. Many Motu stories tell of conflict between the Motu and their neighbors. Stories of the successes of ancestors in raiding neighboring villages are still remembered by some older Motu. Traditional myths tell the origins of the Motu, the development of fire, and the history of the *hiri* (trading expeditions). These myths and others have been written down and published as small booklets.

5 ● RELIGION

Christian missionaries have been active in the area since the earliest Motu-European contact during the 1930s. The vast majority of Motu are Christians. However, some of the traditional beliefs and ceremonies are still maintained in Motu society. The Motu believed in witchcraft and sorcery, but they did not practice it. Instead, they believed that neighboring groups had this power, and the Motu would have to enlist the services of outsiders if they wanted to inflict illness or death on one of their own.

6 ● MAJOR HOLIDAYS

The Motu celebrate Christian holidays. Most Motu participate in the nation's wage-earning work force. Therefore, they also recognize and, in some cases, celebrate the secular (nonreligious) national holidays. The Hiri Festival (commemorating the Motu trade expeditions) is also an important holiday. It gives the Motu a chance to celebrate their traditional heritage and enjoy their traditional dress and entertainment.

7 ● RITES OF PASSAGE

The Motu have experienced the effects of modernization more than many other groups in Papua New Guinea. As a result, many of the traditional aspects of their culture have been lost. The stages of life that were integral to traditional Motu society no longer exist. Only the payment of "bride price" (payment by the groom's family to the bride's family) still exists as part of a rite of passage. The transitions from infant to adolescent, adult, and then onward to death, are marked more in the European manner.

Birthdays are celebrated by Motu who live in Port Moresby.

8 ● RELATIONSHIPS

The choice of language for Motu greetings is the most important aspect of an interaction. Motus will usually greet each other in Hiri Motu, but also use English and Tok Pisin with some frequency. The choice of language directly reflects the nature of the social relationship between the parties involved.

The kinship terminology of the Motu is the Hawaiian type. (A kinship terminology is the set of terms that a person uses to refer to or address a relative.) In American English, one distinguishes between one's mother and one's aunts, but typically does not distinguish between maternal aunts and paternal aunts. In the Motu system, there are no distinctive words for "mother" and "aunt." Instead, both are referred to by the same term. However, the Motus do distinguish between relatives on the father's side and relatives on the mother's side.

9 ● LIVING CONDITIONS

Traditionally, the Motu built their houses in lines that were connected to each other by walkways built over the tidal shallows. A line of houses corresponded to a particular descent group—that is, a group of people related to each other by a common ancestor. Some Motu have chosen to remain in village areas such as these, but have built houses on land. Motu village houses often have corrugated sheet-metal walls, thatched roofs, and plank floors. Some of the Motu who live in traditional villages do not have electricity. They rely on kerosene lanterns for lighting and on battery-operated radios for keeping in touch with the outside world. Urban Motu live in a range of house styles. Wealthy, professional Motu have large houses with all the comforts that most Americans are accustomed to having.

10 ● FAMILY LIFE

The nuclear family is the basic unit of social organization among the Motu. Households were traditionally linked together by a shared walkway and a shared cooking area.

Marriage among the Motu today has changed from when Europeans first encountered them. Today, the Motu are monogamous. In precolonial times, men of status and wealth often had several wives. Motu marriages were arranged in traditional times, and there were many restrictions on potential spouses. Child betrothal (engagement) was quite common. Gift exchange occurred frequently until the final bride price (goods given by the groom's family to the bride's family) was paid and the marriage was finalized. The modern Motu are free to choose their marriage partners. Wealthy Motu families have inflated bride prices, which has lengthened the time it takes for a marriage to become finalized.

11 ● CLOTHING

Traditional clothing for Motu women consisted of a grass fiber skirt. They did not wear any footwear or any covering on their upper bodies, which were frequently tattooed. For ceremonies and other important occasions, both men and women would oil their skin. Feathers, flowers, and the leaves of croton plants were used to decorate women's hair, and were also placed in arm-

bands (worn on the upper arms). Traditional dress is still used by the Motu for ceremonial events such as bride-price payments, weddings, and canoe races. Urban Motus wear Western-style clothing.

12 ● FOOD

The traditional foods of the Motu were fish, yams, and bananas. They also collected shellfish and crabs. The Motu traded with their neighbors and also went on trading expeditions to far-away villages. Nowadays, Western foodstuffs have become staples. Tinned fish and canned Indonesian curry dishes are popular foods. Rice and tea are also important foods that are purchased in shops and grocery stores, where American products such as boxed cereals, soft drinks, and hot dogs are also sold. Although village families often cook together, Motu nuclear families eat separately.

13 ● EDUCATION

Traditional education was structured along sex lines. Boys learned adult male activities from their male relatives; females learned adult female activities from their females relatives. Nowadays, public education is available to the Motu and almost all families take advantage of it. Some Motu go on to college at one of the national colleges or universities, such as the University of Papua New Guinea in Port Moresby.

14 ● CULTURAL HERITAGE

Traditional dances were very impressive. They often were intricate group dances. Men and women wore elaborate face paint and feather headdresses. Dancing was accompanied by drumming, and sometimes, singing. The Motu use hand-held, hourglass-shaped drums called *kundu*. Dancing was discouraged by Christian missionaries. As a result, many of the traditional ceremonial dances are no longer performed and are forgotten. Some dances are still performed on important occasions and for tourists who visit Motu villages.

15 ● EMPLOYMENT

The traditional division of labor in Motu society was along sex lines. Men built houses and canoes, constructed fishing nets, fished, and participated in trading expeditions. Women made the pottery that the men took to trade on the *hiri* (trading) voyages. Women also cooked, fetched water, and gathered foodstuffs. Both men and women tended the garden where limited crops were grown. Today, both men and women seek wage labor outside their villages, usually in Port Moresby. Many Motu hold white-collar (professional) jobs. Traditional industries are all but lost, with only a few still remaining for demonstration at festivals and ceremonies.

16 ● SPORTS

Rugby is both a spectator and participant sport throughout Papua New Guinea. Motu who live or work in Port Moresby watch league (semiprofessional) rugby. Canoe races are an important form of recreation for the Motu. The canoes are modeled on traditional styles, but are constructed of modern materials.

17 ● RECREATION

For Motu who live in or near Port Moresby, movie houses, clubs, and pubs are places for entertainment. The national beauty pageant that crowns "Miss Papua New Guinea" for competition in larger, regional pageants is an important event for those living in Port Moresby. Motu are always well represented in this event.

18 ● CRAFTS AND HOBBIES

Art among the Motu was limited to pottery made by women, and to the elaborate body tattoos of women. Many Pacific societies have given up the practice of tattooing. However, some Motu girls and young women are still being tattooed. Patterns are geometric in nature, with some Christian motifs having become part of the imagery.

19 ● SOCIAL PROBLEMS

Maintaining the distinctiveness of their culture in the face of urbanization and modernization is a challenge for the present-day Motu. The Motu language has lost some ground to the popularity of Tok Pisin among young people. Larger problems are alcohol and drug abuse, and the spread of HIV (the AIDS virus).

20 ● BIBLIOGRAPHY

Groves, M. "Hiri." In *The Encyclopedia of Papua New Guinea,* ed. P. Ryan. Melbourne, Australia: Melbourne University Press, 1972.

Holdsworth, David. *Festivals and Celebrations in Papua New Guinea.* Bathurst, Australia: Robert Brown & Associates, 1982.

WEBSITES

Interknowledge Corp. [Online] Available http://www.interknowledge.com/papua-newguinea/, 1998.

World Travel Guide. Papua New Guinea. [Online] Available http://www.wtgonline.com/country/pg/gen.html, 1998.

Paraguay

■ **PARAGUAYANS** **93**
■ **GUARANÍS** **99**

The people of Paraguay are called Paraguayans. About 90 percent of the population is mestizo (mixture of Spanish and Guaraní Indian). The others are pure Amerindian (native people, about 3 percent), black, or of European or Asian immigrant stock.

Paraguayans

PRONUNCIATION: pahr-ah-GWAY-ahns
LOCATION: Paraguay
POPULATION: 4.1 million
LANGUAGE: Spanish; Guaraní
RELIGION: Roman Catholicism (official)

1 ● INTRODUCTION

Paraguay is a lone, landlocked country. For much of its history, it has deliberately kept itself apart from the rest of Latin America. Tucked away in the south-central part of South America, it is sparsely populated. It is a hot, subtropical lowland that has been dubbed "the empty quarter" of the continent.

When the first Europeans arrived in the sixteenth century, Guaraní-speaking people inhabited most of what is now eastern Paraguay. West of the Río Paraguay (Paraguay River), many other American Indian (Amerindian) peoples, known collectively as "Guaycuru" to the Guaranís, lived in the Chaco territories. The Paraguayans threw out their Spanish governor in 1811 and proclaimed independence. Because the colony was so distant and economically unimportant, the Spanish government did not bother to do anything about it. The new country was left on its own.

Today, Paraguay is a democratic country. (For decades in the past, it was run by a series of brutal dictators.) Paraguay relies on agriculture for much of its export industry. The most important farm products are cassava, sugarcane, corn, soybeans, and cotton, as well as cattle products. It still is one of the least economically developed countries in South America.

2 ● LOCATION

Lying within the heart of South America, Paraguay is surrounded by the much larger neighboring countries of Brazil, Argentina,

PARAGUAYANS

try, they were far outnumbered by the Guaraní people. As a result, the two peoples intermarried. Although many Paraguayans prefer to speak Guaraní, Spanish is the official language of government and business.

Several other American Indian languages, including Lengua, Nivacle, and Ache, are spoken in the eastern parts of Paraguay. Through contact with the Mennonite missionaries, German has become the second language of many of the American Indians.

4 ● FOLKLORE

The historical merging of the Spanish and Guaraní peoples over the centuries has created a unique culture. This is reflected in the folklore, arts, and literature of the country.

5 ● RELIGION

The official religion of Paraguay is Roman Catholicism. However, the Roman Catholic Church is weaker and less influential there than in most other Latin American countries. As a result, a number of irregular religious practices have developed over the years. In fact, in some rural areas, priests are seen as healers and men of magic, rather than as official representatives of the church.

The Mennonites have converted many Chaco Indians since they arrived in the 1930s.

6 ● MAJOR HOLIDAYS

Christmas and Easter are major Christian holidays, as well as the *Día de la Virgen*, on December 8, celebrating the Immaculate

and Bolivia. In area, it is about the same size as California. Although half the country is covered by timber, most of the wood has little commercial value.

Paraguay's population is 4.1 million. Asunción, the capital, is also the largest city, with 500,000 residents. Only 43 percent of Paraguayans live in cities and towns. Most people can claim to be native-born Paraguayans. Ninety percent are *mestizo,* of mixed Spanish and Guaraní ancestry. Many Paraguayans are peasant farmers and make a living by selling their extra crops.

3 ● LANGUAGE

Spanish and Guaraní are Paraguay's official languages. This is a reflection of its colonial history. When Spaniards settled in the coun-

Anne Kalosh

Most Paraguayans in rural areas survive on subsistence crops grown on small landholdings, selling any surplus at local markets.

Conception. The War of the Triple Alliance (fought in the 1860s) is commemorated on March 1. The popular Latin American festival of *Carnival* is celebrated just before Ash Wednesday (in February), the beginning of Lent.

7 ● RITES OF PASSAGE

Through the influence of the Catholic church, baptisms, first communion, and saints' days play an important part in the lives of many families.

8 ● RELATIONSHIPS

A popular social pastime is the drinking of *maté,* a tea made from the leaves of a plant related to holly. It is an important ritual, shared among family, friends, and colleagues. Each time, one person is responsible for filling a gourd almost to the top with the tea. Water is heated, but not boiled, in a kettle and poured into the vessel. Each person then sips the liquid through a silver tube.

9 ● LIVING CONDITIONS

Paraguay's capital city Asunción has preserved much of its nineteenth-century architecture. It has narrow streets full of low buildings. Meanwhile, a steady stream of rural poor people has arrived and caused large shantytowns to develop. Some 40 percent of the population still live in rural areas, where poor sanitation and malnutrition are common.

Paraguay has one of the highest infant mortality rates (the percentage of babies who die in infancy) in South America. Its government aid to the poor ranks very low by both world and South American standards. But the social welfare system does provide some cash and medical care for sickness, maternity, and injury at work, as well as pensions for old age.

Most rural Paraguayans live in one-room houses. Most have dirt floors; reed, wood, or brick walls; and a thatched roof, sloped to carry off the heavy rains. A separate or attached shed serves as a kitchen. Few houses have indoor plumbing.

City dwellers—over 40 percent of the population—have small, pastel-colored houses of brick or stucco, with tiled roofs and iron grillwork on the windows. The poor in the cities live in shacks.

10 ● FAMILY LIFE

Population growth is encouraged, although the abandonment of children and high rates of maternal mortality (the percentage of mothers who die while giving birth) are problems. There is also a high level of births outside of marriage, particularly in rural areas.

Marriage may be performed as both a civil and a religious ceremony.

11 ● CLOTHING

In cities and towns, Paraguayans dress as people do in North America and Europe. Many rural women wear a shawl, called a *rebozo,* and a simple dress or a skirt and blouse. The men usually wear loose trousers called *bomachas,* a shirt or jacket, a neckerchief (neck scarf), and a poncho. Rural people usually go barefoot.

EPD Photos

A popular social pastime is the drinking of maté, *a tea made from the leaves of a plant related to holly. The tea is shared from a gourd and sipped through a metal straw with a strainer on one end.*

12 ● FOOD

Paraguayan food is similar to that of Argentina and Uruguay, although Paraguayans eat less meat. *Parrillada,* grilled meat, is a popular item on restaurant menus. The influence of Guaraní tastes in tropical ingredients can be seen in many Paraguayan recipes.

A common part of almost every meal is grain, particularly corn (maize), and tubers such as cassava. *Locro* is a corn stew, and *mazamorra* is a cornmeal mush.

The national dish and dietary staple is *sopa paraguaya,* which is not a soup, but a kind of corn bread with cheese and onions. Cassava dishes are the main food of the rural poor.

13 ● EDUCATION

Education is compulsory (required) only to the age of twelve. The literacy rate (proportion of people who can read and write) is 81 percent.

The Universidad Nacional (National University) and the Universidad Católica (Catholic University) are located in Asunción. Both also have branches throughout the country.

14 ● CULTURAL HERITAGE

Novelist and poet Augusto Roa Bastos introduced Paraguay to the international literary stage by winning the Spanish government's Cervantes prize in 1990. Other important Paraguayan writers are novelist Gabriel Cassaccia and poet Evio Romero. Very little Paraguayan literature is available in English translations.

15 ● EMPLOYMENT

Most people in rural areas survive on subsistence crops (raising just enough to live on), which are cultivated on small landholdings. They sell any extra produce at local markets. They also add to their incomes by laboring on the large plantations.

There are still small, but important, populations of American Indians in the Chaco and in scattered areas of eastern Paraguay. Until very recently, some of them relied on hunting and gathering for their livelihood. The Nivacle and the Lengua are among the largest groups. Both groups number about

10,000, and many of their members work as laborers on the large agricultural estates.

Many Paraguayans, for either political or economic reasons, live outside the country. They are mainly in Brazil and Argentina. Between 1950 and 1970, more than 350,000 Paraguayans migrated to Argentina to find work. Although the official minimum wage in Paraguay is approximately $200 per month, the Ministry of Justice and Labor is unable to enforce the law that requires this minimum. It is estimated that about 70 percent of Paraguayan workers earn less than the minimum wage.

16 ● SPORTS

As in other parts of Latin America, soccer is the most popular sport, for both playing and watching. Asunción's most popular team, Olímpico, is on a level with the best Argentinian and Uruguayan teams.

Paraguayans also enjoy basketball, volleyball, horse racing, and swimming.

17 ● RECREATION

Theater is popular in Paraguay. Productions are staged in Guaraní as well as Spanish.

The visual arts are also very important and popular. Asunción has many galleries; the most important is the Museo del Barro. It has a wide range of modern works.

Classical and folk music are performed throughout the capital.

Religious holidays are celebrated with festivals that include music, dancing, and parades, as well as athletic contests.

18 ● CRAFTS AND HOBBIES

Paraguay's most famous traditional craft is the production of multicolored spiderweb lace in the Asunción suburb of Itaugua. This cottage industry is practiced by skilled women from childhood through old age. Paraguayan harps and guitars, as well as gold and silver jewelry and leather goods, are made in the village of Luque.

The American Indian communities of the Chaco produce fine crafts of their own.

19 ● SOCIAL PROBLEMS

When Juan Carlos Wasmosy was elected in 1993 as Paraguay's first civilian president after many years, he was nominated by the ruling party only as a figurehead, or symbolic leader with little power. Since then, however, he has clashed with the military. The country's democracy is still fragile.

20 ● BIBLIOGRAPHY

Bernhardson Wayne. *Argentina, Uruguay and Paraguay: A Lonely Planet Travel Survival Kit.* 2nd ed. Australia: Lonely Planet Publications, 1996.

Warren, Harris Gaylord. *Paraguay and the Triple Alliance.* Austin: University of Texas, 1978.

Warren, Harris Gaylord. *Rebirth of the Paraguayan Republic.* Pittsburgh: University of Pittsburgh Press, 1985.

Williams, John Hoyt. *The Rise and Fall of the Paraguayan Republic.* Austin: University of Texas, 1979.

WEBSITES

Ruiz-Garcia, Pedro (The Latino Connection). [Online] Available http://www.ascinsa.com/LATINOCONNECTION/paraguay.html, 1998.

World Travel Guide. Paraguay. [Online] Available http://www.wtgonline.com/country/py/gen.html, 1998.

Guaranís

PRONUNCIATION: gwah-rah-NEES
LOCATION: Paraguay; Brazil
POPULATION: Unknown
LANGUAGE: Guaraní
RELIGION: Traditional indigenous religions

1 ● INTRODUCTION

The Guaranís were once one of the most influential American Indian peoples in the southern part of South America. They were settled in the tropical forests of Paraguay and southern Brazil.

When the Spanish first arrived, many Guaranís helped them in their wars against other American Indian groups. Many Spanish men married Guaraní women during this period. This was the beginning of the long process of intermarriage that produced the Paraguayans of today.

Other Guaraní groups turned against the Spanish and fought to protect their freedom and their way of life. This process continued into the nineteenth century. Many Guaraní groups fell under the control of the Spanish and their cruel *encomienda* system. This system was similar to the old European system of serfdom. It also resembled the British system of indentured servants. In the *encomendia* system, the Guaraní were basically enslaved and were forced to work for Spanish landowners. It was a harsh, exploitative system.

Still other Guaranís joined with Jesuit missionaries (an order of Catholic priests). The Jesuits had become a very powerful force in Latin America. In fact, they often were seen as enemies of the Spanish, even though they were mainly Spanish. Spain feared them because their loyalty was to the Catholic Church, and not to Spain.

The Guaranís who allied themselves with the Jesuits were converted to Christianity and moved into missions. For a time, these missions became powerful institutions in colonial South America. Fearing their increasing power, the Spanish ordered the Jesuits out of South America in 1767. The Guaranís who lived at the missions were pushed out, and many returned to their old way of life in the forests. Those who remained had to fight raids on the missions by colonists, who stole land from the Guaranís and destroyed both cattle and plantations.

The Guaranís also participated, as Paraguayan citizens, in the war against Brazil, Uruguay, and Argentina (1864–70), and in the devastating War of the Chaco (1932–35) against Bolivia, in which many Paraguayan men lost their lives.

2 ● LOCATION

Today the Guaranís who have kept their traditional way of life live in scattered settlements in Paraguay and in southern Brazil. It is thought that the Brazilian settlements date from the nineteenth century. They also made their way into northern Argentina, especially the province of Misiones.

3 ● LANGUAGE

The Guaraní language is still widely spoken in Paraguay. The Guaranís have a "secular," a "secret," and a "sacred" language. All Guaranís speak the secular language. The sacred language is used only by male and

GUARANÍS

he is said to be the father of the Guaraní people.

Pa'í taught his people not only sacred dances and songs, but also farming and ethics. He is the destroyer of evil beings. He created the honeybee as a sweet offering to humankind. He entrusted the care of his creation to four gods. After Ñande Ru created the first earth, it was destroyed by a great flood through the will of the gods. Then the Creator asked the son of Jakaira, the God of Spring, to create another earth. Since that time, the four gods have sent the souls of boys to earth, and the wives of the gods have sent the souls of girls to earth.

5 ● RELIGION

Not all Guaranís have the same beliefs. Among the three major groups that remain today (the Chiripás, the Mbayás, and the Pai-Kaiovás), there are some interesting differences. In general, they believe that every person has an earthly soul and a divine one. Dreams come from the divine soul and are the source of inspiration for the *shamans,* religious leaders. The shamans are the communicators between the divine and earthly worlds. They also have the task of identifying evil-doers and protecting the group as well as curing illnesses.

Some Guaranís believe in reincarnation. Those who have had more Christian influences believe that evil-doers go to a land of darkness, while good people go to the "Land Without Evil."

The Guaraní believe that all living things, including plants, animals, and water, have protective spirits. They also believe in evil spirits.

female elders. They receive divine messages and transmit them to the rest of the group. The secret language is used only by religious leaders. It is called *Ñe'e pará,* meaning "the words of our fathers."

Guaranís often have a Spanish name for everyday use, as well as a secret Guaraní name. It is the task of the group leader to find out the origin of a baby's soul and then give him or her a sacred name.

4 ● FOLKLORE

Guaraní folklore is very rich. Among the *mbyás,* a group of Guaranís who have preserved much of their old literature and tradition, the Creator is called *Ñande Ru.* He gave birth to a son, whom he named *Pa'í Reté Kuaray.* His body was like the sun, and

6 ● MAJOR HOLIDAYS

The Guaranís do not make distinctions between secular and religious occasions. Most feasts and celebrations have religious aspects. Even harvest festivals include sacred ceremonies.

7 ● RITES OF PASSAGE

When a boy becomes an adolescent he undergoes initiation rites with a group of others, apart from the larger group. The rituals are performed under the direction of the shaman. The boy's lower lip is pierced with a piece of wood. He follows a strict diet based on corn for several days. Afterward, he can use adult words and adult ways of talking to people.

During the initiation rites, the boy is instructed in appropriate behavior. This includes working hard, refraining from harming others, being moderate in his habits, not drinking excessively, and never beating his future wife.

When a girl reaches adolescence, she is kept apart for a time under the care of female relatives. Her mother gives her guidance on her future marriage.

Guaranís sometimes have informal marriages. A young man takes a young woman to his parents' house to live for a time, without formal marriage ceremonies. If he wishes to marry her, he asks her father for permission. When a couple forms a family, they are expected to raise their children with kindness and tolerance, and not to hit the children.

8 ● RELATIONSHIPS

Traditional greetings to visitors required the female hosts to wail and mourn, reciting the admirable deeds of the visitor's dead relatives. The guest had to cover his or her face with the hands and show appropriate expressions of sorrow. Some of these traditional greetings have fallen out of use.

Among some groups, there are celebrations that offer young people a way of dating. These celebrations are known as *kotyú*. They are dances that are meant to celebrate important myths. But at the same time, they allow young men to dance with young women and to express their love. During the *kotyú* dances, both formal and friendly, or even romantic, greetings are exchanged.

Two anthropologists did a study of Guaraní songs and literature. They report that an official who came to investigate the condition of a particular Guaraní group was greeted in this way during the dance:

An inhabitant from faraway lands do I see. Oh bird!

In truth, I see, oh bird, an inhabitant

from faraway lands!

This is a greeting from the boys to girls during a *kotyú*, as described by the anthropologists:

Let us, my sisters, give a brotherly greeting,

Oh spotless maidens,

around the Great House

near the Golden Grasses.

9 ● LIVING CONDITIONS

War, conquest, and European diseases have destroyed much of the Guaraní population. The more traditional groups continue to live a lifestyle that satisfies their simple and basic needs, such as food and shelter. Some of these Guaranís live mainly apart from the cash economy and produce only enough to keep themselves alive. There is an active trade in basic implements for hunting, fishing, and cooking.

The traditional extended family unit was part of a clan of as many as fifty or sixty families. This required the construction of large houses with screened-off sections and a large group area. During the Spanish colonial period, government and religious authorities disapproved of these houses. Eventually, most of the Guaranís gave up this mode of living.

The Guaranís in Paraguay live along streams and use bamboo rafts, or occasionally canoes, for transportation. In some jungle areas, they walk long distances, especially during hunting expeditions. The Guaranís in parts of Brazil use dugout canoes.

10 ● FAMILY LIFE

The traditional extended family unit required a cooperative way of living, under the authority of the head of the clan. Guaranís lived in small groups of large rectangular houses built around a square plaza, or courtyard. Today, in many areas, these houses have been replaced by small single-family units.

Some marriage customs are changing. Young people are insisting on having more of a say in the choice of marriage partners. In earlier times, people were betrothed (became engaged) as children. Chiefs also had several wives in earlier times; this is no longer the case.

Some Guaranís keep dogs that they prize as hunting companions, especially in jungle areas where jaguars are still hunted. In some areas, Guaranís keep chickens and other farm animals.

11 ● CLOTHING

Guaranís who live on the reservations in parts of northern Argentina and Paraguay have adopted the clothing of the rural peasant farmers. This consists of plain shirts and trousers and a cloak or poncho.

In distant areas of Brazil, some of the Guaranís still wear traditional ornaments and very little else. Originally, they wore no clothing at all. They used strands of women's hair around their legs in bands as protective ornaments. They sometimes pierced their lower lips. In distant areas, the women still wear black body paint and the men wear black and red body paint. Some Guaranís still wear earrings of shell or gold.

12 ● FOOD

The whole community participates in clearing land to grow crops. When the soil is exhausted, the community moves on. While this traditional method is still in use in some areas, in other places the Guaranís have become more settled.

The staple foods are cassava and corn. Sweet potatoes, beans, pumpkins, and tropical fruits such as bananas and papayas are also grown. Peanuts provide protein, and sugarcane is a delicacy. In the forests, wild honey is sometimes collected.

Chipas are cakes made from corn flour. The Guaranís also wrap corn dough in leaves and cook them under ashes; this dish is called *auimi atucupé*. Cassava is often roasted or boiled.

13 ● EDUCATION

The Jesuits provided the first schools for the Guaranís. After the Jesuits left, many Guaranís took refuge in distant areas and went back to earlier lifestyles. Others went to work as paid peasant farmers on plantations. Still others went into the towns to find work and continued the process of assimilation, becoming like the people around them.

Those that remain today in remote areas, such as some of the Brazilian Guaranís, do not wish to adapt to the Western lifestyle. They also do not want to send their children to school. They fear that this will lead to the destruction of their independent existence.

14 ● CULTURAL HERITAGE

Some Guaraní songs and poems have made their way into the popular culture of the Paraguayans. Some groups, such as the Mbayás, have preserved many of their legends and stories. Traditional instruments include drums, rattles, and flutes. Sometimes important moral and social lessons are given in the form of short plays staged in front of village children.

15 ● EMPLOYMENT

Guaranís farm, hunt, and fish. Some Guaranís are also beekeepers. In wild areas, they hunt the tapir (a kind of wild hog), the anteater, and the jaguar, as well as the agouti (a rabbit-like rodent). They capture parrots by lassoing them with a small noose attached to the end of a pole.

The Guaranís are able fishers, and they still shoot fish with bows and arrows in some areas. They also use traps in the form of baskets or nets made of plant fiber. Fish provides an important source of protein in their diet.

16 ● SPORTS

Sports begin as the games that children play. Guaraní children especially enjoy wrestling and racing. They also play tug-of-war. Some studies report that the ancient Itatín group of Guaranís played games with rubber balls. Adults still play a game with a shuttlecock made out of corn. The aim is to throw it at each other and try to keep it in the air as long as possible.

17 ● RECREATION

Guaranís have always enjoyed celebrations and feasts. Usually they celebrate with generous quantities of a fermented drink called *chicha,* which is often made from corn. A good harvest and a good fishing expedition are also opportunities for celebration.

18 ● CRAFTS AND HOBBIES

Baskets are woven from pindo palm fibers. Some of the Paraguayan Guaranís make bags from leather.

Some still make their own bows and arrows and carve dugout canoes from a single tree trunk. They also weave cotton into white cloth with brown and black stripes. They make their own flutes, sometimes from bamboo. Beads are made and strung into necklaces.

19 ● SOCIAL PROBLEMS

The social problems of the Guaranís vary depending on where they live. Those living in the tropical forests resent the intrusions of Europeans. To keep their simple, sustainable lifestyle, they need to live in small, scattered settlements. These often range over a wide area. This lifestyle clashes with the needs of ranchers and poor farmers, who require land for their operations. Their biggest conflicts, however, are with prospectors searching for oil and minerals.

On the reservations, problems are caused by the economic limitations and the lack of opportunity to preserve the Guaranís' cultural and economic independence.

20 ● BIBLIOGRAPHY

Bernhardson, Wayne. *Argentina, Uruguay and Paraguay: A Lonely Planet Travel Survival Kit.* 2nd ed. Australia: Lonely Planet Publications, 1996.

Steward, Julian Haynes, ed. *A Handbook of South American Indians.* New York: Cooper Square, 1963.

Warren, Harris Gaylord. *Paraguay and the Triple Alliance.* Austin: University of Texas, 1978.

Warren, Harris Gaylord. *Rebirth of the Paraguayan Republic.* Pittsburgh: University of Pittsburgh Press, 1985.

Williams, John Hoyt. *The Rise and Fall of the Paraguayan Republic.* Austin: University of Texas, 1979.

WEBSITES

Ruiz-Garcia, Pedro (The Latino Connection). [Online] Available http://www.ascinsa.com/LATINOCONNECTION/paraguay.html, 1998.

World Travel Guide. Paraguay. [Online] Available http://www.wtgonline.com/country/py/gen.html, 1998.

Peru

■ **PERUVIANS** **105**
■ **ASHÁNINKA** **113**
■ **QUECHUA** **119**

Between 30 and 45 percent of the inhabitants of Peru are Amerindian (native), about 30 percent mestizo (mixed Spanish and Amerindian), 15 percent white, and 3 percent black, Asian, or other. The Asháninka and Quechua are two Amerindian groups, but there are a number of other tribes. There are small groups of Germans, Italians, and Swiss, as well as Chinese and Japanese.

Peruvians

PRONUNCIATION: peh-ROO-vee-yuns
LOCATION: Peru
POPULATION: 24.5 million
LANGUAGE: Spanish; Quechua
RELIGION: Roman Catholicism, intertwined with native beliefs

1 ● INTRODUCTION

Once the seat of the expansive Inca Empire, Peru is a dramatic mix of old and new. After the conquest of the Incas, Peru's capital, Lima, became the center of Spain's colonial power structure in the Americas. The combination of a strong Spanish influence with a rich indigenous (native) heritage has shaped Peru's traditions, politics, and culture.

Peru's political history in the twentieth century has been characterized by swings from democracy to military dictatorship. Most recently, a leftist military government, the result of a military coup (takeover) in 1976, instituted an economic program that promoted agricultural cooperatives, expropriated foreign companies, and decreed worker participation in modern industry. A return to democracy in 1980 lasted until 1992 when a democratically elected president, Alberto Fujimori, ruled as a dictator. Fujimori successfully battled two of Peru's greatest ills—inflation and terrorism. After reopening Congress, he was reelected with popular support in 1995.

2 ● LOCATION

Three times the size of California, Peru has an extremely varied geography ranging from tropical rain forest to arid desert. With Ecuador and Bolivia, it is one of the three Andean countries on the Pacific coast of South America. Peru can be conveniently

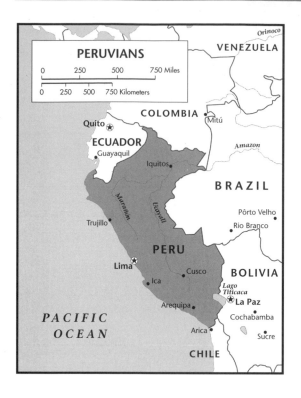

3 ● LANGUAGE

The two official languages of Peru are Spanish and Quechua. Quechua is the language of the Incas. Still widely spoken throughout the Andes, it was made an official language by the military government that controlled the country from 1968 to 1975. The dominant language in urban areas, however, is Spanish. The primary difference between the Spanish spoken in Spain and in Peru is the accent.

In Peru, as in other Hispanic countries, names comprise three parts: the given name, the father's surname, and the mother's maiden name. For example: Pedro (given name) Suárez (father's name) Durán (mother's name).

4 ● FOLKLORE

Many of the beliefs and practices that comprise Peruvian folklore are associated with the native faith and customs that prevailed before the arrival of the Spanish conquerors. For example, the Incas believed that they descended from the Sun God, Inti, and that the reigning Inca was an offspring of the Sun. Though they did not practice human sacrifice, many were headhunters. The Incas believed that the possession of another's head increased the owner's spiritual strength. While headhunting no longer exists, a blending of Amerindian and European beliefs often persists in festivals and other observances.

5 ● RELIGION

Peruvians are fervent Catholics. Catholics comprise 90 percent of the population. No Peruvian town, no matter how small or remote, is without a church. Religious prac-

divided into three basic geographical areas—the Andes mountains *(sierra),* desert, and Amazon rain forest. The tropical rain forest covers 67 percent of Peru's landmass but is rapidly being destroyed by logging companies.

Peru's population of over 24 million people can be subdivided into four groups: white, 15 percent; mestizo or mixed Amerindian and white heritage, 37 percent; indigenous South American Indian (Quechua and Aymara, for example), 45 percent; and black and Asian, 3 percent. The Quechua and Aymara constitute the two main South American Indian tribes. Peru's culture is becoming increasingly *mestijado;* that is, a mix of Western and traditional customs.

Plaza San Martin in Lima, Peru's capital city.

tices carefully intertwine modern and traditional beliefs. The Peruvian version of Catholicism, for example, has incorporated some of the traditional gods and spirits by referring to them as saints or lords. When the Spanish converted the Amerindians to Christianity, they moved many of the Christian holidays to coincide with existing traditional festivals. In so doing, many traditional festivals continue to be practiced, with minor modifications, within the Christian framework.

6 ● MAJOR HOLIDAYS

One of the most colorful festivals is the month-long celebration of the Lord of the Earthquakes in October. Peru is subject to constant tremors and earthquakes, and in the past many of its cities have been severely damaged by them. In October, a weekly procession through the streets of Lima features a painting of Christ that has survived successive quakes, trailed by throngs of followers dressed in purple robes. Strict Catholics dress in purple on these days, whether they are able to attend the procession or not.

A secular holiday that is of great importance to Peruvians is their Independence Day, July 28. This occasion is celebrated with much festivity—dancing, eating, and

© Corel Corporation

Shoppers in an indoor shopping mall in Lima. The residents of the modern suburbs of Lima have living standards comparable to those found in the United States.

birthday may not necessarily be celebrated; the person's namesake saint's day is likely to be observed instead. A novena (nine consecutive days of special prayers) for the dead is usually held in the home of the deceased, with friends invited on the final night. Often a second novena is held later.

8 ● RELATIONSHIPS

It is poor manners to arrive on time if invited to a dinner or a party. Tardiness of an hour or more is expected. If hosts expect the guests to arrive more promptly, they will ask them to observe *hora inglesa* (English time). When being introduced to a woman at a social occasion, the proper greeting is a kiss on the cheek. Men, when introduced to each other, shake hands.

At an informal gathering, when a group of friends are drinking together, it is a sign of friendship to share the same glass. When a large bottle of beer or *pisco* (a Peruvian alcoholic beverage) is opened, the bottle and glass are passed around in a circle. One is expected to serve oneself a small serving, drink it quickly, then pass both the bottle and glass to the next person. To ask for a separate glass would give offense.

The "okay" sign (touching your finger to your thumb) is considered a rude gesture in Peru.

9 ● LIVING CONDITIONS

Approximately one-third of the entire Peruvian population lives in the capital city, Lima. Over half live in urban squatter settlements (occupied without lease or rent). These are known as *pueblos jóvenes* (young towns). Migration to Lima from the Andean region fuels the development of pueblos

drinking. On this day, all homes are required by law to fly the Peruvian flag.

As late as 1966, there were more than 150 national holidays including Sundays.

7 ● RITES OF PASSAGE

Baptism of infants, first communion, and confirmation of children in church are common. Perhaps half of all couples live together without regularizing their unions with a license or a church ceremony. A

Cory Langley

Approximately one-third of the entire Peruvian population lives in the capital city, Lima. Over half live in urban squatter settlements (occupied without lease or rent). These are known as pueblos jóvenes *(young towns). Migration to Lima from the Andean region fuels the development of pueblos jóvenes.*

jóvenes. Uninhabited land is selected and invaded by a group of settlers overnight. The initial housing is usually made out of light reed matting. More-permanent structures are built gradually, bit by bit, as the family can afford to buy bricks and mortar. In addition to poor housing, residents of the pueblos jóvenes suffer from a lack of basic services. While the majority now have electricity in their houses, water is scarce. Unsanitary conditions create serious health hazards.

The residents of the modern suburbs of Lima have living standards comparable to those found in the United States. Suburban houses range from high-rise apartments to grand colonial houses. In periods of drought, however, even these sectors have their water and electricity rationed by the municipality.

10 ● FAMILY LIFE

In countries without a welfare system or social security system, the family bonds together not only as a social unit, but as an economic one as well. The basic household unit includes parents, children, and, in many cases, grandparents or aunts and uncles. In middle-class households, it may also include a live-in servant or nanny to look after young children. Financial difficulties mean that children live at home until they get married as young adults.

Compadrazgo (godparenthood) is an important tie between friends and forges bonds of obligation between two families. Godparents are expected not only to contribute a modest amount of financial support for the godchild, but to provide emotional support and guidance to the family. These interfamily social arrangements expand a family's support network.

Machismo, an attitude of male superiority and sexism, is widespread (*marianismo*, an attitude of female passivity and coyness, is the counterpart of machismo). However, Peruvian women participate actively in important family decisions. Women play an active role both in family and community life. They also make significant contributions to family income.

11 ● CLOTHING

In Andean areas, women wear colorful woven skirts with many layers of petticoats underneath. Solid-colored llama wool sweaters offer protection against the cold Andean night air. Hats are used throughout Peru. Each region has its own style of hat, and it is possible to tell which region an Amerindian is from by his or her hat. Men wear simple trousers and Western-style button-down shirts, and sandals.

As the process of urbanization in Peru has advanced, so has the process of Westernization. Most Peruvians don Western clothes for both everyday and special occasions. Young Peruvians in urban areas prefer jeans, American tennis shoes, and Western-style skirts instead of the traditional alpaca and llama wool clothes worn in the Andean regions. One useful traditional custom that is often retained is the use of a shawl across the shoulders to carry small children.

12 ● FOOD.

Peru has one of the most developed cuisines of Latin America. Many dishes are a delicate combination of South American Indian, Spanish, and African ingredients and cooking traditions. Seafood is the dominant ingredient on the coast, yucca and plantains in the jungle, and potatoes in the Andes.

The national dish of Peru is *ceviche,* a spicy dish of onions and seafood. In ceviche, the fish is cooked not by applying heat but by soaking it for a few hours in lime juice. The acid in the lime juice has the effect of breaking down the protein, thus "cooking" the fish. Sliced onion, hot peppers, and chopped coriander are then added.

Corn-on-the-cob cut into small sections called *choclo* are commonly served as a garnish or addition to different kinds of dishes in Peru. A recipe for ceviche follows.

The high cost of living has led many mothers living in low-income neighborhoods to organize and form communal kitchens. These groups, now recognized by the government, receive subsidized food and cook for one hundred or so people for a small fee.

Recipe

Ceviche

Ingredients

1 pound fresh fillet of red snapper, bass, or bay scallops (Have fish sliced into fillets about ¼-inch thick, and the skin and bones removed.)

Juice of 3 lemons

Juice of 3 limes

1 clove garlic, minced

1 jalapeno pepper, chopped (wear rubber gloves)

½ teaspoon salt

Pinch of white pepper

2 Tablespoons finely chopped fresh cilantro

1 sweet potato

1 ear of corn

½ head of lettuce

1 red onion, sliced thin

Directions

1. Cut fish slices on the diagonal into ¾-inch diamond shapes. (If using scallops, cut them in half if they are larger than about ¾-inch in diameter.)

2. Place the fish into a large, sealable plactic bag or a bowl (Do not use metal).

3. Mix lime juice, lemon juice, garlic, jalapeno pepper, salt, pepper, and cilantro. Pour over fish. Seal bag or cover bowl and refrigerate at least one hour.

4. Place the sweet potato in a saucepan and cover with water and heat until water boils. Lower heat and simmer until the sweet potato about 15 to 20 minutes. Drain and cool, but do not peel until the ceviche will be served.

5. Place the ear of corn into a saucepan and cover with water. Heat until the water boils. Lower heat and simmer until the corn is cooked (about 8 to 10 minutes). Drain and cool to room temperature. Cut cob into 1-inch slices.

6. To serve, arrange lettuce leaves on a nonmetal serving platter. Arrange fish on the center of the platter. Slice sweet potato into ½-inch slices. Arrange the slices, alternating with the corn cob slices, in a circle around the fish. Garnish with rings of red onion.

Adapted from *Recipes from Around the World.* Howard County, Md.: Foreign-Born Information and Referral Network, 1993, p. 10.

13 ● EDUCATION

Peruvian children wear solid gray uniforms to school. Classes are held in two sessions—morning and afternoon—and students attend one or the other. The literacy rate (ability to read and write) in Peru is relatively high, reaching 92 percent for males and 79 percent for females.

The relatively small number of universities in Peru means that it can be difficult to gain admission. Only 3 percent of the population is able to attend university.

14 ● CULTURAL HERITAGE

The different ethnic groups that have migrated to Peru have left a rich musical heritage. Both *musica criolla* of Spanish influence and Andean folk music are popular. A traditional music, recently becoming popular with young Peruvians, is Afro-Peruvian music. This rhythmic music has its roots in the protest songs of the black population of Peru. In the 1980s and 1990s, Afro-Peruvian music has witnessed a strong revival and is now popular in the bars and dance halls of Lima.

Musical shows for tourists feature the *Alcatraz,* a traditional Afro-Peruvian fire dance. Alcatraz dancers tuck a piece of paper into their back pockets or around their waist, leaving a short tail hanging out. A second dancer follows behind with a lit candle trying to set the tail on fire. The first dancer must move his or her hips vigorously to prevent the paper tail from catching fire.

Peru also has a strong literary tradition. One of the most revered contemporary writers in Peru is the novelist Mario Vargas Llosa. Vargas Llosa is known worldwide both for his writings and for his bid for the presidency in 1990. His comic autobiographical narrative, *Aunt Julia and the Script Writer,* was made into a Hollywood movie starring Keanu Reeves in the 1990s. Other outstanding writers include novelist José María Arguedas and Ciro Alegría, dramatists Salvador Bandy and Gregór Díaz, and poets Cesar Vallejo, Cecilia Bustamante, and Cesar Moro.

15 ● EMPLOYMENT

Formal paid employment is difficult to find in Peru. Most families are forced to seek varied and innovative means to generate an income, struggling to earn a living by whatever means possible. Approximately 80 percent of the population are either subsistence farmers (growing little more than their own food) or operate their own tiny enterprise. Both women and children make important contributions to family income, either from small-scale cottage industries in their homes, or as traders outside the home.

Outside urban areas, Peruvians are largely subsistence farmers. The dry Andean terrain makes agriculture a challenge. Steep slopes are farmed by a process of terracing, in which multileveled steps are created to provide flat areas for planting. Potatoes and corn, which adapt well to high altitudes, are the primary crops.

16 ● SPORTS

As in most other Latin American cultures, soccer is the dominant sport in Peru. The love of soccer is one of the few cultural traits that transcends both ethnic and socio-economic boundaries. Even in densely populated urban shantytowns, large pieces of land are often set aside for soccer fields. Middle-class children set up goals and play in the streets.

Lima's two soccer teams, Alianza Lima and Universitaria, have an intense rivalry that has kept Limeños (residents of Lima) fascinated for years. This rivalry has a particular poignancy. In 1987 the plane carrying the members of Alianza Lima crashed when landing in Lima, leaving no survivors.

17 ● RECREATION

Popular culture in Peru is varied. In the evenings, young people flock to both Western-style bars and discos, or to *peñas* where traditional Peruvian folk music is played. In Lima, an old colonial suburb of the city called *Barranco* has become the focus of trendy and artsy activities. Music halls, theaters, book shops, and art galleries attract crowds of middle-class youth.

Also popular in Peru are televised soap operas. Produced largely in Venezuela or Mexico, these evening shows attract a wide following. Soap operas are also produced in magazine format. *Fotonovelas,* as they are called, present soap operas with a series of photos and captions.

18 ● CRAFTS AND HOBBIES

See the article on the "Quechua" in this chapter.

19 ● SOCIAL PROBLEMS

Peru has one of the worst human rights records in the world. The Peruvian government has been battling the Maoist (communist) Shining Path guerrillas since the early 1980s. In its battle to eliminate this violent terrorist group, the military has kidnapped and killed many suspected Shining Path sympathizers. Trade union officials, university professors, and students have all been targeted by the government. The military has been successful in weakening the Shining Path movement, but human rights abuses remain a serious problem.

20 ● BIBLIOGRAPHY

Fiesta! Peru. Danbury, Conn.: Grolier Educational, 1997.

Fisher, John Robert. *Peru.* Santa Barbara, Calif.: Clio Press, 1989.

Hudson, Rex A. *Peru in Pictures.* Minneapolis, Minn.: Lerner Publications Co., 1987.

Jermyn, Leslie. *Peru.* Milwaukee, Wisc.: Gareth Stevens, 1998.

Kalman, Bobbie. *Peru: The People and Culture.* New York: Crabtree Publishing Company, 1994.

King, David C. *Peru: Lost Cities, Found Hopes.* New York: Benchmark Books, 1998.

Lewington, Anna. *Rainforest Amerindians.* Austin, Tex.: Raintree Steck-Vaughan Publishers, 1993.

Lewington, Anna. *What Do We Know about the Amazonian Indians?* New York: P. Bedrick Books, 1993.

Parker, Edward. *Peru.* Austin, Tex.: Raintree Steck-Vaughn, 1997.

Recipes from Around the World. Howard County, Md.: Foreign-Born Information and Referral Network, 1993.

WEBSITES

Interknowledge Corp. Peru. [Online] Available http://www.interknowledge.com/peru/, 1998.

Ruiz-Garcia, Pedro. The Latino Connection. [Online] Available http://www.ascinsa.com/LATINOCONNECTION/peru.html, 1998.

World Travel Guide. Peru. [Online] Available http://www.wtgonline.com/country/pe/gen.html, 1998.

Asháninka

PRONUNCIATION: ah-SHAH-nin-kah
ALTERNATE NAMES: Campa (derogatory)
LOCATION: Peru; Brazil
POPULATION: 45,000
LANGUAGE: Asháninka; Spanish
RELIGION: Native mythical beliefs

1 ● INTRODUCTION

The Asháninka are an ethnic group of the Peruvian Amazon rain forest. They are also known in Peru and abroad by the name "Campa." They consider this name derogatory because it derives from the Quechua *thampa,* which means ragged and dirty. *Asháninka* means "our fellows" or "our kinfolk."

Europeans first attempted to colonize (invade and rule) the area in 1595. In 1742 this period of colonization came to a sudden end with a general Amerindian rebellion led by the legendary Juan Santos Atahualpa. The uprising lasted until 1752 and succeeded in expelling all missionaries and colonists from the area. The Asháninka and their neighbors had control of their land for over a century.

By the mid-nineteenth century the encroachment of agriculture from the Andes and of the rubber-tapping industry from the Amazon brought Europeans back. In 1847 recolonization by Franciscans (a Catholic religious order) and European, Chinese, and Japanese settlers began. Some 5 million acres (2 million hectares) of Asháninka territory, along with the main rivers, were granted to the British-owned Peruvian Corporation forty-four years later. The Asháninka people were then used as laborers. Appalling working conditions together with virus epidemics took a heavy toll.

During the last decades of the twentieth century, the Asháninka territory has been the site of conflicts between the Peruvian Army and rebel groups. Since the beginning of the 1980s, the Shining Path (a communist rebel group) has entered their territory. Since then, guerrilla (rebel) and army actions often result in Asháninka deaths.

2 ● LOCATION

The Asháninka are one of the largest ethnic groups of the Americas. They inhabit mainly the Central Forest in the Amazonian part of the eastern Andean foothills in Peru. Their communities also stretch across the easternmost Peruvian Amazon to the state of Acre in Brazil. Their traditional heartland is the Gran Pajonal, a remote plateau of rolling terrain dissected by river gorges. On the slopes there are *pajonales* (grasslands), created in part by a long history of Asháninka clearing and burning.

Difficult access to the region allowed the inhabitants to remain isolated from outside influences until relatively recently. The degree of integration with their neighbors varies according to the geographic situation.

3 ● LANGUAGE

The Asháninka language belongs to the pre-Andean Arawak linguistic family. The largest language family in South America, it includes several dialects. Most of the population is monolinguistic (speaking one language) until they go to school. If indeed they do go, they learn Spanish. Children are given a provisional name when they start walking. Their official name is decided when they are seven years old.

4 ● FOLKLORE

Among the Asháninka, history and nature are explained through myths and heroes. A great cliff in the Tambo River, for example, used to be a Spanish ship that a powerful hero, Avireri, transformed into a rock. Its sailors became red ants. Other dangerous insects, such as wasps, are also transformations of bad men. As to the origins of their neighbors, it is said that Avireri, the great mythological transformer, turned a murderous hawk and his wife into huge rocks that can be seen in the Ene River. Their feathers became canoes, and each carried Piros, Matsigenkas, Shipibos, and all the other Indian groups that live down the river.

© Corel Corporation

The Asháninka live in the Peruvian Amazon rain forest. Difficult access to the region allowed the inhabitants to remain isolated from outside influences until relatively recently.

5 ● RELIGION

The Asháninka vision of the cosmos is mainly mythical. There is not a figure of a creator but a hero, Avireri, who transformed humans into animals, plants, mountains, and rivers. Their universe is inhabited by the living forms that can be seen, and also by a host of invisible beings. Among the good spirits are the Sun *(Pavá)* and the Moon *(Kashirí)*. There are also evil spirits or *kamári*. The Asháninka have shamans (holy people) or *sheripiári* who are intermediaries between the people and supernatural beings.

The Asháninka have an apocalyptic vision of the world (a vision of doom). They believe that this world is plagued by evil forces and that people will be destroyed. After that, there will be a new world with new people free of sickness or death.

6 ● MAJOR HOLIDAYS

The Festival of the Moon is a celebration of the god Kashirí. According to legend, he is the father of the Sun. Kashirí appeared to a young girl and introduced her and her people to manioc (cassava). He made the young girl his wife, and in giving birth to the Sun she was burned to death. Kashirí began taking his nephews to the forest, where he slaughtered and ate them. When his brother-in-law threatened to kill him, he escaped by rising into the sky. Kashíri continues eating human souls and that explains why the Moon gets fatter every month.

Peru is a Catholic country. Some Indians gradually lose their traditions in the process of acculturation (association with and taking on the dominant culture) and begin to celebrate national holidays.

7 ● RITES OF PASSAGE

Asháninka rites are aimed at protecting the people. Prospective parents, for example, follow a special diet during pregnancy. They refrain from eating turtle meat for fear that this would make their child slow-moving and slow-witted.

When girls reach adolescence, they spend up to six months in isolation. During that time they spin thread. Afterward they are welcomed back to daily life with a wild celebration.

After death a human soul can join the good spirits if the person was sufficiently good in his or her lifetime. However, the Asháninka consider it far more likely that the soul will become an evil ghost. In that case, it will revisit the settlement and attack those living there. That was the reason why, traditionally, the Asháninka would often abandon a settlement after someone died.

8 ● RELATIONSHIPS

Inside Asháninka villages there is a real sense of community. Many economic activities, such as hunting and fishing, are carried out collectively and the take is divided equally among everyone. Intertribal trade has always existed.

9 ● LIVING CONDITIONS

Traditionally a native community housed between 300 and 400 people. Related nuclear families (parents and children) lived in private dwellings surrounding a communal home. Individual houses had two walls made of tree trunks, palm leaf roofs, and raised floors built with pona palm trunks.

Living conditions have changed considerably since the conflicts between the Peruvian Army and guerrillas, as well as the illegal trade in coca. Nowadays, under the raised floor, the Asháninka build trenches where they keep provisions, anticipating attacks. Many Asháninka are refugees, having been forced to abandon their homes and land to save their lives. Asháninka refugees experienced severe malnutrition that had never before been experienced in South America.

10 ● FAMILY LIFE

There are few restrictions on appropriate marriage partners among the Asháninka, apart from immediate family members. To prevent pregnancy, some women eat native plant roots. Polygyny (multiple wives) is practiced, and women used to be traded for goods from other tribes.

11 ● CLOTHING

The Asháninka wear the *chusma*. This is a traditional garment made of a long piece of fabric with an opening in the middle for the head—from front to back for men, and from side to side for women. It is joined on the sides with vertical lines for men and horizontal lines for women. Chusmas are made of dyed cotton and ornamented with feathers and beads. Before contact with Europeans, the Asháninka wore chusmas only for special occasions. On regular days, they would go virtually in the nude, although women often would wear an apron suspended from a string, covering their genitals. Accessories include nasal pendants and pins made of silver, pins for the lower lip, necklaces, feather headdresses, and arm and leg bands. They also paint their bodies and blacken their teeth.

12 ● FOOD

The list of Asháninka crops is long, and ingredients for meals are varied. Crops include yucca, yams, peanuts, sweet potatoes, bananas, pineapples, tuber beans, pumpkins, and peppers. Some communities have added potatoes, maize (corn), and lima beans. Women are in charge of the garden, and men hunt. The Asháninka also keep and eat chickens and their eggs, and they hunt tapirs, boars, and monkeys. To supplement their diet, they collect honey, a root called *mabe,* ants, and several palm fruits. They also fish. Out of necessity, the Asháninka have begun to produce cash crops, like coffee.

13 ● EDUCATION

Education has been badly affected by the social unrest in the area. Since 1990, over seventy rural schools have been closed. Dozens of teachers are reported as having "disappeared," meaning it is not known whether they are dead, have joined the rebels, or are in hiding. Some schools make do with improvised chairs and tables made of tree trunks, and blackboards donated by aid organizations.

14 ● CULTURAL HERITAGE

Music and songs are part of ceremonies and rituals. Asháninka voices, imitations of jungle animal sounds, and stamping of the feet are accompanied by various instruments. Early European accounts of Asháninka instruments included two-headed monkey-skin drums, five- to eight-tube panpipes (hollow pipes of graduated length), bone flageolets (small, end-blown flutes), two-hole transverse flutes, and musical bows.

15 ● EMPLOYMENT

Most Asháninka still live by fishing, hunting, and cultivating small plots of land. Most males spent much of their working time hunting. Although meat is the main source of protein, most of a family's food comes from cultivated plants. Yucca, plantain, peanuts, sweet potatoes, and sugarcane are grown, as well as medicinal herbs. Colonization brought extensive coffee, cacao, rice, and coca plantations to some areas. Selling produce provides some income for the Asháninka. Communities are self-sufficient, and most economic activities are carried out collectively. The product is divided among the families. There is also a long tradition of trade between tribes.

16 ● SPORTS

Since before the arrival of Europeans, the Asháninka made objects that seemed related to sport or games. These included humming tops, bull-roarers, and maize-leaf balls. They also practiced wrestling. In modern times, those who live side-by-side with settlers take part in the spectator sport culture. Soccer is Peru's favorite sport, and it is played even in the most remote regions.

17 ● RECREATION

Contact with Western civilization has brought to some communities new forms of recreation. Radio and television have joined more traditional forms of entertainment such as storytelling, singing, and dancing. In remote areas, where life continues to be similar to the past, the division between work and ceremonies or recreational time is not as sharp. Because many activities are carried out collectively, work also offers a chance for social intercourse.

18 ● CRAFTS AND HOBBIES

The Asháninka traditionally are a seminomadic tribe (one that moves periodically). As a consequence, their material culture is minimal. The few objects they possess are produced with great skill and are decorated artistically. Designs consisting of complex angular, geometric patterns drawn in rectangular panels adorn most objects, from pots and beadwork to musical instruments and clothes. The Asháninka make the fabric for their typical costume, the *chusma*. They use wild cotton and two kinds of weaving frames. The Asháninka make twined baskets, sieves, and mats. Some containers are made of calabashes. Their plates are made of clay and have red designs.

19 ● SOCIAL PROBLEMS

The Asháninka traditional way of life is a casualty of the war between the national army and guerrilla groups. The mountain area of the Asháninka's forest territory was the birthplace of the rebel Shining Path (communist movement). The Asháninka and other Indian peoples of the region have tried to remain outside of the conflict between the national army and the guerrillas, but have often been its victims. Many are refugees in their own land. Those who have been able to remain in their villages have seen their social structure severely affected by political violence. Furthermore, the coca that has been grown in the area for centuries and used since ancestral times for its medicinal qualities has been turned into cocaine in the hands of outsiders. This dangerous and profitable drug attracts those who are interested in the illegal trade.

Asháninka peoples, together with other indigenous tribes, have formed pressure groups. Along with the help of international organizations, they demand justice and defend their human rights. There is still a long way to go before they can also secure Amerindian rights and be free to conduct their own way of life.

20 ● BIBLIOGRAPHY

Fiesta! Peru. Danbury, Conn.: Grolier Educational, 1997.

Kalman, Bobbie. *Peru: The People and Culture.* New York: Crabtree Publishing Company, 1994.

King, David C. *Peru: Lost Cities, Found Hopes.* New York: Benchmark Books, 1998.

ewington, Anna. *Rainforest Amerindians.* Austin, Tex.: Raintree Steck-Vaughan Publishers, 1993.

Lewington, Anna. *What Do We Know about the Amazonian Indians?* New York: P. Bedrick Books, 1993.

LWEBSITES

Interknowledge Corp. Peru. [Online] Available http://www.interknowledge.com/peru/, 1998.

World Travel Guide. Peru. [Online] Available http://www.wtgonline.com/country/pe/gen.html, 1998.

Quechua

PRONUNCIATION: KECH-wah
LOCATION: Peru; Ecuador; Bolivia (Central Andes regions)
POPULATION: About 7.5 million
LANGUAGE: Quechua language
RELIGION: Combination of pre-Columbian and Roman Catholic beliefs

1 ● INTRODUCTION

The Quechua Indians of the central Andes are the direct descendants of the Incas. The Inca Empire, which existed for a century before the arrival of the Spanish, was a highly developed civilization. The Inca Empire stretched from parts of present-day Colombia in the north, southward into Chile. The Incas had an impressive governing structure. The government imposed tribute and taxes on the population which were exacted in the form of labor and in crops. Vast warehouses were used to store food, which was then distributed in times of famine. The Incas also had an immense army, used to continuously expand the empire and conquer new peoples.

The Spanish conquistadors arrived in South America in the early 1500s. When they arrived, the Inca king Huayna Cápac (d.1527) had already died from one of the many European diseases that preceded the conquistadors. The Incas were in a state of civil war when Spanish forces arrived. After the Spanish captured the new Inca king, Atahualpa (1500?–33), the Incas suffered a swift defeat.

Peru attained independence from the Spanish in 1821. Modern-day Peru has struggled to modernize. It has been plagued by problems of hyperinflation, poor governments, and terrorism. Most Quechua still live in the Andean highlands. They rely on subsistence agriculture (growing little more than their own food) and pastoralism (nomadic herding) as did their Inca ancestors.

2 ● LOCATION

Quechua Indians still live in the areas once governed by the Inca Empire in Peru, Ecuador, and Bolivia. The geographical conditions between regions differ dramatically. In mountain valleys there is rich soil and access to water that is suitable for farming. Most Quechua, however, live on the stark, steep slopes of the central Andes. Here the soil is poor, the wind strong, and the weather cold.

About one-third of Peru's 24.5 million inhabitants are Quechua Indians. Migration and urbanization in the past few decades have drawn many Quechua to Lima, the capital city of Peru. There is now a large indigenous and mestizo (mixed-race) population in Lima.

3 ● LANGUAGE

The Quechua language is known by its speakers as *Runa Simi,* or the language of the people. The term *quechua* refers more to the language than to a concrete ethnic group. The Quechua language was the administrative language of the Inca state. It is spoken by millions of people in Peru (about 8 million), Ecuador (nearly 2 million), and Bolivia (about 1 million). Quechua words that have been assimilated into the English language include puma, condor,

QUECHUA

0   250   500   750 Miles

0 250 500 750 Kilometers

rebels. The head disappeared, and they say that it is buried. The myth tells that it is slowly growing its body back and when the body is complete, the Incas will return to rule their land.

Many of the ancient Quechua myths are still preserved in their oral tradition. Most of them narrate the origin of various ethnic groups, or of mountains, rivers, and lakes.

5 ● RELIGION

Quechua religion combines both pre-Columbian and Catholic elements. The most significant pre-Columbian influence that endures is the belief that supernatural forces govern everyday events, such as weather and illness. This belief serves a utilitarian purpose to the agricultural Quechua. By making offerings to the powers that control natural forces, the Quechua feel they can influence events and not merely be helpless in the face of bad weather or disease. When drinking alcohol, for example, it is customary to first offer a drink to Mother Earth, *Pachamama*.

This religious Andean world is populated by gods who have human attributes. Sometimes they love each other and other times they hate and fight each other. For this reason, the Andean religion has two dimensions in the lives of the people. First, in human terms it promotes social cohesion, and second, in transcendental terms it connects gods and humans.

The Quechua have adopted Christianity and also have incorporated it into their indigenous beliefs.

llama, and coca. Unlike most other native South American languages, Quechua is an official language of Peru, accorded the same status as Spanish. Although it rarely occurs, senators and members of congress can give speeches in the Peruvian Congress in Quechua.

4 ● FOLKLORE

The myth of Incarrí perhaps reveals the most about the feelings of the vanquished Inca. After the conquest of Peru in 1532, the Inca rulers retreated from Cuzco to Vilcabamba. There they resisted the Spanish invasion for nearly fifty years. In 1579 the last rebel Inca, Tupac Amaru, was captured and beheaded by the Spanish. The Spaniards stuck his head on a pike and placed it in the plaza of Cuzco as a warning to the

6 ● MAJOR HOLIDAYS

The Quechua celebrate important Catholic holidays such as Christmas and Easter. At the same time, they have not abandoned their ancient holidays. In the ancient Inca capital of Cuzco, the Inca Sun Festival is still celebrated. The Inti Raymi festival, as it is called, draws thousands of tourists from all over the world to witness its spectacular festivities. Donning replicas of Inca tunics, rather than contemporary Andean garb, Quechua Indians reenact the Inca sun-worshiping ceremony. The Inti Raymi festival, which celebrates the June solstice, reflects the Inca's vast knowledge of astronomy. On this occasion, there is much eating, drinking, and dancing. True to Inca traditions, a llama is also sacrificed on this day.

7 ● RITES OF PASSAGE

Major life transitions, such as birth, puberty, and death, are marked by rituals and celebrations that combine Catholic and indigenous traditions.

8 ● RELATIONSHIPS

Courtship and marriage involve a lengthy series of rituals and stages. Most unmarried youths meet (and flirt) during one of the community's many festivals. When a young couple decides that they are ready to consider marriage, the family of the bride is visited by the family of the prospective groom. The groom himself stays home while his parents and godparents discuss the wedding and negotiate what each family will donate to the newlyweds. The engagement is made official at a later date when the bride and groom exchange rosaries. At the wedding, there is a public procession as the bride leaves her home to join her husband's *ayllu* or community. Various other rituals, including fertility rites, follow the wedding.

9 ● LIVING CONDITIONS

The dominant building material throughout most of the Andes is adobe. Adobe has the advantages of being highly durable, free, and widely available. Adobe can be made almost year-round with the rich Andean soil. Traditionally, roofs were made from thatched material. However, now they are more often made of tiles. House-building is a communal affair, based on the ancient Inca system of labor exchange known as *mita*. Neighbors are offered *chicha* (beer), cigarettes, and food in return for their help in the construction of a new home. In exchange, those who participated in the house-building are owed labor that they can claim at any time.

The quality of health care in rural communities is still extremely poor. Most Quechua first turn to a *curandero* (literally, "curer") who provides herbal medicines and treatment.

10 ● FAMILY LIFE

Children in Quechua society play many important roles. From a very young age they participate in economic activities and key household tasks. As in most other subsistence economies, children are essential as they are expected to provide long-term economic security to their parents as they age. An optimum family size is considered to be three or four children. However, due to limited access to birth control, many families have ten or more children. Generally, male children are more highly valued than females, as their economic potential is seen to be greater.

Women play a subordinate role compared to men in the community political structure. Women are less likely to receive a formal education, do not hold significant positions of power within the community, and are excluded from many potentially profitable economic activities. A clear sexual division of labor exists with regard to both agricultural and household tasks. Within the family, women have a say in matters such as decisions about finances or issues surrounding the upbringing of children. However, there is little evidence to suggest that they are free from subordination in that domain either.

11 ● CLOTHING

Traditional Andean clothing reflects Spanish influences. In 1572, the Spanish prohibited the Quechua from wearing native Inca tunics and wrap-around dresses. Andean peoples then adopted the clothing still in use today. Quechua women wear skirts and blouses, with colorful woven shawls around their shoulders. Men wear trousers, shirts, and woven *ponchos* (capes). Sandals are the preferred footwear for both men and women.

The style and color of clothing worn by Quechua Indians varies dramatically from region to region. The Otavalo of Ecuador, an important subgroup of the Quechua, have a very distinctive dress. They wear white trousers and shirts, covered by a solid black poncho. Otavalo men are also famed for their long black braids.

12 ● FOOD

The potato was first domesticated in Peru approximately 4,500 years ago. The potato and quinoa grain remain as two of the main staples of the Quechua diet. Common dishes include meat or potato stews, spiced with hot peppers, coriander, or peanuts. For community feasts, a *pachamanca,* or underground oven, is occasionally used.

Also considered a delicacy is guinea pig. The preferred dish for festivals, guinea pigs are often raised in the house and provide a productive use for kitchen scraps and discarded food. The use of guinea pigs as an important source of protein pre-dates the Incas.

13 ● EDUCATION

Formal education in Peru is required until the age of sixteen. In rural areas, however, the percentage of students who finish their schooling is much lower than in urban areas. This is, in part, because children play a valuable role in household and agricultural tasks and their labor cannot be spared. The schooling received is generally very poor. Teaching methods are based on rote memorization rather than problem-solving skills. Personal initiative is rarely encouraged, and teachers generally have low expectations of what their students can achieve. A further problem emerges for Quechua children, since Spanish is the primary language taught and used at schools.

14 ● CULTURAL HERITAGE

The characteristic music of the central Andes is called *huayno*. The mountain origins of huaynos are reflected in their lyrics

Quechua folk music also includes beautiful, haunting music for panpipes (hollow pipes of graduated length). One of these songs, "El Condor Pasa," was a hit record for the singing duo, Simon and Garfunkel in the 1960s.

As the Incas did not write, there is not a tradition of Quechua literature. In twentieth-century Peru, however, there has emerged a tradition of *indigenista* writers who focus on the life of the indigenous (native) Andean peoples. Jose Maria Arguedas, Cesar Vallejo, and Ciro Alegría have written influential books that portray the oppression of the Quechua throughout the centuries and chronicle their hard life in the Andes. These authors have contributed to a growing Andean nationalism and pride.

15 ● EMPLOYMENT

Most Quechua rely on subsistence farming for their livelihood. Corn, potatoes, and grains are crops that have adapted to the high-altitude environment. Land is still farmed using the Inca method of terracing on steep slopes. This labor-intensive approach to agriculture requires a tremendous amount of time. Little time is left to devote to other economic activities.

Trade is highly developed between different villages and regions. In addition to agricultural products, many communities produce pottery, textiles, belts, hats, and other handicrafts for cash sales. In most communities, there is a weekly market day, which plays an important role in the economic and social fabric of the village.

Cory Langley

Quechua women wear skirts and blouses, with colorful woven shawls around their shoulders. The style of clothing worn by the Quechua varies dramatically from region to region.

that recount daily life in mountain villages and proclaim Andean nationalism (patriotism). Traditional instruments still widely used include drums, flutes, and the *charrango*, a mandolin-style guitar made from an armadillo shell. Huayno singers are increasingly popular in urban areas.

16 ● SPORTS

There are no uniquely Quechua sports. However, as part of a mestizo (mixed background) society, the Quechua participate in a variety of Western sports, such as soccer.

17 ● RECREATION

Socializing is the primary form of recreation in Quechua society. The Quechua celebrate a great many religious festivals, national holidays, and birthdays. Parties and festivals are eagerly anticipated and require many weeks of planning. Many festivals involve up to eight days of drinking, feasting, and dancing.

18 ● CRAFTS AND HOBBIES

The most significant handicraft produced by the Quechua is textiles. Women throughout the Andes can be seen spinning wool almost all day, even while sitting at the market or waiting for a bus. Both llama and sheep wool are used. The "belt loom" still in use by the Quechua dates back to pre-contact (with Europeans) times. The Quechua are skilled weavers. Their products are increasingly in demand for the tourist and export markets.

19 ● SOCIAL PROBLEMS

Male drunkenness is a serious social problem throughout the central Andes. Drinking alcoholic beverages is not only an accepted behavior at the Quechua's many festivals and parties, it is also an expected behavior. Alongside feasting and dancing, becoming drunk is a core part of most social occasions. Unfortunately, this behavior often spills over into daily life. Excessive male drinking has a negative impact on both family relations and family finances. Spousal abuse is a common result of alcoholism.

20 ● BIBLIOGRAPHY

Fiesta! Peru. Danbury, Conn.: Grolier Educational, 1997.

Hemming, John. *The Conquest of the Incas.* New York: Harcourt Brace Jovanovitch, 1970.

Hudson, Rex A. *Peru in Pictures.* Minneapolis, Minn.: Lerner Publications Co., 1987.

Jermyn, Leslie. *Peru.* Milwaukee, Wisc.: Gareth Stevens, 1998.

Kalman, Bobbie. *Peru: The People and Culture.* New York: Crabtree Publishing Company, 1994.

King, David C. *Peru: Lost Cities, Found Hopes.* New York: Benchmark Books, 1998.

Lewington, Anna. *Rainforest Amerindians.* Austin, Tex.: Raintree Steck-Vaughan Publishers, 1993.

Lewington, Anna. *What Do We Know about the Amazonian Indians?* New York: P. Bedrick Books, 1993.

Parker, Edward. *Peru.* Austin, Tex.: Raintree Steck-Vaughn, 1997.

Recipes from Around the World. Howard County, Md.: Foreign-Born Information and Referral Network, 1993.

WEBSITES

Interknowledge Corp. Peru. [Online] Available http://www.interknowledge.com/peru/, 1998.

Ruiz-Garcia, Pedro. The Latino Connection. [Online] Available http://www.ascinsa.com/LATINOCONNECTION/peru.html, 1998.

World Travel Guide. Peru. [Online] Available http://www.wtgonline.com/country/pe/gen.html, 1998.

Philippines

■ **FILIPINOS** 125
■ **HILIGAYNON** 136
■ **ILOCANOS** 142

The people of the Philippines are called Filipinos. There are nine main ethnic groups: Tagalog, Ilocanos, Pampanguenos, Pangasinans, Bicolanos, Cebuanos, Boholanos, Hiligaynon (Ilongos), and Waray-Waray. The Hiligaynon and Ilocanos are covered in this chapter. Numerous smaller ethnic groups inhabit the interiors of the islands, including the Igorot of Luzon and the Bukidnon, Manobo, and Tiruray of Mindanao. There are dozens of hill tribes.

Filipinos

PRONUNCIATION: fih-lih-PEE-nohz

LOCATION: Philippines

POPULATION: 66 million

LANGUAGE: Tagalog (national language); English; Cebuano; Ilocano; Hiligaynon (Ilongo); Bicolano; Waray-Waray; Pampango, and Pangasinan

RELIGION: Roman Catholicism; Philippine Independent Church; Iglesia ni Kristo (Church of Christ); Protestantism; Islam; animism

1 ● INTRODUCTION

The Philippines is made up of thousands of islands with many distinct cultures. For three hundred years, the Philippines was a colony of Spain. Despite speaking several different languages, 90 percent of the population share a common way of life and practice Christianity. The remaining 10 percent consists of many small groups, none of whom are Christian.

As early as 40,000 years ago, the first modern humans roamed the Philippines, which were then still linked to Asia by land bridges exposed during the Ice Age. Agriculturalists arrived from Taiwan between 3000 and 2000 BC. Some of their children and grandchildren migrated to colonize Indonesia, Madagascar, and the Pacific Islands.

The Portuguese explorer Ferdinand Magellan (c.1480–1521) first visited the islands in 1521 on behalf of Spain. Spain saw the islands as a good place to build a base, and sent several expeditions. The Spanish brought the Catholic religion to the people of the islands, and European ways that had both good and bad results. Islanders frequent revolted against Spanish

FILIPINOS

| 0 | 250 | 500 | 750 Miles |
| 0 | 250 | 500 | 750 Kilometers |

government. The election of President Fidel Ramos in 1992 brought the country some stability and launched a period of economic growth.

2 ● LOCATION

The 7,000 islands (1,000 of which are inhabited) of the Philippines comprise a land area equal to that of Italy and a little larger than that of Arizona. If superimposed on the eastern United States, the islands would stretch east-west from New York City to Chicago and north-south from Massachusetts to Florida. There are eleven major islands: Luzon (more than one-third of the total land area); Mindoro; Palawan; Masbate; Panay; Negros; Cebu; Bohol; Leyte; Samar; and Mindanao (another one-third of the land area).

Mountains separated by narrow valleys dominate all the islands. Throughout the country, deforestation (cutting down of forest trees) has reduced the rainforest cover. This has encouraged erosion, which carries silt to the coastal areas and chokes the coral reefs.

The tropical climate is dominated by the monsoon cycle: from June to October the southwest monsoon carries torrential rains to most of the country; from November through February, the northeast monsoon brings warm, dry weather; and from March to May, easterly North Pacific tradewinds afflict the islands with a period of extreme heat and drought. Over twenty typhoons each year cause extreme havoc in the country.

Over 66 million people inhabit the Philippines. Population density is very high at

abuses. On the other hand, Catholic Filipinos stood with the Spanish against invaders and their own rebellious brethren.

In 1896, members of a secret society launched a revolution to end Spanish rule. On June 12, 1898, Filipinos proclaimed their independence. The United States moved to take possession of the islands for their strategic value. A war resulted, dragging on for years and causing the death of an estimated one million Filipinos. American rule introduced mass education in the English language. Japanese invasion and occupation of the Philippines during World War II (1939–45) devastated the country. The United States granted the Philippines independence in 1946.

For the next forty-five years, the Philippines struggled to establish a democratic

570 persons per square mile (220 persons per square kilometer). The population is growing at a rapid rate, due in part to Catholic opposition to the use of birth control. The country's economic difficulties have pushed many people to emigrate in search of work.

3 ● LANGUAGE

Some seventy languages are spoken in the Philippines. The five languages with the greatest number of speakers are:

Tagalog, the basis of Pilipino/Filipino, the national language, spoken by a quarter of the total Filipino population, concentrated in Manila;

Cebuano, spoken by another quarter of the population inhabiting the islands of Cebu, Bohol, southern Leyte, western Negros, and the northern and eastern coasts of Mindanao;

Ilocano, whose speakers comprise about 11 percent of the population found throughout northern Luzon;

Hiligaynon (or Ilongo), spoken by 10 percent of the population on Panay, eastern Negros, and southern Mindoro;

Bicolano, whose speakers represent almost 7 percent of the population and inhabit the long southeastern "tail" of Luzon.

After conquering the country (in 1898), the Americans introduced English as the language of government and education. In 1937, the government decided to promote the use of Tagalog as the national language. It is now called "Pilipino" by most people, although some other ethnic groups resist using that name. Tagalog-Pilipino is taught in schools and is heard in pop music, television programs, and movies, although people continue to use their local languages for everyday purposes. English remains important for professional, academic, government, and business careers.

Among Christians, names of Spanish origin are common. Filipinos generally have three names in the following order: (1) one's personal name; (2) one's mother's surname (usually appearing only as an initial); and (3) one's father's surname. Upon marriage, a woman's name follows a different pattern: (1) her personal name; (2) her father's surname; and (3) her husband's surname.

4 ● FOLKLORE

Many Filipinos believe that beings who can influence human lives for good or ill live around them in mounds of earth (including termite nests and backyard garbage heaps), old trees, and on mountaintops. In appearance, these beings are believed to range from beautiful goddess-like figures such as Mariang Makiling, mistress of a Luzon mountain, to monsters such as the *kapre*, a black-skinned giant. They may also take the form of dwarves and elves (often pictured dressed in archaic European fashions). By far the most widely feared supernatural creature is the *asuwang*, a being who appears as an attractive woman by day. At night, asuwang leaves behind the lower portion of its body in a hiding place and flies about in search of human victims, usually the sick, from whom it can suck the entrails with the aid of a long, tubular tongue. Inexplicable deaths in sleep are often ascribed to attacks by asuwang, although they are frequently also credited to *bangungot*, a fatal nightmare induced by witchcraft. Filipinos expect recently deceased kin to return in some form, as a moth, a strange breeze, or, if resentful of the living, as a wail heard in the night.

The legendary Juan Tamad (John Lazy) appears in a great many folk tales. His extraordinary laziness and stupidity involve him in all sorts of misadventures. He usually ends up being beaten up by his fellow villagers or scolded by his mother. In popular imagination, the opposite of Juan Tamad is Jose Rizal (1861–96), the national hero. Rizal was a doctor, scholar, and novelist who received his education in Europe. He was executed by the Spaniards in 1896, and became the supreme martyr of the Filipinos. There is even a sect comprised of 250,000 people that believes Rizal was the reincarnation of Christ.

5 ● RELIGION

The Spanish colonial settlers in the Philippines were Roman Catholic. Due to their influence, 85 percent of Filipinos are Roman Catholic. This gives the Roman Catholic Church a powerful influence on national life, despite the separation of church and state introduced by the American colonists.

About 5 percent of Filipinos, concentrated in the south of the country, practice Islam, the main religion in neighboring Indonesia and Malaysia. About 3 percent of Filipinos still follow ancestral animist traditions.

Even Catholics believe in supernatural forces. Faith healers and spirit mediums, who use herbs and massage to treat physical ailments, are popular. Catholicism in the Philippines involves looking to patron saints and the Virgin Mary for help in everyday life. Although adult men tend to avoid weekly mass and some Filipinos are skeptical of organized religion, many others express an intense personal religious devotion. Acts of self-mortification such as the world-famous flagellations (self-beatings) and (nonfatal) crucifixions are practiced by a minority of Filipinos.

6 ● MAJOR HOLIDAYS

Christian holidays are the most widely celebrated holidays in the Philippines. Christmas festivities begin on December 16 with the first of the *simbang gabi* or *misa de gallo,* masses held before sunrise every morning before Christmas Day. After Midnight Mass on Christmas Eve, families gather for a feast, the *Noche Buena.* On Christmas Day, parties are held, with children making the rounds, visiting relatives and godparents to pay respect to them and receive presents.

The other highlight of the year is Holy Week (week preceding Easter) in March or April, celebrated in different ways from locality to locality. Many towns hold a *sinakulo,* a traditional musical drama, staged over several nights (and occupying many hours per segment). This drama focuses on the sufferings of Christ but often including scenes from the Old Testament, all the way back to Genesis. Mass on the night before Easter is followed by the reenactment of the meeting of the resurrected

Christ and his grieving mother (represented by life-sized statues carried in procession).

Another important nationwide festival is the *Santacruzan* in May, commemorating the discovery of Christ's cross by Saint Helena (c.248–c.328), mother of Constantine the Great (d.337), the first Christian Roman emperor. These celebrations feature processions in which the daughters of prominent families are splendidly dressed as Reina Elena (Queen Helena), and accompanied by male escorts and a parade of other couples.

On All Souls' Day (November 2), people gather at the graves of family members for a twenty-four-hour vigil. During the vigil, family members pray, clean the graves and decorate them with candles and wreaths. They also eat, drink, and play cards.

Each town has an annual fiesta in honor of its patron saint. Fiestas include public feasting, fairs, brass-band playing, performing arts, social dancing, sporting events (especially cockfights), and beauty contests.

7 ● RITES OF PASSAGE

To ensure the well-being and good fortune of a newborn child, a folk custom requires that the placenta be buried in a place where it will not be stepped on. This custom is still practiced in some rural areas of the Philippines. For Christians, baptism offers an occasion for the parents to choose a relative or friend to serve as godparent. The godparent-godchild relationship is almost like that of a family member.

Around the onset of puberty, boys undergo circumcision, without religious connotations; a simple lecture on hygiene by older female relatives accompanies a girl's first menstruation. Graduations from elementary, high school, and college require major celebrations. Wealthier families give their daughters debuts (special parties to introduce them to society) on their eighteenth birthday; the girl, her close female relatives, and male escorts rehearse set-pieces of ballroom dancing to perform in front of the guests.

Catholic weddings in the Philippines consist of the standard nuptial mass but also include a segment during which a white veil and a cord are draped over the couple's shoulder and an *arias,* an object made of coins, is presented to them (all symbols of unity and prosperity). A couple will have several sponsors (referred to as "wedding godparents"). The ceremony is followed by a reception, to which everyone even remotely connected to the couple and their families is invited.

Funerals are held several days after death to allow relatives of the deceased to arrive from as far away as the United States. The body is kept at home. There are always people keeping vigil over it, usually by playing cards or mah-jong through the night. A procession accompanied by somber music from a brass band accompanies the body to church for the funeral mass and carries the body from there to the cemetery amid dramatic weeping from older relatives. Afterward, mourners gather for nine nights to pray for the departed. Surviving members of the immediate family will avoid wearing brightly colored clothes for some time, often attaching a black ribbon to their clothes. A widow will wear only black for a full year. Family and friends get together again on the first anniversary of the death.

8 ● RELATIONSHIPS

Filipino values aim to promote group solidarity and to emphasize individuals' mutual dependence. A person must have *hiya,* a sense of shame or a social conscience that prevents him or her from violating social norms. Unaccepted behavior damages the reputations of both the individual and his or her immediate family. An individual strives to earn and keep the respect of others, a value called *amor-propio,* Spanish for "loving oneself."

Filipinos are careful to show respect to those of superior status (due to age, education, organizational rank, perceived wealth, etc.). For instance, when speaking (in Tagalog-Pilipino) to an elder, a social superior, or a stranger, a person inserts the particle *po* or *ho* ("sir" or "ma'am") into almost every sentence. A person must show that he or she is grateful for the good others have done for him or her, and must be prepared to repay the act. Some *utang na loob* ("inner debts") can never be repaid, as with a child's debt to its mother for the gift of life.

A common greeting translates as "Where have you just come from?" and "Where are you off to now?" In reply, no one expects to hear more than "Just over there."

It is customary to greet older relatives with a kiss on the cheek or forehead. More traditionally, a younger person bows in front of the elder, take his or her hand, and presses it to the forehead to receive a "blessing."

While passing in front of older people or people of higher status, etiquette dictates that one walk slowly, bowing the head, and either clasping the hands together in front or extending one of the open palms in the direction one is going. One beckons another to come closer with a downward motion of the open palm. Pointing with the fingers is considered offensive; people point pursed lips in the direction they wish to indicate. When catching sight of acquaintances, quickly raising and lowering the eyebrows is sufficient sign of recognition and may substitute for small talk if one is in a hurry. Prolonged staring is considered aggressive, as is holding the arms outstretched. With merely a sharp, clipped hiss, mothers can show displeasure to their children; anyone can use a softer, somewhat more prolonged hiss as a very informal means of catching someone's attention. Physical contact between members of the same sex is a common sign of affection. In embarrassing situations, the reflex is to smile or sometimes also to lower the head and rub the back of the neck.

All guests, even unexpected ones, are served drinks and snacks. It is polite for the guest to appear reluctant to accept what is offered, but the host will insist. The guest leaves a little on the plate to show that the host has provided more than enough. Saying goodbye is usually a lengthy operation. Those returning from long-distance trips are expected to bring back presents *(pasalubong)* for those at home.

Chaperones, often of the same age as the dating couple, and group dates continue to make courting a public affair. Public displays of affection, though no longer taboo, are still subject to social disapproval.

Cory Langley

Filipino children generally live at home until marriage, and often newlywed couples stay with either set of parents for some time. Older children, grandparents, and other relatives help care for younger children; it is common for older children to sacrifice for the younger, such as by working to put them through school.

9 ● LIVING CONDITIONS

Almost half the population lives below the poverty line set by the government. Sharing of resources by more affluent family members and relatives working overseas helps many of the poor. Standards of living also vary dramatically from region to region and between urban and rural areas.

The Spanish colonists settled the Philippines in a pattern called *población*. This is a town laid out in a grid around a church plaza. The población was in turn the center

for a number of *barrios,* villages surrounded by fields. Many of the barrios had remote satellite hamlets (very small villages) known as *sitios.* Sitios have a small chapel that does not have its own priest, but receives occasional visits from the priest from the población.

The *bahay kubo* or *nipa* hut, a two- or three-room structure with bamboo walls and floors and a cogon-grass or palm-leaf roof raised on wooden piles, was the traditional style of housing for the majority of less wealthy Filipinos. Below the house, animals were kept, primarily pigs, chickens, and perhaps a water buffalo. In less-developed parts of the country, this remains the most common type of house. A little less than half of all housing was of this type as of the late 1990s.

In contemporary towns, houses typically have two stories with wooden walls, corrugated iron roofs, and cement foundations. Wealthier residences adopt Spanish elements such as tiled roofs and floors, walls of brick or stone, and iron grillwork on windows, fences, and gates.

Over half of households had electricity in 1990. Drinkable water was available to about 65 percent of households in 1990, and 20 percent of households had a refrigerator . Only about 4 percent of all Filipino household have telephones, but more than 50 percent of those in the capital, Manila, do. Over 50 percent of houses dispose of garbage by burning it in their backyards.

As of the late 1990s, less that 10 percent of households owned a car. In both cities and rural areas, people take tricycles (motorcycles with a passenger car on the side). In rural areas, *kalesas* (horsedrawn carts) are still common. Brightly painted *jeepneys* (originally U.S. military surplus jeeps with back sections lengthened to accomodate passengers) are the cheapest way to get around cities and between towns. Travel between islands is by large passenger ships or by airplane. The traditional *bangka,* an outrigger canoe, is still in common use for fishing and local transport.

10 ● FAMILY LIFE

The family is Filipino society's central institution. The typical household consists of a married couple, children, grandparents, and sometimes servants (common in middle-class households). Children generally live at home until marriage. Newlywed couples stay with either set of parents for some time. Older children, grandparents, and other relatives, help care for younger children; it is common for older children to help their younger siblings by working to put them through school, for example.

Older siblings are addressed with special terms—in Tagalog-Pilipino, *Ate* for an older sister and *Kuya* for an older brother. Filipinos feel equal bonds with relatives from both the mother's and father's sides. Married couples are expected to maintain equal closeness with both spouses' families.

Individuals are free to choose their marriage partners, but family approval is an important consideration. Among Catholics, divorce is illegal. It is legal only among Muslims and other non-Christians.

Filipino men and women have relative equality. Filipino wives manage family finances, giving spending money to their husbands just as to their children. Women are well represented in the professions, government, and business. However, men still hold most of the top positions.

11 ● CLOTHING

The male national costume, the *barong tagalog,* is a shirt, finely embroidered and woven of pineapple leaf fibers. *Indio* (native) women traditionally wore wide-necked, wide-sleeved short blouses and ankle-length tube skirts; in public, they draped a shawl over their shoulders and wrapped a *tapis,* a small piece of cloth, over the skirt. Mestizo (mixed-blood) women preferred fuller skirts (or sometimes ones ending in a long train) and butterfly sleeves. This became known as the terno, the female national costume.

For formal occasions men wear either the barong tagalog or Western-style suits. Women wear either a modified terno or Western-style dresses. Daily casual attire often consists of shorts with or without a tank top for men, and a maong—a loose one-piece dress with wide sleeves and open neck—for women. For younger people, T-shirts and jeans are common.

12 ● FOOD

Boiled rice is almost always included as part of a full meal. All other foods are called *ulam* (accompaniments). The ulam is often dried fish and some sliced tomato or onion. Only the well-to-do include meat as a regular part of the diet. Most Filipinos consume meat only at special celebrations (often in the form of *lechon,* roasted whole pig). Common preparations include soups heavy with vegetables and seafood (such as

Recipe

Adobo Pork

Ingredients

1 onion, chopped
5 cloves garlic
1 tomato chopped (or 1 Tablespoon tomato paste)
1 teaspoon oregano
2 Tablespoons olive oil
½ cup wine vinegar
6 to 8 pork chops

Directions

1. Combine all ingredients except pork chops to make a marinade.
2. Heat a large skillet with a nonstick coating over medium-high heat. Brown pork chops on both sides.
3. Place browned pork chops in a casserole. Pour marinade over pork chops. Cover casserole with lid or heavy aluminum foil.
4. Heat oven to 350°F. Place casserole in oven and bake for about 40 minutes.

The adobo marinade may be used to marinate raw meat for up to twenty-four hours before grilling or roasting.

sinigang and *tinola*); meat or seafood simmered in coconut milk (*ginataan*); Chinese noodle dishes (such as *pansit*); stewed meat dishes of Spanish origin (such as *adobo* or *kaldereta*), or grilled fish. A recipe for adobo is above.

Seasonings tend to be simple. Typical dishes employ garlic, ginger, peppercorns, soy sauce, fish sauce, and shrimp paste. Numerous types of bananas are enjoyed, sometimes even eaten alongside the main meal. Desserts consist of a variety of rice- or cassava-based cakes, and sometimes a Spanish custard, *letseplan.*

The traditional mode of eating has been to scoop up food from flat dishes with the fingers of the right hand. (The left hand is reserved for personal hygiene.) Now, it is considered more refined to eat with a spoon and fork. The fork is held in the left hand and used to push food onto a spoon held in the right hand. Diners do not have their own individual portions served to them. Everyone takes from common dishes laid out in the center of the table.

Breakfast usually consists of leftovers from the previous evening's dinner, such as rice fried with garlic. Alternatively, fresh bread bought from a bakery may be eaten with coffee. The main meal of the day for rural people is lunch. In the city, the main meal is dinner when the entire family can gather together. An afternoon snack, called the *merienda,* is almost a meal in itself (usually without the rice). It is common for those who can afford it.

Smoking is common among men, but uncommon among women. Traditionally, the betel nut was chewed as a mild stimulant, but this is much less common today. Small groups of men often gather at night on the porch of a house to chat and drink beer and eat *pulutan*—snacks ranging from peanuts or quail eggs to grilled fish or shrimp.

13 ● EDUCATION

The literacy rate (percent of the population who can read and write) is more than 90 percent. Elementary school lasts for six

Cory Langley

Filipino boys take a break from their studies. While almost all students attend elementary school, less than two-thirds of all students go on to high school.

years beginning at age seven. It is followed by four years of high school. While almost all students attend elementary school (which is free), less than two-thirds of all students go on to high school, where there are fees. Some families cannot spare the money for fees and travel costs to high schools, which are often a distance away. Also, families need teenage children to help in the fields or otherwise earn income for the family. Many of those who do graduate from high school go on to college. In the 1990s, about 13 percent of the population held an academic degree. Filipinos have a deep appreciation for education, seeing it as a way to enter better occupations such as medicine, law, or education. Many families sacrifice a great deal to send a child to college.

14 ● CULTURAL HERITAGE

The *rondalla,* a traditional music ensemble, consists of plucked and bowed string instruments to accompany social dancing and suitors' serenades. Many communities have a brass band to contribute to the gaiety of fiestas.

The *tinikling* is a folk dance where a couple executes intricate figures while skipping through two bamboo poles being clapped together at an accelerating pace.

When the Spanish arrived, Filipinos were using an alphabet derived from India, carving messages on palm leaves or bamboo. Word play ranged from riddles (bugtong) to extended debates in poetry (balagtasan), an integral part of courtship. Long verse narratives, from retellings of Christ's Passion to heroic tales set in mythical lands, came to be composed in native languages. Today, most literature in native languages is confined to stories (nobela) appearing serially in comics.

15 ● EMPLOYMENT

About one-third of Filipino workers are employed in agriculture. Most agricultural workers do not own the land they work, but work either as tenant farmers or plantation laborers. The staple crops are rice, maize (corn), and sweet potatoes. In rural areas, wet-rice fields dominate the landscape. In some places, these rice fields are planted as terraces climbing steep mountainsides. The principal cash crops are coconuts, bananas, pineapples, sugar, tobacco, and abaca (hemp).

16 ● SPORTS

Sipa is an traditional game in which two teams of one to four players each hit a wickerwork ball with their knees, legs, or feet over a net or across a circle. Introduced by the Americans, baseball and basketball are popular. The professional basketball league pits teams identified by the companies that own them, rather than with cities as in the United States. Fond of watching boxing, many Filipinos also practice arnis, a martial art using bamboo rods three feet (one meter) long. Cockfighting (two roosters battling each other in a ring) commands a fanatical following. Held during Sundays, public holidays, and fiestas in mini-stadiums, cockfights are the occasion for intense gambling.

17 ● RECREATION

Two in three households have a radio. One in three households has a television. Domestically produced programming is strong on talent shows, comedies, family dramas, and romance stories.

Traditional theater consisted of the comedia or moro-moro, verse-plays depicting warfare between Christians and Muslims, usually ending in the conversion of the Muslims. The zarzuela, a Spanish-derived operetta sung in local languages, has been popular since the late 1800s.

Film tickets are comparatively cheap, and cinema attendance rates are among the world's highest. The Philippines possesses a lively film industry, producing comedies, action films (frequently punctuated with shoot-outs and kung fu), and melodramas. American television programs and movies attract a wide audience.

Children commonly play sungka, a game of skill in which players move cowrie (a type of seashell) shells around a course of two rows of seven holes carved in a wooden board. Every neighborhood has chess enthusiasts, and the Philippines has produced many world-class players. Card games and mah-jongg, a Chinese game similar to rummy that is played with ivory tiles, regularly involve gambling.

18 ● CRAFTS AND HOBBIES

A variety of crafts are practiced by individual Filipino ethnic groups, including woodcarving; weaving textiles, baskets, and mats; and tie-dying.

19 ● SOCIAL PROBLEMS

Under the civil war conditions during the regimes of Ferdinand Marcos (governed 1965–86) and his successor, Corazon Aquino (governed 1986–92), human rights abuses were common, with government forces, insurgents, and anti-insurgent vigilantes victimizing noncombatant civilians as a matter of course. Under the Ramos regime in the late 1990s, the more prominent problem was violence by criminal elements, and by supposedly noncriminal elements such as corrupt law-enforcers and elected officials. Filipinos have little faith in their justice system since the wealthy and powerful are able to buy the verdicts they want.

20 ● BIBLIOGRAPHY

Federal Research Division. *Philippines: A Country Study.* Washington, D.C.: Library of Congress, 1993.

Gochenour, Theodore. *Considering Filipinos.* Yarmouth, Maine: Intercultural Press, 1990.

Tarling, Nicolas, ed. *The Cambridge History of Southeast Asia.* Vols. 1 and 2. Singapore: Cambridge University Press, 1992.

WEBSITES

Embassy of the Philippines, Washington, D.C. [Online] Available http://www.sequel.net/RpinUS/WDC/, 1998.

World Travel Guide. Philippines. [Online] Available http://www.wtgonline.com/country/ph/gen.html, 1998.

Hiligaynon

PRONUNCIATION: hil-uh-GUY-nuhn
LOCATION: Philippines (Western Visayas)
POPULATION: 5.4 million
LANGUAGE: Hiligaynon
RELIGION: Pre-Christian belief system, coexisting with Catholicism

1 ● INTRODUCTION

Long before the 1600s, the fertility of the Western Visayas region in the Philippines permitted the Hiligaynon people to develop one of the archipelago's most advanced societies. They engaged in international trade (as evidenced by large finds of Chinese porcelain) and created fine work in gold and semiprecious stones.

Large-scale sugar production for the world market created a small group of elite citizens, most of whom were mestizo (mixed race). They enjoyed an opulent lifestyle on vast plantations. With the drop in the price of sugar in the 1980s and 1990s, the region entered a steep economic decline.

2 ● LOCATION

The Western Visayas region of the Philippines includes Panay island, Negros Occidental, and Romblon. The region's population numbered 5.4 million in 1990, all speakers of Hiligaynon Ilongo or closely related dialects. Hiligaynon speakers constitute approximately 10 percent of the national population. They inhabit one of the major rice-producing areas of the Philippines. The landscape consists of broad plains stretching between mountain ranges.

Large rivers deposit the volcanic sediments that make the lowlands fertile.

3 ● LANGUAGE

The Hiligaynon language is the language of Iloilo province, which has come to be spoken throughout the Western Visayas region. Other regions of Panay have their own distinct speech forms (Capizeño, Aklanon, and Kiniray-a, the last spoken in interior villages), but these are mutually intelligible with Hiligaynon (speakers of one can understand the other). Hiligaynon intonation is noted for its gentle lilt under which, it is said, a curse may go unrecognized. The narrow straits link Panay and western Negros, and Hiligaynon is spoken on both shores. Mountains separate western from eastern Negros, where the people speak Cebuano, a language that the Hiligaynon people cannot readily understand.

4 ● FOLKLORE

The *Maragtas* epic, an imaginative nineteenth-century reworking of Panay folk memories, tells of the migration to the Philippines in AD 1250 of the Bornean *datus* (chiefs) Puti, Sumakwel, Bangkaya, Balakasusa, Paiburong, Dumangsil, Lubay, and Dumalogdog. They had led their followers there to escape the tyranny of the Srivijayan empire. The datus bought the coastal lands of Panay from the indigenous (native) people with gold, pearls, and other ornaments (the native people moved inland).

5 ● RELIGION

Among the Hiligaynon, a pre-Christian belief system coexists with the Catholic one brought by the Spaniards. The two exert

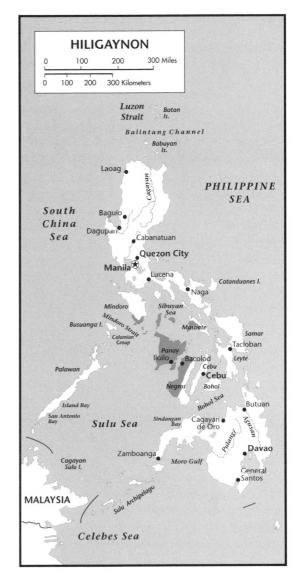

mutual influence on each other, as when the Santo Niño, the image of the Child Jesus as World Sovereign, is bathed to summon rain or attract good luck. The native beliefs divide the universe into three parts: the upperworld, middleworld, and lowerworld. The upperworld houses at its peak the *udtohanon*, which is God and his favorite angels who will pass the final judgment but are otherwise remote from human affairs. Lower down in the upperworld reside the *langitnon,* angelic beings who live above the clouds. In the *awan-awan* (between the clouds and the earth but still in the upperworld) live the spirits of the wind, rain, thunder, lightning, typhoons, and whirlwinds; supreme among them is the *tagurising* who lives where the sun rises. The middleworld (the earth) is the home to the *dutan-on,* spirits expelled from the upperworld for rebelling against God; they are identified according to where they first landed, for example, in trees, the river, or the sea. The underworld includes hell, in front of whose gate is a hollow pit where the *engkanto,* the malevolent (evil) spirits, live with their reptilian pets; the underworld regions are connected to the middleworld through a tunnel called the *bungalog.*

Each community has specialists who are able to communicate with spirits and heal diseases thought to be caused by spirits. They also recover lost objects, predict the future, and discover the causes of misfortunes. The most important of these specialists is the *baylan,* a medium whom a spirit has befriended and granted powers. To increase the power of his rituals, the baylan often adds Latin prayers and Catholic sacred objects.

6 ● MAJOR HOLIDAYS

The Hiligaynon celebrate *Santacruzan* with parades and feasting each May. The holiday commemorates the time when St. Helena (c.248–c.328) discovered the cross on which Christ was believed to have been crucified.

7 ● RITES OF PASSAGE

Persons wanting to marry consult with their siblings and other relatives before approaching their parents for consent and support. The boy's family arranges a meeting with the girl's family to discover if the girl has already been promised to another; this serves as a public announcement to discourage other suitors. The boy's family employs a spokesperson to learn whether the girl's parents have accepted the proposal. If they have, the arrangements, including the prospective groom's term of bride service, are arranged at another meeting, the *padul-ong,* after which the engagement becomes binding and the girl is no longer to be seen in the company of other boys.

On the night before the wedding, both sides attend a party at the bride's parents' house. The church ceremony itself includes ritual acts that are meant to ensure the wife's subservience and fertility. Formerly, a *sinulang* (a machete dance) accompanied the couple out of the church. Arriving at the house, the couple proceeds straight to the family altar to ensure future prosperity; a feast follows. The marriage is not consummated until the second night at the groom's parents' house; on the third day, the couple returns to the bride's parents' house to live.

When a person is dying, relatives say prayers for the deliverance of his or her soul and to ward off evil spirits (men wave machetes in the yard). The body is washed with water mixed with ginger or bark juice and is laid out in the house next to an improvised altar and a tin can in which mourners put contributions. The deceased's family refrains from making excessive noise, fighting, combing their hair, and bathing until three days after the burial. Only unmarried men may take the body out of the house; water is thrown on the threshold so that another death will not follow. The entire funeral procession must return to the house of the deceased and wash their hands and feet.

Nine days of prayer follow the burial; as many as nine more days may be added, depending on the family's wealth (as all attending must be served food and drink). At a midnight ceremony on the ninth night, all family members must be awake to bid farewell to the spirit of the deceased. On the death anniversary, nine days of prayer again take place. On the ninth night, a *patay-patay* (a dummy of the dead) is set up, consisting of pillows laid on a wooden trunk upon which the deceased's clothes are laid.

8 ● RELATIONSHIPS

Hiligaynon share the general Filipino behavioral values such as *hiya* (*huya* in the Hiligaynon language). Violating norms (such as insulting spiritual mediums) will earn *gaba,* supernatural punishment. Those who humiliate others will suffer the same amount of humiliation in turn, called *ulin.*

9 ● LIVING CONDITIONS

Houses are raised 9 to 13 feet (3 to 4 meters) off the ground; walls are of plaited (braided) bamboo, and roofs are of *nipa* or coconut palm leaves or *cogon* grass. *Sulay,* bamboo, or timber props, are placed against all sides of a house to keep it from being blown away by typhoons. The room for receiving guests is separated from the rest of the house by a wall; a sofa and two side

Cory Langley

In public, husbands are the dominant partner; inside the house, however, the wives reign supreme.

chairs occupy the space immediately inside the front door. Small children of both sexes sleep together, but once they are older, boys sleep near the door and girls sleep in a bedroom at the back. Animals are kept under the house, and rice is stored there (if not in a separate granary structure). The house lot is enclosed with a bamboo fence or a hedge of ornamental plants; fruit tree groves and gardens are nearby.

10 ● FAMILY LIFE

Hiligaynon family structure conforms to the general Filipino pattern. In wealthier families, the Spanish terms papa and mama, or even the English mommy and daddy, are preferred over the native *tatay* and *nanay*. Educated people may address their spouses with such English expressions as honey or darling (often shortened to "ling") rather than the native *nonoy* (for the husband) or *neneng* (for the wife). Uncles and aunts are addressed as "tay + [name]" (Papa + [name]) and "nay + [name]" (Mama + [name]), respectively.

A peasant couple share work responsibilities. For example, a husband plows while the wife plants; he fishes but she sells the catch. Husbands are the dominant partner outside the house (in public or in the fields), whereas wives reign supreme within the house. Spouses refrain from showing affection publicly, exchanging only casual greetings. While village people disapprove of a man taking a mistress, saying it will bring bad luck, elite men take mistresses for the sake of prestige.

Family members lavish much attention on a child but also discipline him or her from an early age. Children will gang up on a sibling to whom the parents show favoritism. As they get older, sons become more formal with their mothers, and daughters with their fathers. (With puberty, daughters become closer to their mothers.) At the age of seven, a boy will start to help his father with farming or fishing.

Parents discipline children by telling them frightening tales (mentioning the *aswang* or names of old people) or by spanking or whipping them with a stick. All children are punished, even if only one child initiated the misbehavior.

11 ● CLOTHING

For fieldwork, men wear worn-out short pants and often go shirtless. On formal occasions, however, they wear long pants, shirts, and shoes (otherwise they go barefoot).

Married women wear either a *bestida* (dress) or a *patadyong* (tube skirt) with a blouse. Traditional weaving is nearly extinct, but was a thriving industry before the nineteenth-century import of British manufactured cloth. For *pangalap* (magical protection), many older men wear tattoos (a crucifix, initials, or female figures). At the time of the Spanish arrival, all the people living in the Visayan region wore elaborate tattoos, earning them the name *Pintados*, "the painted ones," from their conquerors.

12 ● FOOD

The eating pattern is either three meals a day or two meals (at 10:00–11:00 AM and 4:00–5:00 PM). Between-meal snacks consist of rice cakes, boiled roots, or bananas. Family members eat at their own convenience but are encouraged to eat together. Ordinarily, people eat with their hands while sitting on the floor; silverware and tables are reserved for the use of guests. Men do not eat breakfast unless, as a gesture of hospitality, they are joining visitors who are being served breakfast.

Around 6:00 PM, men gather for *tuba* (palm wine) drinking sessions in the tree groves between houses (some women may also join them).

13 ● EDUCATION

Almost all Hiligaynon are literate (can read and write). Most children attend elementary school, which is free, for six years. High school provide four more years of education. Only about 70 percent go on to high school, because not all families can afford to pay the required fees. Attending high school may involve travel to a school some distance away.

14 ● CULTURAL HERITAGE

The Hiligaynon have an epic, the *Hinilawod.*

15 ● EMPLOYMENT

The Western Visayas region is dominated by two very different types of agriculture: rice cultivation by small holders, and sugar cultivation in large plantations. Swidden (shifting-cultivation) farming is still practiced in the highlands.

Tobacco has become increasingly important. Other crops grown include maize (corn), bananas, coconuts, sweet potato, cassava, *singkamas* (similar to turnips), squash, tomatoes, beans, and red peppers. Fishing is an alternative means of livelihood. Some Hiligaynon engage in various forms of petty trade: *libod,* making the rounds of one's village, selling a product; *pahumay,* selling from one's house; *tinda,* selling at fiestas and other local events; and *tiyanggi,* operating a small variety store (*sari-sari* in Tagalog-Pilipino).

16 ● SPORTS

Tumbang patis, popular with both boys and girls, involves two or more children throwing rocks at a tin can while someone who is "it" watches the can, putting it back in place when hit; if a player is caught retrieving the stone he or she has thrown, he or she becomes "it." Other popular games include: "gunfighting" with bamboo popguns; beetle- and spider-fighting; and *huyup-huyup,* blowing rubber bands out of a circle for bets. Young children catch dragonflies, dig holes in the ground, pile sticks, measure sand with bottle caps, and pull empty coconut shells or sardine cans on strings.

17 ● RECREATION

The Hiligaynon, like all Filipinos, enjoy watching television and going to the movies. Children play board games and team sports like chess and soccer.

18 ● CRAFTS AND HOBBIES

Hiligaynon practice weaving baskets, place mats, and textiles.

19 ● SOCIAL PROBLEMS

Hiligaynon people view the government and the justice system as corrupt, because wealthy people are able to bribe officials to receive the verdicts they desire.

20 ● BIBLIOGRAPHY

LeBar, Frank M., ed. *Ethnic Groups of Insular Southeast Asia.* Vol. 2, *The Philippines and Formosa.* New Haven, Conn.: Human Relations Area Files Press, 1972.

WEBSITES

Embassy of the Philipines, Washington, D.C. [Online] Available http://www.sequel.net/RpinUS/WDC/, 1998.

World Travel Guide. Philippines. [Online] Available http://www.wtgonline.com/country/ph/gen.html, 1998.

Ilocanos

PRONUNCIATION: ee-lo-KAHN-ohs
LOCATION: Philippines (northern Luzon)
POPULATION: 1.8 million
LANGUAGE: Ilocano
RELIGION: Roman Catholicism; Philippine Independent Church; Iglesia ni Kristo (Church of Christ); Protestantism; Islam; animism

1 ● INTRODUCTION

When the Spanish first encountered them in 1572, the inhabitants of Ilocos (then called "Samtoy") were living in large villages at sheltered coves or rivermouths and were trading with the Chinese and Japanese. Although massive churches in a distinctive style give evidence of Spanish-Ilocano collaboration, the colonial period was marked by frequent revolts; the most famous of these was that led by Diego and Gabriela Silang during the British occupation of Manila in 1762–63.

Ilocanos were prominent in the nationalist movement, and many rose to high office in the central government. The greatest of these Ilocano "success stories" (as far as it went) was President Ferdinand Marcos, who ruled from 1965 to 1986.

2 ● LOCATION

The four provinces of the Ilocano homeland (Ilocos Norte, Ilocos Sur, La Union, and landlocked Abra) stretch from Cape Bojeador at the northwestern tip of Luzon down to the Gulf of Lingayen. Most of the population is concentrated along a narrow coastal plain that has only a few good harbors. This environment is harsh, forcing Ilocanos to be hard-working and thrifty. Many Ilocanos have left their homeland to seek employment elsewhere.

The population of the four provinces is about 1.8 million. Ilocano speakers, however, numbered 11 percent of the national population of 66 million, or 7.26 million people. Among all Filipino groups, the Ilocanos are the most famed as migrants, settling since the nineteenth century in sparsely populated expanses of the northern Central Plain of Luzon (provinces of Pangasinan, Tarlac, and Nueva Ecija) and of the Cagayan Valley in the northeast. In addition, many Ilocanos have established themselves in Manila and other major cities of the country, as well as in frontier lands on Mindanao. Ilocano men left to find work as migrant laborers on sugar plantations in Hawaii and on farms in California in the first decades of the twentieth century. They were the first Filipinos to immigrate to the United States. In the Philippines, every Ilocano town has a number of men known as "Hawaiianos," returned migrants from the United States. These migrants courted their future wives in their home country by letter.

3 ● LANGUAGE

The Ilocanos speak a Western Austronesian language of the Northern Philippine group, whose closest relatives are the languages of neighboring mountain peoples. Ilocano has become the lingua franca of northern Luzon, as Ilocano traders provide highland peoples with their primary link to the commerce of the outside world.

4 ●FOLKLORE

According to one Ilocano origin myth, a giant named Aran built the sky and hung the sun, moon, and stars in it. Under their light, Aran's companion, the giant Angalo, could see the land, which he then molded into mountains and valleys. The giants found the world they had created windswept and desolate. Angalo spat on the earth, and from his spit emerged the first man and woman. He placed them in a bamboo tube that he tossed into the sea. The bamboo washed up on the shore of the Ilocos region, and from this couple came the Ilocano people.

Like other Filipinos, Ilocanos recognize an array of supernatural beings, such as the *katawtaw-an* (the spirits of infants, who died unbaptized who in turn victimize newborns). The *karkarma,* the souls of living persons, leave the body at death but linger in the house until after the post-funerary offerings of food are made to the deceased; in the form of the scent of perfume, the odor of a burning candle, or a strange draft of wind, they are believed to visit relatives who have failed to come to the sickbed of the deceased. The *al-alia,* the spirit doubles of humans, appear at their human doubles' death as the groaning of the dying, the cracking of glass, the rattling of beds, and the banging of doors, or in the form (at night) of a grunting pig, howling dog, or a crowing chicken. These signs remind the living to pray to God for the forgiveness of the deceased's sins (otherwise, the al-alia may visit misfortunes upon them).

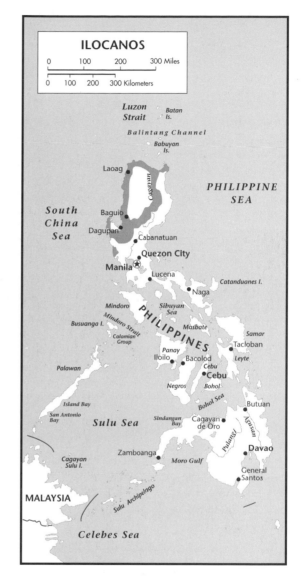

5 ●RELIGION

Filipinos were converted to Roman Catholicism by Spanish colonial settlers. Catholicism in the Philippines combines belief in patron saints with belief in supernatural forces. Many people consult faith healers for herbal treatments of physical ailments.

6 ● MAJOR HOLIDAYS

Ilocanos celebrate national and religious holidays.

7 ● RITES OF PASSAGE

Although free to choose their own marriage partners, young people seek the approval of both sets of parents. When a couple decides they'd like to marry, the first step is for the young man to ask for the consent of his own parents. His parents will pay the dowry and finance the wedding. Next, the future groom makes a formal announcement *(panag-pudno)* to the young woman's parents of his intention to marry their daughter. The groom's parents then visit the future bride's parents, to set the date for the wedding. For this, the parents consult a *planetario,* an almanac identifying auspicious (good-luck) days. At a further meeting *(palalian* or *ring-pas),* the young man and his relatives come to the young woman's house to finalize the wedding arrangements; each party employs a spokesperson who negotiates for his or her side in formal language. The families set the choice of wedding sponsors (an equal number, ranging from ten to fifty people for each side), the dowry (land for the couple, or the money to buy such land), the *sagut* (the wedding dress, jewelry, and accessories that the groom is to provide for the bride), and the *parawad* (cash that the groom gives the bride's mother as a reward for raising his bride).

The wedding feast follows the church ceremony. At the feast, the bride and groom go through an entertaining ritual. First, the groom offers the bride a plate of mung beans (symbolizing fertility). The bride refuses the dish several times before finally accepting it. Then the bride offers the beans to the groom who in turn refuses the dish until an old man calls an end to the ritual. (The pleadings and feigned refusals greatly amuse the onlookers.) Another highlight is the *bitor:* guests contribute cash to the newlyweds either by dropping money onto plates held by two men seated on a mat (representing the bride and groom, respectively) or by pinning bills to the couple's clothing while the two dance. After the wedding, offerings of rice cakes are made to the spirits of departed family members.

To announce a death formally, a piece of wood *(atong)* is lit in front of the deceased's house and is kept burning until after burial, at which time it is extinguished with rice wine. The corpse is kept in the house. It is dressed in its best clothes and a kerchief is tied around the jaw; a basin of water mixed with vinegar is placed under the bed to remove the odor of death. Money is placed in the coffin to pay the "ferry man" who takes the soul to the other world. In the days before burial, relatives keep vigil over the body, wailing and recounting the deceased's good deeds (sometimes, professional mourners perform the lamentation *(dung-aw).*

Before the funeral itself, each of the relatives pays their last respects by kissing the deceased's hand or raising it to his or her forehead. Extreme care is taken in transporting the body from the house to the church; any mishap could cause premature death for the attendants. After the church ceremony, the relatives pose as a group for souvenir photos with the coffin. Everyone in the procession to the cemetery must return to the deceased's home by a different route from the one taken there. Upon arrival, they must wash their faces and hands in order to remove the power of death.

8 ● RELATIONSHIPS

Ilocanos share the same basic values as other Filipinos, such as *bain,* which corresponds to *hiya* or *amor propio* ("face" or sense of shame). The fear of gossip and the desire to avoid the envy of others serve as strong pressures for conformity. Before pushing through with his or her own plans, a person feels *alumiim,* the need to figure out how others will react first in order to avoid embarrassment. It is essential to show *panagdayaw,* proper respect for the sensitivities of others. This requires that individuals speak about themselves only in the humblest of terms. Although Ilocanos are group-oriented, they also value a certain individualism *(agwayas)*: one should not reveal his or her inner intentions to others, since it is unwise to be too trusting.

A person is expected to overcome life's challenges through his or her own hard work, limiting his or her dependence on others to obtaining aid from close kin. However, Ilocanos do form savings associations (including as many as fifty women in a neighborhood), mutual-aid associations (financing members' major celebrations), and labor-exchange arrangements.

Life-passage parties and fiestas provide teenagers their main opportunity to chat and joke. For a young man to initiate a courtship is a serious matter, since the only proper end is marriage. On his first visit to the house of a young woman, the young man takes one or two companions with him so that he can get their opinion. During the second visit, the companions excuse themselves to allow the young man to confess his feelings to the young woman. Love notes are an important means of courtship.

9 ● LIVING CONDITIONS

Raised two to three feet (0.6 meters to 1 meter) off the ground, houses have beams of wood, walls of bamboo, and roofs of rice straw or *cogon* grass. Sometimes, newly married children may live in roofed extensions. On the *bangsal,* a landing on the staircase, guests wait before being admitted, and wash or wipe their feet before entering the receiving room. Curtains or bamboo partitions separate the living room from the bedroom areas (most have beds but prefer sleeping mats). A separate storage room also serves for a place to change clothes. Outhouses provide toilet facilities.

10 ● FAMILY LIFE

The structure of the Ilocano family (average size, six to seven persons) conforms to the general Filipino pattern. The father is the formal head of family, backing up the mother who disciplines the children and manages the house finances. The eldest child divides the chores equally among siblings. Grandparents tend to be more indulgent of grandchildren than the parents themselves.

11 ● CLOTHING

Dress inappropriate for one's age or perceived wealth or status attracts gossip such as *mabiag ti ruar ngem matay ti uneg* (outwardly alive, but inwardly dying); *uray napintas no inutang* (even if it is nice, it is acquired through credit). Still one should

The bitter melon resembles a dimpled cucumber, and has large seeds at its center. It is available at some specialty markets in the United States.

12 ● FOOD

Ilocano food essentially resembles that elsewhere in the country, but Ilocanos are especially fond of *bagoong* (a salty shrimp or fish paste). One regional specialty that has entered national cuisine is *pinakbet*—eggplant, bitter melon, okra, and green beans cooked with bagoong, tomatoes, and a little water (dried or broiled fish, meat, or shrimps can be added to improve the taste).

Other favorites are *dinardaraan*—cooked pig's blood (*dinuguan* in Tagalog-Pilipino); and *kilawen*—the lean meat and intestines of water buffalo, cow, sheep, or goat, eaten raw or partially cooked with a sauce of vinegar, salt, hot pepper, and pig's bile.

Eating with their hands, family members squat around the food laid out on the floor or take food and eat in different parts of the main room. As food is regarded as a symbol of God's grace, there should be no noise, laughing, singing, or harsh words (including parents scolding children) while eating is going on. One should not drop food on the table or floor, or the food "will be angered and leave the household." Similarly, no one should leave the house while someone is still eating, for God's grace will go with him or her, out of the home.

13 ● EDUCATION

Iloconas are almost all literate (can read or write).

14 ● CULTURAL HERITAGE

The Ilocanos have an epic, the *Biag ni Lam-ang* (Life of Lam-ang), which, however, exists only in the form of a highly Hispanicized metrical romance composed in the

dress well for special celebrations. Everyday wear, especially at home, consists of short pants for boys, and dusters, loose skirts, shirts, and short pants for girls. Those working in the fields wear long-sleeved shirts, long pants, and wide-brimmed hats as protection against the sun and mud.

During the rainy season, people wear a headress of *labig* leaves extending well down the back. Older women wear their hair long and knotted in a bun, while men keep it short and apply pomade on special occasions.

nineteenth century. Ilocos is also the only place in the country where the Spanish *zarzuela* (operetta) is still performed.

15 ● EMPLOYMENT

Almost all farmers (the major occupation) own the land they till, except for those who are tenants of farms owned by urban professionals. The staple crop is rice, though poorer people must mix cheaper maize (corn) with their rice. Root crops are also grown both as a supplement to the diet and for sale. Watered by wet-season rains or irrigation, wet-rice fields range from small plots that can only be worked with a hoe or dibble stick to those large enough for a water-buffalo–drawn plow. Dry-rice agriculture is also practiced in the hilly areas between the flatlands. Crops grown for market include tobacco and garlic (both Ilocos specialties), as well as onions, and vegetables. Petty traders may travel as far as Manila to sell such products.

Farmers fish during the lull between planting and harvesting, usually in nearby offshore waters, rivers, or fish ponds. An important part of the catch are *ipon,* small fish for *bagoong* (fish paste).

Cottage industries include salt-making; *basi* wine-making (from molasses); pottery-making (twenty different types are produced in San Nicolas); weaving (at one time using locally grown cotton; a goddess is said to have bequeathed the art to the people of Paoay town); basket- and mat-weaving; woodworking; and silversmithing (recycling old Spanish or Mexican coins).

EPD Photos

Bagoong, a pink fish paste that turns brown when cooked, is a key ingredient in Ilocano cuisine and an important product in the economy.

16 ● SPORTS

One uniquely Ilocano game is *kukudisi*. A stick (the *an-anak*) is placed on a baseline scratched into the ground. One player makes the stick jump in the air; the other player tries to catch it before it hits the ground. If the latter cannot do so, a second, longer stick (the *in-ina*) is laid across the baseline; the player then tries to hit it with the an-anak. The next two phases of the game involve competing to see who can hit the an-anak (which has been tossed in the air and stuck into the baseline, respectively) with the in-ina the farthest.

17 ● RECREATION

Children enjoy such games as *balay-balay* (playing house), hide-and-seek, team-tag, jumping "hurdles" (sticks or outstretched arms or legs), jacks, and chess.

18 ● CRAFTS AND HOBBIES

Ilocanos engage in the same hobbies as all Filipinos. These include weaving, wood-carving, and playing chess.

19 ● SOCIAL PROBLEMS

Ilocanos, like all Filipinos, feel their government is corrupt. Wealthy citizens frequently bribe officials to get the verdict they want.

20 ● BIBLIOGRAPHY

Jocano, F. Landa. *The Ilocanos: An Ethnography of Family and Community in the Ilocos Region.* Quezon City: Asian Center, University of Philippines, 1982.

LeBar, Frank M., ed. *Ethnic Groups of Insular Southeast Asia.* Vol. 2, *The Philippines and Formosa.* New Haven, Conn.: Human Relations Area Files Press, 1972

WEBSITES

Embassy of the Philippines, Washington, D.C. [Online] Available http://www.sequel.net/RpinUS/WDC/, 1998.

World Travel Guide. The Philippines. [Online] Available http://www.wtgonline.co.uk/country/ph/gen.html, 1998.

Poland

■ **POLES** **149**

Before World War II (1939–45), over 30 percent of the people living within the boundaries of Poland were non-Poles. As a result of World War II, and of the boundary changes and population transfers that followed, only about 2 percent of Poland's population today is non-Polish. Ukrainians, Lithuanians, Belarusans, Germans, and Slovaks are the most numerous minorities.

Poles

PRONUNCIATION: pOAls
LOCATION: Poland
POPULATION: 38.5 million
LANGUAGE: Polish
RELIGION: Roman Catholicism (90 percent)

1 ● INTRODUCTION

In AD 966, the Poles converted to Christianity and formed their first state. During the first seven centuries of its history, Poland expanded to become one of Europe's largest countries. After uniting with Lithuania in the fourteenth century, Poland was the center of a huge multi-ethnic empire. The sixteenth and seventeenth centuries are considered the Golden Age of Polish history. This was when the nation pushed eastward to take over its Slavic neighbors, dreaming of a kingdom that stretched from the Baltic to the Black Sea.

By the end of the eighteenth century, neighboring countries destroyed Poland. Over time, its territories were divided among the Austrian, Prussian, and Russian empires. By 1795, Poland no longer existed as a separate government. This sitution continued for more than a century.

Reunited and restored to independence after World War I (1914–18), the country was able to sustain a parliamentary democracy for only a few years. It was overwhelmed by invasions from both Nazi Germany and the Soviet Union in 1939. The country then entered into the darkest period of its long history. More than 6 million of its people died during World War II (1939–45). After the war, a communist government was imposed by the Soviet Union. It lasted almost fifty years.

In 1990 Lech Walesa (b.1943), a former labor leader and the hero of Polish independence, was elected president. Today Poland

POLES

Poland's population of 38.5 million is highly homogenous, meaning most people are of the same ethnic group. The country does have minority groups, including Ukrainians, Germans, and Belorussians.

3 ● LANGUAGE

Polish is a Slavic language that uses the Roman alphabet. When pronouncing words, the stress is usually on the second-to-last syllable.

Some common everyday words are: *tak* (yes), *nie* (no), *jak* (how), *dobrze* (OK), *dzien dobry* (good morning), *czesc* (hello), and *prosze* (please).

4 ● FOLKLORE

There are many legends associated with Easter and Christmas, which are very important holidays in Poland. For example, a legend of the Christmas spiders tells of when Jesus was a little boy and came upon a poor farmhouse. He heard a family of spiders crying because there was not enough money to buy decorations for the Christmas tree. The spiders let him in and he blessed the tree. Within minutes it was decorated in silver and gold webs. This is why tinsel is used to decorate Christmas trees.

5 ● RELIGION

The Poles are deeply religious. Roman Catholicism is the religion of some 90 percent of the population. It has an important influence on many aspects of Polish life. In 1978, a Pole, Cardinal Karol Wojtyla (b.1920), was chosen to become Pope (John Paul II), the first Polish person to be so honored.

is a parliamentary democracy. In 1997 it was picked to be one of the first countries of Eastern Europe to join the North Atlantic Treaty Organization (NATO).

2 ● LOCATION

Poland is bordered on the east and southeast by Ukraine and Belarus, on the northeast by Lithuania and Russia, on the south by the Czech Republic and Slovakia, on the west by Germany, and on the northwest by the Baltic Sea. The capital city is Warsaw.

Poland consists almost entirely of lowlands that are part of the North European Plain. The climate varies, with cold, snowy winters and warm summers. Forests occupy more than one-fourth of the total land area.

Cory Langley

With the school day over, this boy feeds the pigeons in a busy city square. Education is compulsory from age seven through age fifteen and is free through high school. In addition to the traditional focus on Polish history and culture, there is a strong emphasis on foreign languages and computer skills.

Poland has 2,500 convents with 28,000 nuns, and over 500 monasteries. The Catholic University in Lublin and the Academy of Catholic Theology in Warsaw are the leading church-controlled institutions. The city of Czestochowa, with its Black Madonna, is one of the most important pilgrimage centers in Europe. Other Christian denominations besides Catholicism include Russian Orthodox and the Uniate faith, which combines aspects of Catholicism and Russian Orthodoxy. There are also a variety of Protestant churches.

6 ● MAJOR HOLIDAYS

There is a famous Polish saying, "Every day is good for celebration." Important public holidays include New Year's Day (January 1), Good Friday (in March or April), All Saints' Day (November 1), Corpus Christi Day (in June), and Worker's Day (May 1). Constitution Day (May 3) is also an important holiday in Poland.

Polish Catholics have an interesting annual tradition of pledging their vows to the Blessed Virgin Mary. The Mother of God, or Bogurodzica, is the patron of

Poland. People often visit Czestochowa, where the shrine of the Black Madonna is located, to renew their vows to her.

The church calendar is based on two cycles, which end in the two biggest religious celebrations: Christmas (*Boze Narodzenie*) and Easter (*Wielkanoc*). There are also many saints' feast days, which are especially numerous for the Virgin Mary.

Although it is not an official holiday (banks and government offices remain open), St. John's Eve in June is a popular day of festivities. Originally a pagan celebration designed to drive out devils, it is now celebrated with great bonfires around which young people dance and over which boys try to leap. They carry buckets of water to douse the girls.

7 ● RITES OF PASSAGE

Occasions such as baptism, first communion, and marriage are cause for festive celebrations.

A Polish wedding always promises a good time. Some traditional rituals associated with a Polish wedding include long blessings by the parents before the actual ceremony, and greenery on the bride's headpiece symbolizing her virginity. These customs are not always practiced today. Many Poles have adopted Western-style wedding traditions. Wedding anniversaries are very special among Polish couples. The tenth wedding anniversary is the occasion for a major celebration.

Lively wakes are held after Polish funerals, with toasts and tributes to the deceased. In the past, Poles wore black for a year following the death of a family member. Today, a black armband is worn instead.

8 ● RELATIONSHIPS

Poles greet each other by shaking hands. Men and women often shake hands. Usually the man waits until the woman has extended her hand first. In general, Poles are more conservative and formal than Westerners, but they are known for their hospitality. When responding to a dinner invitation, it is considered polite to bring a bouquet of flowers for the lady of the house.

Common Polish polite expressions include *przepraszam* (excuse me), *Jest pan/pani bardzo uprzejmy* (Sir/madam you are very kind), and *dziekuje* (thank you).

9 ● LIVING CONDITIONS

The average life expectancy for Poles is about seventy years. The infant mortality rate is fourteen per one thousand live births. Government-funded medical care is available to all Poles. However, facilities do not measure up to Western standards, and there are not enough doctors to care for patients (1 doctor for every 480 patients and 1 hospital bed for every 144 people). Alcoholism is a major health problem in Poland.

Poland faces a serious housing shortage, and young couples often live with parents for the first years after they marry. In addition to being scarce, housing is also very expensive. In the villages, brick and stone structures with fireproof roofs have replaced the traditional wooden houses with thatched roofs.

Most families do not own cars, although car ownership is on the rise. Hitchhiking is both legal and encouraged. Hitchhikers can buy books of coupons, which they give to any driver who picks them up. At the end of every year, the drivers then use these coupons to enter contests and win prizes. Most cities have efficient bus and streetcar systems, and there are air and rail links to major cities.

10 ● FAMILY LIFE

Families in urban areas typically have one or two children, while rural families often have three or four. Traditionally, the Polish father is a stern authority figure, with the mother mediating between him and the children. The nuclear family (father, mother, and children) is usual. Aged parents or unmarried brothers and sisters may be part of the household. Single-parent households are becoming more common.

In most families, both parents work. Children assume considerable responsibility for themselves at an early age, helping cook, clean, and care for younger brothers and sisters. Grandparents also play a significant role in childrearing. Mother's Day is a big occasion for Polish children. They often put on performances for their mothers at school.

11 ● CLOTHING

Poles wear modern Western-style clothing and generally dress conservatively. As a rule, women do not wear pants. Clothing is very expensive, so wardrobes tend to be small. It is still common to wear handmade clothing. Young people like jeans and sweatshirts with American slogans or logos. Jeans are also popular among people in the arts and around universities. In rural areas,

Cory Langley

Poles wear modern Western-style clothing and generally dress conservatively. Young Poles like to wear jeans and sweatshirts with American slogans or logos.

older women can still be seen wearing full skirts, thick stockings, and headscarfs.

12 ● FOOD

Meat is integral to Polish cuisine. Beef, pork, ham, and sausage make up many national dishes, such as *bigos* (sauerkraut with spicy meat and mushrooms), *flaki* (tripe, or sheep's stomach, boiled or fried), *golonka* (pig's leg), and *pierogi* (dough filled with cheese, meat, or fruit). Common fish include pike, carp, cod, crayfish, and herring. The Poles are known for their thick, hearty soups, including *borscht* (beet soup), *botwinka, chlodnik,* or *krupnik.*

EPD Photos

This young American student is enjoying a plate of cheese pierogi topped with a dollop of sour cream.

13 ● EDUCATION

Poland has a 98 percent literacy rate (ability to read and write) and a 97 percent attendance level in its schools. In 1773 a national education commission was established. The system still operates today. Education is compulsory from age seven through age fifteen and is free through high school. Polish children spend many hours in school.

In addition to the traditional focus on Polish history and culture, there is a strong emphasis on foreign languages and computer skills. Students who pass an entrance exam may attend one of Poland's ten universities or a technical institute or other type of institution. Higher education is also free. Poland has ninety institutions of higher education. The Jagiellonian University in Cracow, founded in 1364, is the second-oldest university in Central Europe.

14 ● CULTURAL HERITAGE

During the repressive communist era, art and theater were used to protest against the government.

Poland's musical heritage includes such greats as Frederic Chopin (1810–49), Ignacy Jan Paderewski (1860–1941), and Artur Rubinstein (1887–1982).

Poland has ten symphony orchestras, seventeen conservatories, over one hundred music schools, and almost one thousand music centers. In Warsaw, nightly operas, ballets, chamber concerts, and recitals are a popular recreational activity. Warsaw is also the home of the Jazz Jamboree festival—the oldest and biggest jazz performance in Eastern Europe.

Sour cream and bacon bits are condiments necessary for almost every dish. Typical desserts include stewed fruit, fruit dumplings, pancakes with fruit or cheese, and jam donuts called *paczki* (POONCH-key).

Poland has several varieties of vodka. It is a favorite drink, which Poland claims to have discovered. Bottled beers made locally area are popular, as are soft drinks made of strawberry and apple. Pepsi and Coke are also commonly drunk. Tea is consumed with everything.

Village musicians often play at weddings and festivals. Their sound is a combination of the fiddle, pan pipes, accordion, and a single-reed bagpipe.

Writers are considered important people in Poland. Adam Mickiewicz, a nineteenth-century poet, is the national poet. Many streets and squares are named after him. The following Polish-born writers have won Nobel Prizes for literature: Henryk Sienkiewicz, Wladyslaw Reymont, and the poet Czeslaw Milosz. Twentieth-century poets such as Julian Przybos and Julian Tuwim have celebrated Polish uprisings and written verse opposing the communist regime.

15 ● EMPLOYMENT

In the days of communist bureaucracy, the policy was to create jobs even where there was no need for them. Over half the urban population used to work in state offices.

Today, about a quarter of the labor force is employed in agriculture and over a third in industry. It is anticipated that foreign trade problems could cause the loss of around 70,000 jobs, as the steel mills adjust to decreased production targets.

16 ● SPORTS

Some popular sports include swimming, gymnastics, hockey, volleyball, and soccer. On some Saturday mornings part of a street may be closed off for a soccer game. Soccer, which is played at every school, is also the biggest spectator sport. "Streetball," similar to basketball, is played by children in the parks.

Skiing is Poland's most popular winter sport. The beautiful ski resort of Zakopane

Cory Langley

An artist sells his paintings on a sidewalk in Krakow.

(which means "a place buried in the ground") is the most popular ski getaway for Poles. A popular saying goes "when life gets unbearable, there is always Zakopane."

17 ● RECREATION

Popular family activities include watching television and listening to American pop music. Poland's cities are famous for theater and cinemas, opera houses, jazz and classical concerts, and discos. Outdoor activities include hiking, motorcycle racing, horseback riding, and hunting. Poland's spas are also popular leisure-time areas. The largest is Ciechocinek.

18 ● CRAFTS AND HOBBIES

Among folk art specialties from particular regions are paintings on glass by the Zakopane mountain folk, red-sequined Cracow folk costumes, the black pottery of Kielce, lacework from Koniakow, rainbow-colored cloth from Lowicz, and paper cutouts from Kurpie. The small village of Zalipie is famous for the flower paintings on its wooden houses, wells, wagons, and chairs.

19 ● SOCIAL PROBLEMS

Social tensions are caused by the disparity in income between the poor and the wealthy. Other problems include housing shortages and inadequacies in the national health care system.

20 ● BIBLIOGRAPHY

Curtis, Glenn E. *Poland: A Country Study.* 3rd ed. Washington, D.C.: Federal Research Division, Library of Congress, 1994.

Heale, Jay. *Cultures of the World. Poland.* New York: Marshall Cavendish, 1994.

Meras, Phyllis. *Eastern Europe: A Traveler's Companion.* Boston: Houghton Mifflin, 1991.

Otfinoski, Steven. *Poland.* New York: Facts on File, 1995.

Shoemaker, M. Wesley. *Russia, Eurasian States and Eastern Europe 1993.* Washington, D.C.: Stryker-Post Publications, 1993.

Taras, Ray. "The End of the Walesa Era in Poland," *Current History* (March 1996): 124–28.

WEBSITES

Embassy of Poland, Washington, D.C. [Online] Available http://www.polishworld.com/polemb/, 1998.

Embassyof Poland in London. [Online] Available http://www.poland-embassy.org.uk/, 1998.

Polish Airlines. [Online] Available http://www.fuw.edu.pl/index.eng.html, 1998.

Portugal

■ **PORTUGUESE** 157

The Portuguese people represent a mixture of various ethnic strains. In the north are traces of Celtic influence. In the south, Arab and Berber influence is considerable. Other groups—Lusitanians, Phoenicians, Carthaginians, Romans, Visigoths, and Jews—also left their mark on the Portuguese people. The present-day Portuguese population all comes from the same ethnic background, with no national minorities.

Portuguese

PRONUNCIATION: por-che-GEEZ
LOCATION: Portugal
POPULATION: 10.5 million
LANGUAGE: Portuguese
RELIGION: Roman Catholicism; Islam; Judaism; Protestantism

1 ● INTRODUCTION

Portugal was one of the first European nations to be unified into a single country. It gained independence from Spain with the accession of King Alfonse I in 1143. The country is located in southwestern Europe. Due to colonization and emigration, there are Portuguese-speaking peoples living in North and South America, Asia, Africa, and Australia.

The Portuguese Age of Discovery began in the fifteenth century. This marked the beginning of a vast overseas empire which expanded for over three centuries. Portugal's wealth and importance declined after the loss of Brazil in 1822. In 1910, the monarchy was eliminated and a republic was declared. This was replaced by the dictatorial rule of António Salazar (1889–1970) in 1926.

The Salazar government was finally overthrown in 1974. A democratic government was established and a new constitution was adopted in 1976. During this period Portugal granted independence to its remaining colonies, including Angola and Mozambique. In spite of continuing poverty, especially in rural areas, the nation has seen numerous advances since the 1970s.

2 ● LOCATION

Portugal occupies about one-fifth—and most of the western coast—of the Iberian Peninsula (the rest of it is Spain). It is bordered on the south and west by the Atlantic

PORTUGUESE

0   100   200   300 Miles

0   100   200   300 Kilometers

FRANCE

Bay of Biscay

Paris

Nantes

Bordeaux

Bilbao

Oporto

ANDORRA

PORTUGAL

Madrid

Barcelona

Lisbon

SPAIN

Balearic Islands

Sevilla

Málaga

Gibraltar (UK)

COMMON WORDS AND PHRASES

English	Portuguese
good morning	bom dia
good afternoon	boa tarde
good evening	boa noite
yes	sim
no	não
please	por favor
thank you	men say "obrigado;" women say "obrigada"
goodbye	adeus

4 ● FOLKLORE

The Portuguese are a deeply superstitious people. Their formal Catholicism is mixed with pre-Christian practices and beliefs. Offerings to saints—intended to promote healing—hang on strings near many church altars. Images on these offerings depict whatever is to be (or has been) healed. These include hands, heads, breasts, babies, and animals.

Popular superstitions involve the phases of the moon, the healing power of fountains, and the evil eye, which is the power to inflict bad luck on someone. The evil eye is feared in a number of situations. Ceremonies surrounding death and the occult abound. Portuguese widows are expected to wear black for about seven years, and many wear it for the rest of their lives. The loss of a parent is mourned for up to three years.

5 ● RELIGION

The overwhelming majority of Portuguese (97 percent) are Roman Catholics. Catholicism is at the center of Portuguese life. Portugal's holidays, its moral and legal codes, health and education systems have been greatly impacted by its Catholic heritage. While only about a third of the population attends church regularly, almost all Portu-

Ocean and on the north and east by Spain, its only neighbor.

Portugal's population of 10.5 million people is ethnically homogeneous. This means that nearly all the people are of the same ethnic group. There is a small Muslim population of guest workers from North Africa and small Jewish and Protestant communities composed mainly of foreigners. There are also as many as 100,000 Roma, sometimes called Gypsies, mostly in the Algarve region.

3 ● LANGUAGE

Portuguese is a Romance language that is most closely related to the Spanish dialect Galician. Over time it was modified by the language of the Muslim Moors living in lands taken over by Portugal.

Susan D. Rock

School children walking in Lisbon, Portugal. Although education is free and compulsory to the age of fifteen, traditionally many children drop out after primary school to begin working.

guese are baptized and married within the church and receive its last rites when they die. Religious observance is greater in the northern part of the country than in the south.

Churches occupy a prominent physical location in almost every Portuguese village. Many Portuguese make pilgrimages *(romarias)* to religious shrines. The most famous such shrine is the one at Fátima where the Virgin Mary is said to have appeared before three children in 1917. The cult of the Virgin is very powerful in Portugal, and images of Mary and Christ are commonly seen even in such non-religious places as labor union offices.

There are small numbers of Muslims, Jews, and Protestants.

6 ● MAJOR HOLIDAYS

Most holidays celebrated in Portugal are those of the Christian calendar. Those with the status of national holidays are Shrove Tuesday (in February or March), Good Friday (in March or April), Corpus Christi (in June), All Saints' Day (November 1), the Immaculate Conception (December 8), and Christmas (December 25). Secular holidays include New Year's; Liberty Day (April 25), which commemorates the death of the national poet, Luiz Vaz de Camões, in 1580; Portugal Day (June 10), which celebrates the 1974 Revolution; Proclamation of the Republic Day (October 5), celebrating the founding of the Republic in 1910; and Restoration of Independence Day (December 1).

In rural areas, villagers honor their patron saint during the annual *festa*. This celebration is both religious and secular. There is a procession, and people fulfill their religious vows *(promessas)* for the occasion. The festivities may last several days and often include such non-religious elements as picnics, dancing, fireworks, and bullfights.

7 ● RITES OF PASSAGE

Portugal is a modern, industrialized, Christian country. Because of this, many of the rites of passage that young people undergo are religious rituals, such as baptism, first communion, confirmation, and marriage. Also, a student's progress through the education system is marked by many families with graduation parties.

8 ● RELATIONSHIPS

When the Portuguese greet each other, they kiss on both cheeks. Those who live in the northern part of the country, which has been isolated from foreign influences, are formal, conservative, and reserved among strangers. In the south people are generally more casual, relaxed, and friendly. In the north, many people are referred to by nicknames *(alcunhas),* which are an important part of their identities.

9 ● LIVING CONDITIONS

Over half of all Portuguese rent their homes. Rural villagers often live without

Susan D. Rock

Houses along a cobblestone street in an older section of Lisbon.

electricity or running water. Migration to the cities made an already existing shortage of urban housing worse. It also resulted in the growth of shantytowns *(bairros da lata)* which lack sewage systems. In response to this situation, the Portuguese government has instituted a $2 billion program to clear these slums and build low-income housing units.

Almost all sectors of Portuguese society have access to modern medical care. Portugal's national health service was inaugurated in 1979. While infant mortality rates were cut nearly in half between the mid-

1970s and mid-1980s, the government program is still insufficient to meet the nation's health care needs. It is supplemented by church-supported services. While home birth was common as recently as the 1960s, today almost all Portuguese women have their babies in hospitals.

10 ● FAMILY LIFE

The nuclear family headed by a father is the ideal throughout Portugal. But in reality families vary considerably according to class and region. Middle- and upper-class Portuguese, and those in the southern part of the country, are more likely to conform to the tradition. Women stay at home to raise children and run the household while men engage in business or the professions.

Among the poor, especially in the northwest, the relationship between husband and wife is a more equal one. Households are headed jointly. In farming families, women may work the fields alongside their husbands. Fishermen's wives may help repair nets or sell the day's catch. Due to high rates of male emigration, a relatively large number of women in the north never marry. Many have traditionally managed their own farms and remain financially independent.

The position of women in Portugal improved greatly after the end of the military dictatorship in 1974. The 1976 constitution guaranteed them full legal equality. By the early 1990s, women accounted for more than half of all persons enrolled in higher education and 37 percent of the country's physicians.

11 ● CLOTHING

Western-style clothing is the norm, and people in the cities, especially in the city of Lisbon, dress well. However, traditional clothes—such as berets and loose-fitting shirts for men and black shawls for women—may still be seen in some rural areas.

12 ● FOOD

Fish is the main staple of the Portuguese diet. Cod is the most popular. The average Portuguese eats about 100 pounds (45 kilograms) of it every year. It is prepared so many different ways in Portugal that there is said to be a different recipe for every day of the year.

Other commonly eaten seafoods include sardines, salmon, sole, sea bass, and hake, as well as eel, squid, octopus, and lamprey. Practically every Portuguese meal is accompanied by soup. The most popular is *caldo verde* (green soup), made with *couve galega* (Galician cabbage), sausage, potatoes, and olive oil. Another popular soup is *sopa alentejana,* simmered with bread, garlic (another staple of the Portuguese diet), and other ingredients. *Caldeirada,* a fish stew, is another popular national dish.

Portugal's varieties of succulent fruit, which vary regionally, provide some of its best desserts. These include peaches, strawberries, oranges, figs, plums, pineapples, and passionfruit. Of the sweet dessert offerings, the most common is *arroz doce,* a cinnamon-flavored rice pudding. Flan, a custard with caramel topping, is also very popular.

Susan D. Rock

In the south, the people in Portugal's Algarve region find employment in agriculture, fishing, and the tourist industry. Fishing is most important in the coastal villages.

13 ● EDUCATION

Education is free and compulsory to the age of fifteen. Many children, however, drop out after primary school to begin working. Secondary education is completed either at state-run high schools or at technical or professional institutes. The twelfth grade (at age eighteen) consists of preparatory study for university or technical college.

An estimated 2 percent of the population continue their education beyond the secondary level. Portugal's main universities are located in Lisbon, Porto, Aveiro, Coimbra, and Braga. There is also a government-supported adult education program, as well as hundreds of private schools, most supported by the Catholic Church.

14 ● CULTURAL HERITAGE

Portugal's most famous poet was Luiz Vaz de Camões (1524–80), who wrote during Portugal's Age of Discovery. He was also an explorer himself. His epic poem, *Os Lusiadas (The Lusiads),* is based on the life of the famous explorer Vasco da Gama (c.1460–1524). In modern times, the poems of Fernando Pessoa (1888–1935) are popular. Freedom of expression has thrived in the period since the 1974 revolution. It has seen the publication of books that used to be banned as well as new ones by women writers such as novelist Olga Goncalves. Portuguese-Africans, including Angolan Jose Luandino Viera, have also become popular writers.

The Age of Discovery produced the Manueline style in architecture. This style expressed the national passion for exploration and the sea through the use of sailing images in buildings. Famous examples of this style include the Tomar and Batalha convents.

Also unique to Portugal are the decorative tiles known as *azulejos*. Adopted from Spain, they were modified by the Portuguese, who added a variety of colors, most notably the blue, or azure, from which they get their name.

In music, Portugal is known for its *fado* songs. These plaintive songs reflect the fatalistic Portuguese spirit of melancholy and nostalgia known as *saudade*. Performers of *fado* (which, roughly translated, means "fatc") are known as *fadistas*.

15 ● EMPLOYMENT

Portuguese are known for being reliable and hard working. Industry employs about a third of the country's labor force. Nearly half work in service jobs. This is partially accounted for by the rapid growth in civil service employment since 1974. Employment varies by region.

In the Portuguese islands, the Azores and Madeira, the main occupation is agriculture. Madeira's embroidery industry employs about 70,000 women. In the south, the people in Portugal's Algarve region find employment in agriculture, fishing, and the tourist industry. Fishing is most important in the coastal villages. Cash-crop agriculture (wheat, corn, rice) employs most people in the Alentejo region in the southeast. Heavy industry, including steelworking, shipbuilding, and iron production, is concentrated in the Lisbon-Setubal region to the south. Other occupations include forestry, furniture making, food processing, winemaking, and pulp and paper production.

16 ● SPORTS

Soccer (called football) is the foremost sport in Portugal, as in much of Europe. Golf has grown increasingly popular, and the country now boasts more than twenty world-class golf courses. Tennis is widely played as well, and auto racing becomes the focus of attention during the annual Grand Prix of Portugal held in September.

17 ● RECREATION

One of the most popular recreational activities in Portugal is bullfighting *(Tourada)*, with *cavaleiros* (bullfighters) dressed in eighteenth-century costumes. These costumes include tricornered hats, silk jackets, and riding breeches. In contrast to the violent bullfights in Spain and parts of Latin America, in Portugal the bull's horns are sheathed to avoid injuries, and bulls are not killed at the end of the event.

Another well-known national pastime is dancing. The fandango and other popular folk dances are enjoyed throughout the country. Other forms of recreation include horseback riding, fishing, hunting, skiing, and water sports.

18 ● CRAFTS AND HOBBIES

Traditional craft industries can be found throughout Portugal. The people of the south are renowned for their rug making. Other regions are known for fine embroidery, black pottery, and basket weaving. Characteristic folk art is also seen on floats carried in religious pageants.

19 ● SOCIAL PROBLEMS

Violent crime is rare in Portugal. Murders generally occur in the context of personal conflicts rather than during the commission of other crimes, such as robbery. Many illegal drugs are shipped through Portugal because of its strategic location in relation to Western Europe and South America. There is no serious domestic drug problem, however. Emigration has served as a release for social tensions and discontent, helping to keep the crime rate low.

20 ● BIBLIOGRAPHY

Ballard, Sam, and Jane Ballard. *Pousadas of Portugal.* Boston: The Harvard Common Press, 1986.

Cross, E., and W. Cross. *Portugal.* Chicago: Children's Press, 1986.

Gall, Timothy, and Susan Gall, eds. *Junior Worldmark Encyclopedia of the Nations.* Detroit: UXL, 1996.

Hubbard, Monica M., and Beverly Baer, eds. *Cities of the World: Europe and the Middle East.* Detroit: Gale Research, 1993.

Kaplan, Marion. *The Portuguese: The Land and its People.* London: Viking, 1991.

McCarry, John. "Madeira Toasts the Future." *National Geographic* (November 1994): 90–113.

Moss, Joyce, and George Wilson. *Peoples of the World: Western Europeans.* Detroit: Gale Research, 1993.

Porter, Darwin. *Frommer's Comprehensive Travel Guide (Portugal '94–'95).* New York: Prentice Hall Travel, 1994.

Severy, Merle. "Portugal's Sea Road to the East." *National Geographic* (November 1992): 56–93.

Solsten, Eric. *Portugal: A Country Study.* Washington, D.C.: U.S. Government Printing Office, 1994.

WEBSITES

Investments, Trade and Tourism of Portugal. [Online] Available http://www.portugal.org/, 1998.

World Travel Guide, Portugal. [Online] Available http://www.wtgonline.com/country/pt/gen.html, 1998.

Qatar

■ **QATARIS** **165**

The native population of Qatar (about 100,000) descends from Bedouin (or Bedu) tribes. Pakistanis, Indians, Iranians, and Gulf and Palestinian Arabs are among the leading immigrant groups.

Qataris

PRONUNCIATION: KAHT-uh-reez
LOCATION: Qatar
POPULATION: 100,000
LANGUAGE: Arabic; English
RELIGION: Islam (Sunni Muslim)

1 ● INTRODUCTION

Qataris live on a small peninsula that juts due north into the Persian Gulf, in the area generally known as the Middle East. Qatar is one of the "oil states," a country that moved quickly from poverty to riches with the discovery of oil reserves.

There is archaeological evidence that the land now known as Qatar was inhabited by humans as long ago as 5000 BC. Pearling in the oyster beds just offshore began back in 300 BC. The Islamic revolution arrived in Qatar in AD 630, and all Qataris converted to Islam.

The Qatari people lived fairly traditional lives until oil was discovered. World War II (1939–45) delayed production of the oil until 1947. Since that time, Qataris have become some of the wealthiest people in the world. Qatar became fully independent on September 3, 1971.

2 ● LOCATION

A peninsula in the Persian Gulf, Qatar is about the size of Connecticut and Rhode Island combined. The north, east, and west sides of the peninsula are bordered by the Gulf waters. To the south lie Saudi Arabia and the United Arab Emirates. Qatar and Bahrain have long disputed ownership of the Hawar Islands, which lie between the two states.

The climate in Qatar is generally hot and dry. In the winter months it gets somewhat cooler, but much more humid. Temperatures can go as high as 110°F (43°C) in the summer (between May and October). In the winter, the humidity can reach 100 percent. A hot desert wind blows almost constantly all year long, bringing with it frequent sand- and duststorms.

Little plant or animal life exists in Qatar. The Gulf waters support a greater amount and variety of life. Sea turtles, sea cows, dolphins, and an occasional whale can be found there. Shrimp are harvested in large numbers.

The population of Qatar is somewhere between 400,000 and 500,000 people. Of those, 75 to 80 percent are foreign workers. There are only about 100,000 native-born Qataris. Most people in Qatar live in the cities. Eighty percent of the total population lives in the capital city of Doha. Doha is on the east coast of the Qatar peninsula.

3 ● LANGUAGE

The official language of Qatar is Arabic. Many Qataris are also fluent in English, which is used as the common language for business.

"Hello" in Arabic is *Marhaba* or *Ahlan,* to which one replies, *Marhabtayn* or *Ahlayn.* Other common greetings are *As-salam alaykum,* "Peace be with you," with the reply of *Walaykum as-salam,* "And to you peace." *Ma'assalama* means "Goodbye." "Thank you" is *Shukran,* and "You're welcome" is *Afivan.* "Yes" is *na'am* and "no" is *la'a.* The numbers one to ten in Arabic are *wahad, itnin, talata, arba'a, khamsa, sitta, saba'a, tamania, tisa'a,* and *ashara.*

Arabs have very long names. They consist of their given name, their father's first name, their paternal grandfather's first name, and finally their family name. Women do not take their husband's name when they marry, but rather keep their mother's family name as a show of respect for their family of origin.

4 ● FOLKLORE

Many Muslims believe in *jinns,* spirits who can change shape and be either visible or invisible. Muslims sometimes wear amulets around their necks to protect them from jinns. Stories of jinns are often told at night, like ghost stories around a campfire.

5 ● RELIGION

At least 95 percent of the total population of Qatar is Muslim (followers of Islam). Native-born Qataris are all Sunni Muslims of the Wahhabi sect. Wahhabis are a puritanical branch of Islam which is prevalent in Saudi Arabia. A somewhat more moderate form is found in Qatar.

6 ● MAJOR HOLIDAYS

As an Islamic state, Qatar's official holidays are Islamic ones. Muslim holidays follow the lunar calendar, moving back by eleven days each year, so their dates are not fixed on the standard Gregorian calendar. The main Muslim holidays are Ramadan, the month of fasting from dawn until dusk each day. *Eid al-Fitr* is a three-day festival at the end of Ramadan. *Eid al-Adha* is a three-day feast of sacrifice at the end of the month of pilgrimage to the prophet Muhammad's birthplace at Mecca (the pilgrimage is known as the *hajj).* The First of Muharram is the Muslim New Year. *Mawoulid An-Nabawi* is Muhammad's birthday. *Eid al-ism wa al-Miraj* is a feast celebrating the overnight visit of Muhammad to heaven.

Friday is the Islamic day of rest. Most businesses and services are closed on Fridays. All government offices, private businesses, and schools are also closed during Eid al-Fitr and Eid al-Adha.

7 ● RITES OF PASSAGE

Qataris mark major life transitions such as birth, puberty, marriage, and death with Islamic ceremonies and feasting.

8 ● RELATIONSHIPS

Arab hospitality reigns in Qatar. An Arab will never ask personal questions. To do so is considered rude.

Food and drink are always taken with the right hand. When talking, Arabs touch each other much more often, and stand much closer together, than Westerners do. People of the same sex will often hold hands while talking, even if they are virtual strangers.

Members of the opposite sex, even married couples, never touch in public. Arabs talk a lot, talk loudly, repeat themselves often, and interrupt each other constantly. Conversations are highly emotional and full of gestures.

9 ● LIVING CONDITIONS

Qatar has engaged in a rapid modernization program since the 1970s, when income from the oil industry rose dramatically. All villages and towns can now be reached by paved roads, which are well maintained.

There is little public transportation available in Qatar. Nearly everyone drives a car. Housing, utilities, and communication services are all modern (many Qataris have cellular phones). Health care is up-to-date and free to all Qataris. Health clinics, both public and private, are located throughout the country.

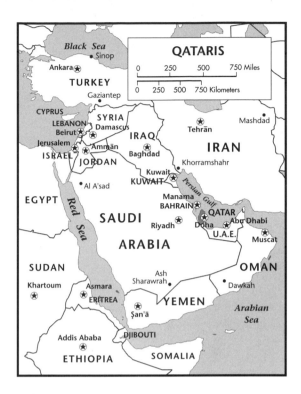

The two largest cities, the capital city of Doha and the west-coast city of Umm Said, have water-main systems that provide running water to all residents. In other places, water is delivered by tankers and stored in tanks in gardens or on roofs, or is pumped into homes from deep-water wells. All foreign workers are provided with free housing. Even the formerly nomadic Bedu (or Bedouin) now live in air-conditioned houses built by the government. The government also provides social welfare programs for the sick, elderly, and disabled.

10 ● FAMILY LIFE

The family is the central unit of Qatari society. Qataris are only recently removed from a tribal way of life, so tribal values and customs still prevail.

11 ● CLOTHING

Qataris wear traditional Arab clothing. For men, this is an ankle-length robe called a *thobe* or *dishdasha,* with a *ghutrah* (a large piece of cloth) on the head which is held in place by an *uqal* (a woven piece of rope). Women tend to wear very colorful long-sleeved, ankle-length dresses, with a black silk cloak called an *abaya* covering them completely in public. Some older Qatari women still wear a face mask, called a *batula,* but this custom is dying out.

12 ● FOOD

Rice is the staple food for Qataris. It is usually fried (or sautéed) first, then boiled. Saffron is often added during the frying stage to make the rice yellow. Bread is served at almost every meal, especially pita bread.

Hummus, a spread made from ground chickpeas, is also eaten at most meals. *Hamour,* a type of fish caught in the Gulf, is frequently served baked, or cooked with rice. Mutton (sheep) is the favorite meat. Pork is forbidden by Islam, as is alcohol.

Shellfish, particularly shrimp which are caught in great numbers off Qatar's shores, is a popular dish. Tea and coffee are the beverages of choice. Tea is never drunk with milk added. Coffee is always made from Turkish beans and is often flavored with saffron, rosewater, or cardamom. Coffee and tea are usually sweetened with sugar.

13 ● EDUCATION

Education is highly valued by Qataris. Attendance at primary and secondary schools is 98 percent, and the literacy rate is more than 65 percent and rising. In the public school system, education is compulsory from age six to age sixteen. It is free all the way through the university level. The government even provides full scholarships (including travel costs) for university students who wish to study abroad.

Recipe

Hummus bi Tahini (Chick Pea Dip)

Ingredients

1 19-ounce can chick peas (garbanzo beans), drained, reserving the liquid
¼ cup sesame seed paste (tahini)
1 clove garlic
½ teaspoon salt
¼ cup lemon juice
olive oil (optional)
lemon wedges as garnish
parsley sprigs as garnich
pita bread as accompaniment

Directions

1. Combine drained chick peas, sesame seed paste, garlic clove, salt, and lemon juice in the bowl of a food processor. Add a small amount of the reserved liquid.
2. Process for 2 to 3 minutes, adding more liquid as necessary to give the desired consistency.
3. Transfer the dip to a small bowl. Drizzle with olive oil if desired.
4. Garnish with lemon wedges and parley sprigs.
5. Cut pita bread into wedges and serve.

Adapted from Salloum, Mary. *A Taste of Lebanon.* New York: Interlink Books, 1992, p. 21.

Over 40,000 students, both boys and girls, are enrolled in primary and secondary schools. Another 400 or so study in vocational training institutes and religious schools. Adult education was introduced in 1957. Forty adult education centers now provide literacy courses to about 5,000 adult students. Qatar University was founded in 1973 and offers state-of-the-art degree programs in many subjects. Computer courses are required for all university students.

14 ● CULTURAL HERITAGE

Arab music is much like the Arab language. Both are rich, repetitive, and exaggerated. The *oud* is a popular instrument; it is an ancient stringed instrument that is the ancestor of the European lute. Another traditional instrument is the *rebaba,* a one-stringed instrument. A traditional Arab dance is the *ardha,* or men's sword dance. Men carrying swords stand shoulder to shoulder and dance, and from among them a poet sings verses while drummers beat out a rhythm.

Islam forbids the depiction of the human form, so Qatari art focuses on geometric and abstract shapes. Calligraphy is a sacred art. The writings of the Koran (or Quran) are the primary subject matter. Muslim art finds its greatest expression in mosques. The Islamic reverence for poetry and the poetic richness of the Arabic language are the basis of much of Qatar's cultural heritage.

15 ● EMPLOYMENT

The most profitable industries in Qatar are oil and natural gas production. The government runs both. Other industries include cement, power plants, desalinization plants (making drinking water out of sea water by removing the salt), petrochemicals, steel, and fertilizer.

The government is trying to encourage private industry by offering grants, low-interest loans, and tax breaks to private entrepreneurs. There is almost no agriculture in Qatar, although irrigation systems are being developed to increase the amount of arable land. Fishing continues to be a way of life for many Qataris, one that they have followed for thousands of years.

16 ● SPORTS

Qataris love outdoor sports, both on land and on water. Football (what Americans call soccer) has become the most popular sport, although auto racing is also a favorite. Basketball, handball, and volleyball are modern sports that are beginning to catch on. Tenpin bowling and golf are also enjoyed by some Qataris. The traditional sports of horse- and camel-racing and falconry are still pursued passionately in Qatar.

17 ● RECREATION

Qataris enjoy playing chess, bridge, and darts. There are no public cinemas or theaters, except for the National Theater, in Qatar.

18 ● CRAFTS AND HOBBIES

Goldsmithing is an ancient art among Qataris that continues to be practiced today.

19 ● SOCIAL PROBLEMS

Rapid modernization in the last few decades has created a huge generation gap between the pre-oil boom elders and the post-oil boom young people. Older people who grew up in Qatar before oil wealth do not understand or like many of the changes that modernization has brought. They often lament the loss of the "good old days."

Young people, on the other hand, have grown up in the more industrialized era of high technology and are comfortable with it, seeing only the benefits and none of the losses. The two generations often find it very difficult to communicate with each other.

20 ● BIBLIOGRAPHY

Abu Saud, Abeer. *Qatari Women, Past and Present.* New York: Longman, 1984.

Background Notes: Qatar. Washington, D.C.: U.S. Department of State, Bureau of Public Affairs, Office of Public Communication, April 1992.

Post Report: Qatar. Washington, D.C.: U.S. Department of State, 1991.

Rickman, Maureen. *Qatar.* New York: Chelsea House, 1987.

Salloum, Mary. *A Taste of Lebanon.* New York: Interlink Books, 1992.

Vine, Peter, and Paula Casey. *The Heritage of Qatar.* London: IMMEL Publishing, 1992.

Zahlan, Rosemarie Said. *The Creation of Qatar.* London: Croom Helm, 1979.

WEBSITES

ArabNet. [Online] Available http://www.arab.net/qatar/qatar_contents.html, 1998.

World Travel Guide, Qatar. [Online] Available http://www.wtgonline.com/country/qa/gen.html, 1998.

Romania

■ **ROMANIANS** 171
■ **ROMA** 178

Ethnic Romanians constitute 89 percent of the population of Romania. Two important ethnic minorities are Hungarians (7.5 percent of the total population) and Germans (0.5 percent), both concentrated in the Transylvania region. The number of Roma (Gypsies), is officially estimated at about 400,000, but may be much higher.. For more information on Hungarians, see the chapter on Hungary in Volume 4; on the Germans, see the chapter on Germany in Volume 4.

Romanians

PRONUNCIATION: roh-MANE-ee-yuhns
LOCATION: Romania
POPULATION: 23 million, of whom 89 percent are ethnic Romanians
LANGUAGE: Romanian
RELIGION: Christianity (Romanian Orthodox Church; Greek Catholic Church; Protestantism)

1 ●INTRODUCTION

The territory that comprises Romania today was inhabited by the Dacians and Getae as early as the sixth century BC. These ancestors of the Romanians organized a separate country known as Dacia, which developed and prospered to the time of King Decebalus (AD 87–106). The Romans conquered Dacia in AD 106. The victory over the Dacians was considered so important in Roman history that a monument was erected in the Forum at Rome to commemorate the event.

From 106 to 271, Dacia was a Roman province. As a border province, however, Dacia became increasingly difficult to defend against invasions from the east. The Romans retreated from Dacia in 271, ceding the country to the invading Goths. After the Goths left in 375, and the Huns left in the sixth century, there was a slow but steady infiltration of Slavs among the Romanians.

In 1601, Michael the Brave was able to unite briefly all the Romanians under one rule. Though short-lived, this unification contributed to the strengthening of Romanian identity.

The Ottoman Empire imposed its rule over the Romanian principalities for nearly 300 years. With the help of Russia, which defeated the Turks, the Romanians were given more freedom and granted a new con-

ROMANIANS

0   100   200   300 Miles

0   100   200   300 Kilometers

BELARUS
Minsk
Homyel
POLAND
Rivne
Kraków
UKRAINE
Kiev
Dnipro
SLOVAKIA
Bratislava
MOLDOVA
Chișinău
Budapest
Cluj-Napoca
Odesa
HUNGARY
ROMANIA
Pécs
CROATIA
Danube
Bucharest
Constanța
BOSNIA-
HERZEGOVINA
Belgrade
Black
Sea
Sarajevo
YUGOSLAVIA
BULGARIA
Varna
Pristina
Sofia
Skopje
ALBANIA
MACEDONIA
Tirana
Salonika

nation and Nicolae Ceaușescu (1918–89) became its president. Under his harsh dictatorship, the country had serious economic problems, including food shortages and lack of consumer goods.

During the years of communism, the living standard of the average citizen worsened and the economy was poorly managed. Many people were imprisoned and many others fled the country. Over 500,000 Romanians emigrated to Western Europe, the United States, Israel, and elsewhere.

In December 1989, security forces opened fire on demonstrators in the city of Timișoara. A state of emergency was declared, but the protests continued to spread throughout the country. Ceaușescu was overthrown and he was found guilty of genocide and executed.

After the execution of Ceaușescu and the ousting of many Communist Party officials, a ragtag government made up mostly of former communists took over, headed by Ion Iliescu. Inflation rose, living standards suffered, and corruption continued. Iliescu was was finally voted out in November 1996, with Emil Constantinescu as the first non-communist president in over fifty years.

stitution in 1829. In 1881, Romania became a monarchy, and King Carol I ruled until his death in 1914.

Romania fought on the side of the Allies during World War I (1914–18). With the defeat of the Austro-Hungarian Empire, the provinces of Transylvania, Banat, and Bucovina were awarded to Romania in 1918, thus uniting most of the Romanians in one country for the first time in its history.

At the start of World War II (1939–45), Romania was allied with Nazi Germany, but it switched sides in August 1944 and joined the Allies as Russians entered the country. With the forced abdication of King Michael V (b.1921), Romanian communists gradually took control of the country. In 1965, Romania officially became a communist

2 ●LOCATION

Romania is located in Eastern Europe at the mouth of the Danube River as it flows into the Black Sea, which forms the country's eastern border. Romania is bordered on the north by Ukraine and Moldova, on the south by Bulgaria and Yugoslavia (Serbia), and on the west by Hungary. It is slightly less than 92,000 square miles (238,000 square kilometers) in area, about the size of New York State and Pennsylvania combined. The Carpathian Mountains run from north to south through the middle of the country. Romania has hot summers, cool autumns, and cold winters with snow and winds.

Romania has a population of about 23 million people, with ethnic Romanians accounting for 89 percent of the population. The remaining population includes Hungarians (7.5 percent), Germans (0.5 percent), Roma (also known as Gypsies), and various other minorities.

3 ● LANGUAGE

The Romanian language is a modern Romance language, just like Italian, French, Spanish, and Portuguese. It is closest in structure to the Latin spoken in the first centuries AD by ordinary Romans.

4 ● FOLKLORE

One of the greatest repositories of Romanian folklore is their traditional Christmas carols, which have been passed down through many generations.

5 ● RELIGION

The ancient Dacians gradually accepted Christianity and established churches under the Eastern Orthodox Patriarch of Constantinople. Even though there was a Slavic influence, the Romanian Orthodox Church retained its Latin heritage and remains the predominant religion of Romanians. There are smaller numbers of Greek Catholics (Uniates), Roman Catholics, and Protestants.

David Johnson

A Romanian mother and her child.

6 ● MAJOR HOLIDAYS

Romanians celebrate the major Christian holy days; Christmas (December 25) has more customs and observances than any other holy day. Easter (March or April) is most joyous religious holiday, following a six-week Lenten preparatory season and solemn Holy Week rituals.

Romanians ring in the New Year with partying, singing, and drinking. Some New Year's Day customs have prevailed throughout the centuries, dating from pagan Roman times, such as the *pluguşotul* (plow). Boys dressed in sheepskin outfits pull a small plow through the village, wishing everyone a prosperous new year.

David Johnson

Family from Burla, Suceava, Romania. Romanians are family-oriented and try to bring up their families in the highest moral Christian spirit. Traditionally, Romanians had large families, as many hands were needed to work the fields.

7 ● RITES OF PASSAGE

When an infant is baptized, there is always a celebration at the home of the child's parents. At baptism, children are given the name of a saint, usually one whose feast day is nearest to the date of birth.

When young people decide to marry, they ask for the blessing of their parents. The girl usually has a dowry that her parents start when she is very young. It may consist of household linens, rugs, tablecloths, personal items, kitchen utensils, and family heirlooms.

After the marriage date is set, the groom sends out emissaries to personally invite friends and relatives to the wedding. Male members of the wedding party usually come to church on horseback, while the bride is brought in a carriage bedecked with flowers and peasant embroideries. After the nearly one-hour church ceremony, the bride and groom drink wine from the a common cup, signifying their union.

When someone dies, the body is washed and deodorized but not embalmed. It is then laid in a wooden coffin and brought to the deceased's home for the wake. Prayer services are held before the open coffin two or three evenings before the funeral service. After the funeral ceremony at the church, the closed coffin is taken to the cemetery and is interred. Mourners return to the deceased's home for a meal.

8 ● RELATIONSHIPS

Romanians are influenced by the Romanian Orthodox Church, which emphasizes humility, love, and forgiveness in one's relationships. Romanians typically offer warm greetings and a willingness to serve others.

9 ● LIVING CONDITIONS

The typical one-story Romanian house usually includes a waiting room with an oven and a pantry. Some homes have a living room with a fireplace and at least one bedroom. More-prosperous rural Romanians may have a large enclosed yard with a garden, hay barn, stable, pigsty, chicken coop, corncrib, and outhouse.

Romania has undergone many changes in the last fifty years. There was a large migration from villages to cities. During the years of the communist regime, some villages disappeared as inhabitants moved to the cities, where plain high-rise apartments were built to accommodate them. Such buildings line the outskirts of most of Romania's major cities.

Life expectancy is sixty-seven years for males and seventy-three years for females. Infant mortality is 25 deaths per 1,000 births. There is 1 hospital bed per 100 persons, and 1 doctor per 559 persons. There is a scarcity of hospitals, clinics, and other facilities. Some children are abandoned and end up in orphanages, which have a difficult time caring for them.

10 ● FAMILY LIFE

Traditionally, Romanians had large families. Children are brought up to respect their parents. Divorce is not common but occurs more frequently in the cities than in the villages.

11 ● CLOTHING

Among the most visible and attractive articles of clothing are the Romanian traditional costumes, especially the blouse, which varies greatly from one district to another. The traditional Romanian male costumes were just as varied as the women's, but less elaborate. The trousers and the long shirt were mostly white. The men wore a leather belt or a wider one with pockets.

Today, Romanians wear the same Western-style clothing that is commonly worn throughout Europe.

12 ● FOOD

Romanian cooking has Hungarian, Serbian, Turkish, and Russian influences. There are also traces of French, Viennese, and other Western European cuisines.

Mamaliga (cornmeal mush) is one of the staples of the Romanian diet. It is usually served as a side dish and sometimes in place of bread.

Pork is the favorite meat of the Romanians, much more so than beef. Pigs are usually slaughtered before Christmas, smoked, made into sausage, and preserved for use throughout the year. Pork products such as bacon, ham, spare ribs, chops, and various cold cuts are also favorites of the Romanians. Stews, roasts, and casseroles

Cory Langley

Romania boasts a literacy rate approaching 100 percent.

flooded the market with their literary works. These included well-known poet Vasile Alexandri (1821–90), novelists such as Costache Negruzzi (1808–68) and Alexandru Odobescu, storytellers such as Ion Slavici and Liviu Rebreanu (1885–1944), dramatists such as L. Caragiale (1853–1912) and Barba Delavraucea, and and historians such as Alexandra D. Xenopol and Nicolae Iorga (1871–1940).

The traditional Romanian musical instrument is the violin. Others include the wooden saxophone and the cimbalom (a type of dulcimer). Later, orchestras added the bass fiddle, the piano, the clarinet, and the accordion. Romanians also play panpipes.

Among the most popular styles of folk songs are love songs and patriotic songs. There is no other form of popular poetry more prevalent than the traditional carols, which have been passed down from one generation to the next

with vegetable, salads, sour pickles, and sauerkraut make up the usual main course.

13 ● EDUCATION

At present the literacy rate is nearly 98 percent, with compulsory education for ten years.

14 ● CULTURAL HERITAGE

In the middle of the nineteenth century, literary magazines and books started to be published in growing numbers. Many poets, novelists, historians, essayists, and writers

One of the most common and generalized folk dances is the *hora* (circle dance), danced by men and women holding hands. A popular dance is the *sârba,* with dancers holding each other by the shoulder in a semicircle.

15 ● EMPLOYMENT

Villagers with their small plots raise enough food for their own needs. Urban dwellers, who must buy all their food, have a more difficult time because of scarcities, inflation, and low salaries.

16 ● SPORTS

As in many European countries, the preferred sport is soccer. Romania has a number of professional teams, which compete with other countries. Each larger town has its own stadium, and some of them accommodate tens of thousands of spectators. Besides soccer, Romanians also enjoy basketball, boxing, rugby, tennis, and volleyball.

Calisthenics, exercising, and other gymnastics are a part of the school curriculum. Some of the best students are specially trained to compete in international events such as the Olympics.

17 ● RECREATION

Romanians enjoy a leisurely walk on the weekend where one stops to chat with friends and acquaintances.

Romanians also enjoy folk dance groups, amateur theatrical groups, music ensembles, and a host of other entertainers. There are many movie houses that show local productions and imported films with Romanian subtitles. Solo entertainers and all kinds of groups tour the country and present all kinds of entertainment to enthusiastic audiences.

Romania has many radio stations, television stations, live theaters, opera houses, cabarets, and entertainment establishments. Western influence, especially American, is increasingly noticeable in Romanian music, dance, and film.

18 ● CRAFTS AND HOBBIES

Traditional handmade crafts were not only useful but also decorative, with colorful and intricate designs. Women traditionally sewed, knitted, and crocheted, while men carved geometric designs or painted wooden articles and ceramics.

Besides the textiles and wooden articles, Romanian peasants also wove rugs with unusual designs and colorful schemes. Pottery was usually decorated with circles, spirals, stylized flowers, and other imaginative patterns.

A most unusual form of Romanian folk art are icons painted on glass. The image is painted backwards on a piece of glass, so it can be seen correctly when viewed from the front side.

19 ● SOCIAL PROBLEMS

Alcoholism is sometimes a problem, especially among men. Crime and vandalism are becoming serious problems, especially in the cities.

20 ● BIBLIOGRAPHY

Augerot, Joseph E. *Modern Romania*. Columbus, Ohio: Slavica, 1993.

Basderant, Denise. *Against Tide and Tempest: The Story of Romania*. New York: R. Speller, 1966.

Carran, Betty. *Romania*. Chicago: Children's Press, 1988.

Matley, Ian M. *Romania: A Profile*. New York: Praeger, 1970.

WEBSITES

Embassy of Romania, Washington, D.C. [Online] Available http://www.embassy.org/romania/, 1998.

World Travel Guide. Romania. [Online] Available http://www.wtgonline.com/country/ro/gen.html, 1998.

Roma

PRONUNCIATION: ROW-mah
ALTERNATE NAMES: Gypsies; Vlach Roma; Rom; Romanichals; Cales; Kaale; Kawle; Sinti/Manouches
LOCATION: Dispersed population in Europe; parts of Asia, North, Central and South America, Australia, New Zealand, North and South Africa, the Middle East, and elsewhere.
POPULATION: 6–10 million
LANGUAGE: Romani dialects; also the language of the host country
RELIGION: Hinduism with Christianity or Islam (host country religion)

1 ● INTRODUCTION

The Roma people originated in India. By the eleventh century AD they were located in the area called Gurjara, in what was then the Rajput Confederacy. A group called *Dom* belonged to the aboriginal peoples of India but had adopted the Hindu religion and an Indo-Aryan language derived from Sanskrit. Some groups of *Dom* were nomadic entertainers and artisans.

In the tenth century, a Muslim kingdom arose in what is now Afghanistan, with its capital at Ghasni. In 1017, its ruler, Mahmud Ghazni, launched a series of massive raids into India. He and successive rulers entered India, plundering and massacring the people, carrying off thousands of slaves, and laying waste to the countryside. The Rajputs fought back, during which groups of people were displaced or forced to move out of desolated areas. At some point during the eleventh century, the ancestors of the Roma made their way into the Upper Indus Valley from Gurjara and spent some time in this region.

The ancestors of the Roma then left India and entered northwestern China. From there they followed the ancient trading routes which led them to Persia, then through southern Georgia, Armenia, and finally to the Byzantine Empire. From the Byzantine capital, Constantinople (now Istanbul), they reached Romania by at least the fourteenth century. Some groups remained in Romania but many moved on, traveling both west and east. By the end of the fifteenth century, Roma could be found as far west as the British Isles and Spain and as far east as Poland and Lithuania.

At some point during their migration from India, scholars believe their original name, *Dom* (or *Domba* in the plural), changed to *Rom* (singular) and *Roma* (plural).

2 ● LOCATION

Since the fifteenth century, Roma have been a dispersed ethnic population in Europe. Roma in the Romanian-speaking principalities, later including Transylvania, were once enslaved and are known as Vlach Roma (the "ch" in Vlach is pronounced as k or as *ch* in Scottish *loch*). After their emancipation in 1864, many made their way into Central and Western Europe and the Balkans, eventually reaching North, Central, and South America by the 1890s. Today the Vlach Roma are the most numerous and most widespread group of Roma.

In Western Europe, because of persecution in most countries, Roma were forced to become nomadic (moving from place to place). This characteristic gave rise to the tradition in popular literature of the roving "Gypsy." In the past, colonial powers deported or transported Roma to their colonies in Africa, the West Indies, the Americas, and Australia.

Roma from many groups have more recently migrated from Europe to the Americas, Australia, New Zealand, Africa, and elsewhere. They take on the nationality of their host countries and consider themselves American Roma, Canadian Roma, Australian Roma, South African Roma, and so forth.

3 ● LANGUAGE

The speakers normally refer to their language as *Romani*, *Romani chib*, or *Romanes*. There are many dialects, some of which go by different names, such as Romnimus (in Wales), Kaale (in Finland), or Calo (in Spain). Romani has its own unique grammar, as opposed to adopting the grammar of the country in which its speakers live. As an example, note the following comparative sentences:

English
I am going into the village to buy a horse from the non-Roma man.

Inflected Romani
Jav ando gav te kinav grast katar o gadjo.
(These words are of Sanskrit/Indian origin)

English Romani
I'm *jall* in' into the *gav* to *kin* a *grai* from the *gorjo*.

Spanish Romani
Voy en el gao para quinelar un gras del gacho.

Romani uses many idiomatic expressions, proverbs, and sayings, often with metaphorical qualities. This situation makes it difficult to write dictionaries of Romani with word-for-word equivalents. For example, "He is retiring" in English would be expressed in Romani as *Beshel lesko kam* (His sun is setting). "What are you thinking?" is expressed as *So si tut ando shoro*, which means "What do you have in your head?"

Roma usually take Christian names like those of the people around them, such as Milano, Yanko, or Zlatcho for men, and Mara, Tinka, or Pavlena for women. The Vlach Roma have no surnames. Other groups adopt last names similar to those of the people among whom they live. The Vlach Roma also do this for identity papers, driver's licenses, and other documents, but do not use these names among themselves.

4 ● FOLKLORE

Roma folktales and legends are known as *paramichia*. A legendary hero among the Vlach Roma is Mundro Salamon or Wise Solomon. Other Roma groups call this hero O Godjiaver Yanko. Mundro Salamon is a wise man who uses his mental powers and cunning to escape from those who would harm him or to save others from danger. A typical Mundro Salamon story runs as follows:

One day Mundro Salamon learned that the Martya, or Angel of Death, was about to come and claim the soul of the village miller who was his friend. He went to the Martya and asked her to spare the miller's life because he had small children to support, and the people of the village needed him to grind their corn. She refused, so Mundro Salamon tricked her. "How could you take his soul," he asked her, "if he locked himself in a room?" "I would simply dissolve into smoke and slip under the door," she told him. "Rubbish," Salamon replied. "You mean you could slip inside this peashooter I am whittling for the miller's son?" To prove it, the Martya dissolved into smoke and entered the peashooter. Salamon then plugged both ends of the peashooter, trapping the Martya inside. He locked the peashooter inside a metal box, rowed out to the sea in a boat, and dumped the box over the side. For seven years nobody died, until one day two fishermen casting their nets caught the metal box and retrieved it. They smashed it open, found the peashooter, and unplugged it, allowing the Martya to escape.

Now she began to search for Salamon to get her revenge. But Salamon had anticipated she might escape and had taken precautions. He had shod his horse backwards so that the prints of the horseshoes led the Martya to look for seven years in the wrong direction. She then realized her blunder and spent another seven years looking in the right direction. She finally found Salamon, now an elderly man. "Now I'm going to make you suffer," she told him. "For seven years I will freeze you in ice. Then, for another seven years I will roast you in fire. Then, for seven years I will turn you into rotten pulpwood and you will be nibbled on by maggots. Only after this will I put you out of your misery and take your soul." "Rubbish," Salamon said mockingly. "How can you take my soul? You don't have the power. You're bluffing me." "I'll show you," the Martya screamed, and blew three times on his face. Salamon died smiling. He had outwitted the Martya even in death!

5 ● RELIGION

Roma religious beliefs are rooted in Hinduism. Roma believe in a universal balance, called *kuntari*. Everything must have its natural place: birds fly and fish swim. Thus hens, which do not fly, are considered to be out of balance (and therefore bad luck), as are frogs, which can go into the water and also walk on land. For this reason, Roma traditionally do not eat hens' eggs and avoid frogs. The Roma also believe it is possible to become polluted in a variety of ways, including breaking taboos involving the upper and lower halves of the body. A Roma who becomes polluted is considered out of balance and must be restored to purity through a trial before the Roma tribunal of elders. If declared guilty, he or she is usually given a period of isolation away from other Roma and then reinstated. In severe cases of pollution, a Roma can be outlawed from the group forever, but this is rare today. Children are exempt from these rules and from pollution taboos until they reach puberty.

The surrounding host-culture religions are used for ceremonies like baptisms or funerals for which the Roma need a formal religious institution. Except for the elders who are the spiritual leaders, there are no Roma priests, churches, or bibles except among the Pentecostal Roma, who are a small and new minority. Despite a 1,000-year separation from India, Roma still practice Shaktism, the worship of a god through a female consort. Thus, while Roma worship the Christian God, they pray to Him through the Virgin Mary or Saint Ann.

ROMA

0   100   200   300 Miles
0 100   200   300 Kilometers

6 ● MAJOR HOLIDAYS.

Roma celebrate the holidays of the various countries in which they live. The Vlach Roma and many other groups celebrate Christmas (December 25) and Easter (March or April). In Romania, there are holidays commemorating the emancipation of Roma slaves. In Muslim countries, Roma often observe Muslim religious holidays.

Christmas and Easter, among the Vlach Rom, are always celebrated by feasts. Sometimes family heads will get together and pool their resources to hold one large feast for the entire community. There will be music, dancing, singing and socializing. At Easter, each family will dye Easter eggs a special color and place them in a large bowl. These are given, one each, to every guest. There is also a ceremony called *chognimos,* or egg-whipping, where the visitor or guest will bring an egg and hold it in the palm of his hand. The host will do the same, and they will slap their palms together, usually cracking or crushing both eggs. This is believed to bring *baxt,* or good karma.

7 ● RITES OF PASSAGE

When a baby is born, the mother and her baby are considered polluted and are separated from the rest of the household and from other Roma for a predetermined period, which varies among clans and groups. Once this period is over, godparents are selected from the Roma community. They take the baby to a church for the actual baptism ceremony. They also give the baby a small gold cross. When the godparents return with the baptized baby there is a feast called *bolimos.*

At puberty, *shave* (boys) and *sheya* (girls) are initiated into the world of adults. Boys are taught to drive and to work with their adult male family members at the family trade. Girls are instructed by female adults in women's work and strictly chaperoned when they go to movies or shopping. Roma girls do not go on dates and must be chaperoned outside the home. Boys have more freedom and are allowed to go to dances and socialize with non-Roma teenagers. Teenagers enter adulthood when they marry, which is generally at fifteen or sixteen for girls and from sixteen to eighteen for boys. The young married person becomes a *Rom* (male adult Roma) or a *Romni* (female adult Roma). The bride, or *bori,* must serve a period of apprenticeship in the home of her in-laws until the mother-in-law is satisfied that she is following the laws of respect and pollution to the family's satisfaction.

When adults become middle-aged, they graduate to the ranks of the elders: men become spiritual leaders of the community and sit as judges on the tribunal of elders. It is believed that after women go through menopause, they can no longer pollute men. They too become spiritual elders who advise the younger women.

After a death, there is a one-year mourning period called *pomana,* with feasts for the dead held at three-month intervals. The Roma believe that their deceased join their ancestors and watch over the actions of the living. The spirits of the ancestors are called as witnesses at solemn events like the swearing of oaths at the tribunal of elders, where they are assumed to be spiritually present and able to send a *prekaza* (jinx) to any Roma who is lying. Roma do not discuss their dead.

8 ● RELATIONSHIPS

When a guest arrives, the Roma host will say "Welcome! God has sent you!" The guest or guests must also be served food and drink. The usual greeting is a handshake, although Roma men often embrace relatives and close friends and kiss them on the cheek. Women also embrace and kiss when they meet. When family or friends visit, the host will often provide entertainment and ask his sons to play music and his eldest daughter to dance. Women must appear modestly dressed before guests and at group gatherings.

Roma body language varies in different countries, but most Roma are very expressive and impulsive. They make use of gestures, use their hands when talking, wink, snap their fingers, and indulge in mimicry. When talking about somebody else, they will imitate his or her voice or mannerisms.

Whereas most modern cultures have two concepts of cleanliness (clean and dirty), the Roma have three: *wuzho,* or clean; *melalo,* dirty with honest dirt; and *marime,* which means polluted or defiled among the Vlach Roma (other groups use different words). While non-Roma are concerned with visible dirt, Roma are concerned with beliefs about ritual pollution.

Another central belief regarding cleanliness involves the upper and lower halves of the body. Roma do not take baths but shower standing up, since the lower part of the body is considered an agent of pollution. The body above the waist is considered clean, and the head is the cleanest and purest area of all. Clothing worn above the waist must be washed separately from clothing worn below the waist (also, men's clothing cannot be washed with women's clothing). Roma wash their hands constantly—after touching their shoes or doorknobs, or doing anything considered necessary but potentially defiling.

If a Roma person is declared to be polluted, he or she may not socialize with other Roma nor have any dealings with them, since Roma believe that the pollution can spread from one person to another and contaminate the entire community.

9 ● LIVING CONDITIONS

The living conditions of Roma vary enormously, from the wealthier, technologically advanced countries like the United States and Canada to impoverished, third-world countries. In any society, Roma usually live at a somewhat lower standard than the non-Roma.

Roma adapt well to societies where there is a surplus of consumer goods that they can buy and sell, or where there is scrap they can collect to recycle. While many Roma are nomadic, especially in Europe, others are sedentary. They might settle in trailer camps, living in horse-drawn wagons or travel trailers, or in modern apartments. Others live in houses in Eastern European villages. Conditions are especially bad in Slovakia, where many Roma live in dilapidated shacks. Others live in shantytowns, or *bidonvilles,* in France and Spain, which are often bulldozed into oblivion by the town councils while the occupants are at a local feast. Many Roma in Western Europe are squatters, occupying condemned buildings while trying to find more suitable accommodations. In the United States, many Roma own their own homes or rent decent living accommodations. In Central and South America, many are still nomadic and live in tents. In Portugal, Roma travel with horses and wagons and sleep in tents.

Nomadic Roma are often healthier than those who lead sedentary lives. The Roma diet was evolved for a nomadic and active people, and when they settle down and still eat the same types of foods, they often become overweight and suffer from health problems. Women generally live longer than men, who often die in middle age from heart attacks. Roma life can be stressful because of constant problems arising from their lifestyle, which is often misunderstood by the law-enforcement agencies who move them on when they are traveling or, when they are sedentary, harass them over by-laws, work permits, and licenses. In Eastern Europe, there is a high mortality rate among Roma children and infants. Perhaps 80 percent of the orphans in Romania are Roma children suffering from diseases like AIDS (transmitted by infected medical syringes).

Except in rural areas of the less developed countries, most Roma use cars, trucks, and travel trailers. In countries like the United States, they fly to visit relatives or to attend weddings. In Europe, they travel by train, bus, or in their own cars and trailers. The Roma in the United States and other developed nations see the car as a status symbol and try to own an impressive vehicle. They often buy expensive jewelry, watches, home furnishings, and appliances as well as luxurious carpets. In Europe, Roma caravans are often full of expensive china dishes.

10 ● FAMILY LIFE

Roma families are usually large and extended. The nuclear family is rare and unmarried adults are looked upon with suspicion. To be unmarried means to be out of balance, according to the Roma beliefs. Among the Roma, women are equal to men, but each sex has its own traditional role. The men go out to work and earn the larger sums of money, which tend to come in sporadically, while the women earn the day-to-day expenses needed to run the household. The Roma woman is the absolute ruler of the home. The eldest daughter, or *she bari*, also has a special role in the family. She replaces the mother in the role of housekeeper when the mother is sick or absent, and is responsible for the meals, housecleaning, and the care of her younger siblings. Men do a limited amount of cooking and housework.

Pets are rare among the Roma. Watchdogs may be kept outside. Cats, which can jump and climb, are taboo.

AP/Wide World Photos

Roma family selling flowers in Bucharest, Romania.

11 ● CLOTHING

There is no traditional male Roma costume. Women among the Roma wear a traditional costume composed of a full, ankle-length skirt tied on the left side at the waist, a loose, low-cut blouse, a bolero vest, and an apron. In the United States, the bandana of the married woman is often replaced by a thin strip of ribbon. In Europe, the full traditional female costume is still in common use among the Vlach Roma and other more traditional groups. Roma men like to dress well and often adopt a particular style. Roma men wear expensive suits but seldom wear ties, except for Western-style bolos (string ties). In Europe, men in some groups wear a *diklo*, a type of neckerchief, often with a fancy ring which they use to tighten it. Most Roma men like fancy belt buckles and lots of jewelry. Women also wear jewelry.

For everyday wear, Roma dress casually. Men wear business suits without ties. Hats are popular among older Roma men, who wear them indoors as well as outdoors. Teenagers and younger men adopt the local styles, such as baseball caps, sneakers, and windbreakers. Girls may wear jeans, but if guests arrive, they change into a dress.

12 ● FOOD

Roma food differs from one country to another. Roma enjoy stuffed cabbage rolls and stews. In the past, nomadic Roma always kept a stewpot simmering in the camp. Hedgehogs (porcupines) are a delicacy among some nomadic Roma.

The two basic dietary staples of the Roma are meat and unleavened bread, called *pogacha*, augmented by salads and fruit. Roma drink a lot of tea, prepared with slices of fruit and sugar. Lambs are roasted outdoors on revolving spits and sprinkled with beer.

There are many taboos surrounding food. Certain foods like peanuts can only be eaten at a *pomana* or funeral feast. Bread cannot be burned, and any food that falls on the floor is polluted and must be destroyed. Horsemeat is forbidden to all Roma. Food served at a funeral feast must be eaten before sundown or given away to strangers.

13 ● EDUCATION

Until this century, a formal education was virtually unheard of in the Roma commu-

nity. Even today, the illiteracy rate is high. In Eastern Europe, some Roma have become doctors, journalists, teachers, nurses, and technicians. Some Roma, however, see formal education as assimilating their children—schools are viewed as dangerous places and agents of pollution.

Once children of both sexes reach puberty, they are usually taken out of school, and the boys begin to work with their male elders. In Europe, most schools aim at assimilating Roma children into the dominant culture of their country.

14 ● CULTURAL HERITAGE

The Roma have a strong cultural heritage, which is expressed mainly in music and dance. The roots of Roma music go back to India and show traces of all the musical cultures to which the Roma have been exposed in their migrations. Roma music from certain countries has become world renowned. Foremost is the Flamenco of the Spanish Roma, who are called Cales. Flamenco displays Roma, Moorish, and Spanish influences.

Hungarian Roma music, played on violins and cimbaloms, can be heard in many Hungarian restaurants, even in the United States and Canada. Russian Roma music has also become famous. Under the czars, Roma choirs performed for the royal family and the nobility, while other musicians played for army officers and businessmen at restaurants and inns.

15 ● EMPLOYMENT

Since their arrival in Europe, Roma have been self-employed artisans, entertainers, and middle men dealing in various commodities. Roma traditionally became horse trainers, animal dealers, and ratcatchers. The Roma economy has been built around self employment and the perpetuation of old skills, plus the acquisition of new skills to adapt to new technological developments.

16 ● SPORTS

Sports in general do not appeal to the Roma, although certain regional games can be found, such as Roma wrestling in Romania. Many Roma enjoy horse racing and will patronize local racetracks. Roma men and teenagers also like to play billiards, often for money with non-Roma. It is a status symbol among American Roma teenagers to be a good billiard player. In Europe, Roma participate in mainstream sports, and there are a few Roma soccer teams.

17 ● RECREATION

Roma, especially children and teenagers, enjoy going to the movies. The television, if there is one, is usually left on so that the children may watch it. Since Roma often have little to do with non-Roma, except for business, many form their ideas of non-Roma culture from what they see on television. Teenagers may adopt the slang they hear from teenagers on television or copy their way of dressing, but for the most part, the surrounding mainstream culture contravenes Roma taboos.

18 ● CRAFTS AND HOBBIES

While some individuals have excelled as painters or sculptors, and in other art forms, the majority of Roma practice few handicrafts. Some Roma men make belts or leather clothing, and women may do elabo-

rate embroidery work, while both sexes create artifacts, such as baskets, for sale.

The carving and fretwork (cut-out woodwork) designs seen on the Roma wagons in England became world famous and were later copied by European Roma in some countries. Today, some of the ornately carved versions are made for European collectors by Roma craftsmen.

19 ● SOCIAL PROBLEMS

In Slovakia, the Czech Republic, Romania, and Hungary, Roma have become the target of prejudice and discrimination. There have been ethnically motivated killings of Roma in Slovakia and the Czech Republic, while in Romania, mobs have burned Roma homes and driven the Roma from villages. In some countries, the Roma are stereotyped as romantic misfits or backward savages who should be civilized and assimilated into the general population.

20 ● BIBLIOGRAPHY

Gropper, R. C. *Gypsies in the City: Cultural Patterns and Survival.* Princeton, N.J.: The Darwin Press, 1975.

Hancock, I. *A Grammar of Vlax Romani.* London & Austin: Romanestan Publications, 1993.

McDowell, Bart. *Gypsies: Wanderers Of The World.* Washington, D.C.: National Geographic, 1970.

Tong, D. *Gypsy Folktales.* New York & London: Harcourt Brace Jovanovich, 1989.

Yoors, J. *The Gypsies.* New York: Simon & Schuster, 1967.

WEBSITES

Embassy of Romania, Washington, D.C. [Online] Available http://www.embassy.org/romania/, 1998.

World Travel Guide. Romania. [Online] Available http://www.wtgonline.com/country/ro/gen.html, 1998.

Russia

■ **RUSSIANS** 187

■ **CHECHENS** 199

■ **CHUKCHI** 206

■ **MORDVINS** 211

■ **NENTSY** 216

■ **TATARS** 221

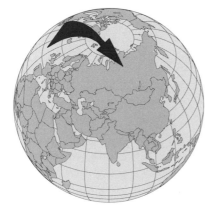

The people of Russia are called Russians. A little more than 80 percent of the population are Russian by ancestry. About 3 percent of the population is Ukrainian. For more information on Ukrainians, see the chapter on Ukraine in Volume 9.

Russians

PRONUNCIATION: RUSH-ens

LOCATION: Russian Federation

POPULATION: 150 million [total population of country: 80 percent are ethnic Russians]

LANGUAGE: Russian

RELIGION: Russian Orthodox; Baptist; Seventh-Day Adventist; Jehovah's Witness

1 ● INTRODUCTION

Ethnic Russians account for about 80 percent of the Russian Federation's population, but the country is very diverse. There are many language groups represented by over one hundred different ethnic groups. Besides the Russians, this article also contains profiles on five other ethnic groups, each from different linguistic, geographic, and cultural backgrounds: the Chechens (a Caucasian group), the Chukchi (Paleo-Siberian), the Mordvins (Finno-Ugric), the Nentsy (Samoyedic), and the Tatars (Turkic).

The Russians are primarily eastern Slavs, but many also have a Finnish, Siberian, Turkish, or Baltic heritage. Since the Russians have spread over such a large territory, many culturally distinct subgroups have developed because of ethnic mixing or isolation.

The Slavic ancestors of the Russians may have first settled in the area north of the Black Sea. The culture and religion of this early Russian state was influenced by the Byzantine (or Eastern Roman) empire.

During the Mongol occupation (c. 1240–1480), the Mongols made the Russians pay them tribute and taxes, but the Mongols let the ruling princes and the Russian Orthodox Church remain in power. The period of Mongol rule disrupted cultural links with the rest of Europe and is part of the reason why Russia was not influenced by the Renaissance, Reformation, or Industrial Revolution when those events occurred in Western Europe.

After a dozen years of power struggles, in 1613 the Russian nobility elected Michael Romanov as the new *tsar* (emperor—the empress was called *tsarina*). The Romanov dynasty produced Tsar Peter I (1672–1725, better known as Peter the Great), considered the greatest tsar in Russian history. During the reign of the Tsarina Catherine II (who ruled 1762–96, also known as Catherine the Great), the Russian Empire added substantial territory through conquest.

For centuries, serfdom was a way of life for most Russian peasants who did not own any land. Serfdom was a form of bonded labor similar to slavery, except that a serf belonged to the master's land. Whenever land was sold, the serfs who worked on that land became the property of the new owner. After the Russians defeated Napoleon's army in the War of 1812, Tsar Alexander I (who ruled 1801–25) eventually abolished serfdom in a few small areas near the Baltic Sea.

In 1825, a group of army officers called the Decembrists organized the first revolt against the imperial government. Although the revolt failed, its memory served to rally the people in later years. In 1861 Tsar Alex-ander II (ruled 1855–81) freed the serfs, but in 1881 he was assassinated by terrorists. Industrialization helped improve the economy, but a financial crisis in 1899, crop failures, and an embarrassing defeat in the 1905 war with Japan led to more civil unrest and strikes by organized labor. Millions of Russian peasants were moving from the country into cities, which made it possible for them to get politically organized. At the start of the twentieth century, many Russians had come to believe that the imperial government was incapable of properly running the country.

During World War I (1914–18), the Russians found themselves fighting in a useless war that plunged the nation into deeper economic and social problems. Tsar Nicholas II (who ruled 1894–1917) gave up the throne, and a temporary government briefly had loose control. Then the Bolsheviks, led by Vladimir Lenin (governed 1917–24), took over the government. In 1918, Lenin had the entire royal family executed. Russia was called the Soviet Union after that time.

The Soviet era lasted from 1917 to 1991. In the 1920s and 1930s, the Soviet government under Josef Stalin (governed 1924–53) instituted policies of terror and persecution to keep its power. The government wanted to control all property and information in order to keep people in line. Millions of Russians were eventually imprisoned, exiled, or executed on made-up charges and suspicion. An estimated 20 million Soviet citizens died during 1928–38 from Stalin's reign of terror and from preventable famine.

The most profound event during the Soviet years was World War II (1939–45), which Russians call "the Great Patriotic

RUSSIANS

War." An estimated 27 million Soviet citizens died in the war, half of whom were civilians or prisoners. After World War II, the Soviet Union quickly rebuilt its military and became a rival of the United States. During the 1950s and 1960s, the Soviet Union, under the leadership of Nikita Khrushchev (governed 1953–64), and the United States began building nuclear weapons to use against each other in the event of warfare.

During the 1970s, there was political and economic stagnation (lack of movement or progress) in the Soviet Union. In the mid-1980s, widespread reforms began under the leadership of Mikhail Gorbachev (governed 1985–91), and those reforms brought a new optimism to the Russian people. However, the Soviet administration had always relied on a strong central government to control the people, and the reforms and the economic problems eventually caused the Soviet Union to split apart.

When the Soviet Union ceased to exist in 1991, the Russian people were filled with hope for a bright future. They had their first chance in history to freely choose their own leadership through democratic elections. During the 1990s, however, the people realized that the transition from central planning (socialism) to a market economy (capitalism) would not be quick and painless.

2 ● LOCATION

By 1800, Russia extended into much of Eastern Europe and Central Asia, and even had territorial claims in North America. At that point, Russia was the largest country in the world to cover a single land mass. Russia is still the largest country in the world, covering about 12 percent of the world's land surface. Today, many of the country's eighty-nine administrative regions are considered ethnic homelands and have various degrees of independence and control over their own affairs. For this reason, the country as a whole is known as the "Russian Federation."

During the Soviet years, most Russians were not allowed to leave the Soviet Union. But many did settle outside of Russia in the other republics of the Soviet Union, especially in urban or industrial areas. Since the end of the Soviet era, there has been a massive movement of Russians to and from the Russian Federation. Many ethnic Russians in the other former Soviet republics have moved to Russia because some of those new governments have pressured them to leave. Some Russians have left the homeland altogether since now they are free to emigrate.

3 ● LANGUAGE

Modern Russian is an Eastern Slavic language. During the tenth century, two Orthodox monks, Cyril and Methodius, created a new alphabet in order to translate the Bible into the Russians' native language. The Cyrillic alphabet, as it is called, is used in Russian and some other Slavic languages.

Common male first names include Aleksander, Boris, Dmitri, Ivan, Leonid, Mikhail, Sergei, and Vladimir. First names for women typically end with an "a" or "ya" sound and include Anastasia, Maria, Natalya, Olga, Sophia, Svetlana, Tatyana, and Valentina.

Examples of everyday Russian words include *Kak delah?* (How's it going?), *da* (yes), *nyet* (no), *pozhaluistah* (please), *spaseebo* (thank you), and *do sveedanniya* (goodbye).

4 ● FOLKLORE

Traditional Russian fairy tales are just as likely to have a sad ending as a happy one. A fairy tale hero is usually a prince or a simpleton, such as Ivanushka Durak. Famous evil figures in Russian fairy tales include Baba Yaga, a witch who lives in a house supported by chicken legs; and Koshchey the Immortal, a dragon that can only be killed if the egg that holds the essence of its death is found. Animal tales deal with funny encounters between animals that have human qualities.

The origin of one of the world's most famous Christmas traditions began with St. Nicholas of Myra, a patron saint of Russia. According to legend, Prince Vladimir (who declared Christianity the official religion of Russia in AD 988) personally selected the generous Nicholas to be the advocate of the people and protect the oppressed. From Russia, the fame of St. Nicholas spread to other peoples.

© Corel Corporation

A souvenir sign in both Russian and English.

5 ● RELIGION

In AD 988, Prince Vladimir proclaimed Christianity as the religion of his realm in order to ally his kingdom with the powerful Byzantine Empire. Russian Orthodoxy grew out of this Byzantine influence. A typical Russian Orthodox church usually has many icons (images of persons who are revered as holy). Magnificent ceremonies on holy days are a well-known part of the Russian Orthodox tradition. The congregation typically stands during the service (many churches have no pews) and move to various stations around the sanctuary.

During the Soviet era, religious intolerance became official policy, and some 85 percent of all churches were shut down and the property seized. This was because the communists were atheists who saw the Russian Orthodox Church as a player in the corrupt imperial system of the tsars. The tsars claimed that their authority was God-given and they were supported by the Russian Orthodox Church. The Soviet government encouraged discrimination against those with spiritual beliefs, and Russians were even imprisoned and killed for their faith. Many religious activities were conducted secretly during that time.

Since the end of the Soviet Union, many of the closed churches have begun to reopen. For many, Russian Orthodoxy is a

© Corel Corporation

People in line to visit Lenin's Tomb in Moscow's Red Square.

cultural as well as a religious institution, and it serves as a link to a pre-Soviet heritage. The Russian Orthodox Church survived the Soviet era and for many Russians is a symbol of the Russian national spirit and identity. There has also been a recent interest among Russians in faiths more common in the West (such as Baptist, Seventh-Day Adventist, and Jehovah's Witness).

Superstition and mysticism have also long been a part of Russian spiritual culture. Russians today are often very open to the possibility of psychic phenomena, mental telepathy, and UFOs (unidentified flying objects).

6 ● MAJOR HOLIDAYS

Orthodox Christmas occurs on January 7 (the Russian Orthodox Church still follows the old Julian calendar, which differs from the modern Gregorian calendar by thirteen days). Epiphany, which occurs twelve days after Christmas, is a major holy day in the Russian Orthodox Church. Easter (in March or April) is the most important religious holiday and is highly revered by the Russian Orthodox Church with elaborate rituals and extravagance.

Russians also celebrate holidays that became prominent during the Soviet era. New Year's Day is a major holiday among modern Russians, and usually the week preceding January 1 is full of festivals. Women's Day is celebrated on March 8, and women usually get gifts and do not work on that day. May Day, on May 1, is no longer International Workers' Solidarity Day as it was during the Soviet era, but is now a festival known as Labor and Spring Day. Victory Day on May 9 commemorates the end of World War II in Europe and is usually observed as a time to solemnly honor those who died during that war.

7 ● RITES OF PASSAGE

Completion of high school or university are important moments that mark the passage into adulthood. Entrance into military service was also revered in the same way. Weddings are usually followed by a trip in a special black limousine (marked with two large interlinked rings on the top) to pay respect and leave flowers at a local memorial.

8 ● RELATIONSHIPS

In public situations, Russians can be very reserved and formal. In private and informal settings, they are very friendly and sincere. Russians use patronymics (where the father's first name forms the root of the child's middle name) in formal and business situations. For example, the patronymic for the son of Pavel (Paul) is "Pavlovich," and "Pavlovna" for a daughter. Adult acquaintances and casual friends usually talk to each other using the first name combined with the patronymic.

Veterans are highly honored in Russia, particularly anyone who defended or aided the Soviet Union during World War II.

Cory Langley

Most urban Russian families have only one or two children. Parents often make tremendous personal sacrifices to help their children succeed.

9 ● LIVING CONDITIONS

During the Soviet years, Russians received health care from a large state-run system that provided services free of charge. In theory, the socialist system was supposed to serve everyone fairly, use the most recent technology, promote preventive medicine, and be open to recommendations from the public. In reality, however, resources were distributed unequally. Political leaders received the best care and rural areas got

Cory Langley

Many Russians wear fur hats during the frigid winter months.

poor equipment and inexperienced personnel. Although medical care was free, many health care professionals moonlighted to make extra money because official health care usually involved long lines and waiting lists. Although the number of doctors doubled from the 1960s to the 1980s, health indicators such as illness rates and life expectancy worsened during that time.

10 ● FAMILY LIFE

Russian women typically get married between the ages of nineteen and twenty-two, while men are usually between twenty and twenty-four years old at marriage. Dur-

ing the Soviet era, nonreligious marriages became common, and new Soviet marriage customs developed. Couples who decided to marry would have to register at a local office, where they would be assigned a wedding date that allowed them enough time to reconsider.

Although Russian society favors large families, the birth rate among Russians has been low since the 1970s, due to economic uncertainty and a high frequency of abortions among Russian women. This was especially true during the Soviet years, when contraceptives were often unavailable. Most urban Russian families have only one or two children, but rural families frequently have more.

Russian adults typically do not hesitate to assist any child in need, and parents will often make tremendous personal sacrifices for their children. It is also common for Russian adults to scold any misbehaving child, regardless of relation. Since so many households have only a single child, Russian parents are often accused of raising a generation of spoiled children.

11 ● CLOTHING

Most Russians wear Western-style clothing on a daily basis and for special occasions. Jeans and other types of practical work clothes are often worn as well. Russians usually try to appear as neatly groomed and dressed as possible when out in public. Many Russians do not possess a large wardrobe, but will often try to have just a few garments of high quality.

Traditional costumes are usually only seen during cultural performances or sometimes in the country. Young Russian girls often wear huge bows in their hair. Older women often wear a large kerchief or scarf over the head and tied under the chin. This headcovering is often referred to as a *babushka,* named after the Russian word for "grandmother." Men and women wear fur hats to keep warm during the frigid winter months.

12 ● FOOD

Russians typically drink *chai* (hot tea). A typical Russian meal has four courses: *zakuski* (appetizers), *pervoye* (first), *vtoroye* (second), and *sladkoe* (dessert). Zakuski usually include fish, cold cuts, or salads. Alcoholic drinks such as *pivo* (beer), vodka, *konyak* (brandy), or *kvass* (made from rye) are customarily served during a formal meal. *Ikra* (caviar), a famous Russian appetizer made from harvested sturgeon eggs, is also a part of formal Russian cuisine. *Borshch* (borscht) is a traditional everyday Russian soup, made with red beets and beef, usually served with a dollop of sour cream. *Blini* are small crepes served with different types of fillings; *pirozhki* are fried rolls that usually have a meat or vegetable filling. *Morozhenoye* (ice cream) is a popular year-round treat. *Kartoshki* (potatoes) are often served at meals, either boiled, mashed, as pancakes, or as a *kugel* (baked pudding).

13 ● EDUCATION

After Russian children are about one year old, they go to a day nursery called a *yasli* until they are about three years old. From age three to age six or seven, Russians attend *detski sad* (kindergarten). Elementary school (grades one to four) is called *nachalnaya shkola.* At age eleven, Russian chil-

Cory Langley

From age three to around age six, Russian children attend detski sad *(kindergarten). The school day features breaks for outdoor exercise year-round.*

dren enter the fifth grade and stay in *srednaya shkola* (high school) through the tenth grade, usually at age seventeen. After the ninth grade, a student may follow one of three educational paths: vocational school, professional training at a *tekhnikum* (secondary specialized school), or two years of general high school as preparation for university studies. In order to go to a high school, students need to pass an exam in language and mathematics at the end of the ninth grade.

Attending a university or science institute is difficult because there is much competition just to get in. There is a series of special examinations, and many students will spend a whole year studying for those tests. A program of college takes five years for a master's degree (there is no equivalent to a bachelor's degree in Russian universities) or six years for a medical degree.

Children are exposed at an early age to systems that stress or value collective efforts. Students in schools often perform in groups and are graded as a team rather than as individuals. Teachers often tell students their grades out loud, so that each person knows what grade the others received.

14 ● CULTURAL HERITAGE

Russian epic songs, known as *byliny,* were traditionally sung by peasants and date back to before the sixteenth century. Some of the byliny are probably over a thousand years old. One of the typical Yuletide observances by Russians is the singing of *kolyadi,* carols that have their roots in pagan culture. The verses typically come from old songs about the sun, moon, and stars.

The most well-known folk instruments are probably the *balalaika* (a triangular guitar with three strings) and the *garmon'* (concertina). Some instruments, such as the *gusli* (psaltery), *gudok* (similar to a rebec, a primitive violin), and *rog* (horn) have been a part of Russian folk music for over a thousand years.

Classical Russian literature is an important part of Russian culture. Poetry recitals,

going to plays, and discussing novels are all popular activities for Russians. These activities are enjoyed by Russians of all social levels, not just by an educated few. Russians often revere their poets, playwrights, and authors as popular celebrities.

15 ● EMPLOYMENT

During the Soviet years, the government controlled labor by setting wages and terms of employment. The problems that came with government control over the labor market, however, were huge. Production goals were set by the state and were supposed to replace profit as a motive. Consumer goods were often given a low priority for production, which meant that there were often shortages of everyday items. Workers had no incentive to be productive, while factory managers had little motivation to operate efficiently. A popular saying by workers during the Soviet years summarizes the situation: "We pretend to work, and they pretend to pay us."

With the collapse of the Soviet Union, many workers found themselves unemployed. As a result, unemployment and homelessness became visible in post-Soviet society. However, private businesses and money-making opportunities have also risen out of this situation.

16 ● SPORTS

Soccer and hockey are popular team sports that Russians enjoy playing as well as watching. Sports societies and organizations were prominent in the Soviet years, and the government promoted participation in a wide variety of sports. The role of sports in Russian life makes international competi-

Cory Langley

Since the collapse of the Soviet Union, the Russian economy has seen high inflation and instability. Some older Russians living on pensions are struggling to make ends meet.

starts in kindergarten, and children study the strategies and techniques of champions before they begin serious competition at around age ten. There are thousands of Russian children who have achieved the International Chess Federation's rank of chess master.

17 ● RECREATION

Russians are fond of outdoor activities. It is not unusual to see people outdoors playing chess or musical instruments and singing, even during the cold winters. The circus is traditionally a popular form of entertainment among Russians.

Russians also have a strong ballet tradition, which started in 1738 and was patterned after the classical French style. During the 1800s, many new ballets were choreographed using traditional Russian themes and compositions. Russian ballet is known for its elaborate choreography and stages.

18 ● CRAFTS AND HOBBIES

Traditional Russian folk art often uses elaborate designs on everyday objects. The designs are sometimes simply spirals or other patterns, but they might also be scenes from fairy tales or of famous people or places. Perhaps the best-known lacquered Russian folk art piece is the *matryoshka,* a series of wooden dolls that nest inside each other. The dolls usually show a woman in traditional dress, but in recent years other themes have included modern political figures, celebrities, and holiday designs.

tions, such as the Olympics, very important social rallying events.

Skiing and ice skating are popular recreational activities. Tennis has become increasingly more popular since the mid-1950s. Gymnastics and acrobatics are also prominent, perhaps due to the influence of ballet and the circus on popular culture. Baseball, basketball, and golf have been growing in popularity as well.

Russian society reveres *shakhmahty* (chess) as a sport. During the Soviet years, chess masters became highly respected members of society and often received special privileges and honors. Chess instruction

19 ● SOCIAL PROBLEMS

Since the collapse of the Soviet Union, Russians have been confronted with many of the old social problems that existed during the Soviet era, as well as with a new set of problems brought about by the rapid changes in society. The change to private ownership created new opportunities but also resulted in high unemployment in many areas. Because of high inflation and economic instability, many elderly persons who live on a government pension are now very poor. Life expectancy and health rates have plunged as well.

Ethnic hostilities have flared up in some parts of Russia that were conquered either by the Soviet government or during the imperial Russian era. When the Soviet government collapsed, there was enough instability for some areas to gain partial independence or even try to break away completely from the Russian government. The fiercest fighting of this type occurred in Chechnya, a region in the Caucasus Mountains near Georgia. Between 1994 and 1996, thousands of Russian troops were sent into the area, and many people on both sides were killed.

Alcohol abuse has traditionally been a problem for the Russians. Alcoholism was prevalent during the Soviet years and is still a problem today. Family violence is often a consequence of alcoholism.

Crime rates have risen rapidly in Russia since the end of the Soviet Union, which has made the economic situation even worse. Much of the crime problem is due to the threats and violence caused by organized crime, which has gained considerable power in some areas. Organized crime is also aided in some places because of corruption among local officials. Russians often look down on the "new rich," who are assumed to be criminals.

Unemployment is high for women, and prostitution has become a popular way for women to make money. Many teenage girls believe that a career in prostitution will pay more than most legitimate professions ever would, regardless of education. About one-fourth of Russia's prostitutes have received some sort of higher education.

20 ● BIBLIOGRAPHY

Arnold, Helen. *Russia.* Austin, Tex.: Raintree Steck-Vaughn, 1996.

Bickman, Connie. *Russia.* Edina, Minn.: Abdo & Daughters, 1994.

Brown, Archie, Michael Kaser, and Gerald S. Smith, ed. *The Cambridge Encyclopedia of Russia and the Former Soviet Union.* Cambridge: University Press, 1994.

Murrell, Kathleen Berton. *Russia.* New York: Alfred A. Knopf, 1998.

Schomp, Virginia. *Russia: New Freedoms, New Challenges.* Tarrytown, N.Y.: Benchmark Books, 1996.

Streissguth, Thomas. *A Ticket to Russia.* Minneapolis, Minn.: CarolRhoda Books, 1997.

WEBSITES

Embassy of Russia, Washington, D.C. Russia. [Online] Available http://www.russianembassy.org/, 1998.

Interknowledge Corp. and Russian National Tourist Office. Russia. [Online] Available http://www.interknowledge.com/russia/, 1998.

World Travel Guide. Russia. [Online] Available http://www.wtgonline.com/country/ru/gen.html, 1998.

Chechens

PRONUNCIATION: CHECH-ens
LOCATION: Chechnya territory between Russia and Georgia
POPULATION: Unknown
LANGUAGE: Chechen
RELIGION: Islam

1 ● INTRODUCTION

The Caucasus Mountains stretch along a line 600 miles (1,000 kilometers) long between the Black Sea and Caspian Sea, and the region includes the southwestern corner of the Russian Federation. The Caucasus region has a long history of conflict and bloodshed among its peoples. The ethnic complexity of the Caucasus is unequalled in Eurasia, and there are nearly sixty distinct peoples living in the area, and fifty languages originate from the region. Many of these groups are quite small in population, yet they have been able to retain their distinct languages and cultures. The Caucasus is the most politically unstable region of the former Soviet Union. Since 1989, the region has been the site of five wars, including two within the territory of the Russian Federation: the North Ossetian–Ingush war (1992) and the Chechen–Russian war (1994–96).

The Chechens live in a small territory called Chechnya that lies within the Russian Federation along the border with Georgia. The Caucasus Mountains protect them not only from enemies but from outside influences in general. The Chechens therefore have retained many traditional customs and practices.

The Chechens were threatened throughout the nineteenth and twentieth centuries, especially by Russian domination. In the 1920s (the early years of Soviet government), the Chechens were allowed to express and develop their national culture. This period of relaxation ended by the late 1920s, and during the 1930s many Chechen political and cultural leaders were arrested, exiled, or executed.

Soviet suspicion of the Chechens led to the brutal deportation of the entire Chechen population in the spring of 1944. In the course of a few days, the people of Chechnya were rounded up by the Soviet army and secret police, loaded into boxcars, and transported to remote regions of Kazakstan, Central Asia, and Siberia. Many died on the way, and many more died in their harsh new living conditions. Survivors were denounced as traitors and suffered severe discrimination.

In 1956, the Chechens were permitted to return to their homeland. Although they had spent over a decade in exile, most Chechens returned to their native territory. Upon return, many discovered that ethnic Russians had taken over their land. Clashes and hatred between Chechens and Russians living within Chechen territories have persisted to the present. The bitterness between the two groups made the long-standing Chechen resentment of Russia even worse.

Chechen nationalism gained strength from the 1960s to the early 1980s. During the mid- to late 1980s, the Soviet government became more tolerant. However, this relatively free political climate provided the Chechens with opportunities to discuss the possibility of splitting from the Soviet

CHECHENS

0   50   100 Miles

0   50   100 Kilometers

In 1996, a ceasefire treaty between the two sides put a stop to the fighting. However, the treaty did not resolve the issue of Chechnya's independence. Instead, the treaty postponed the issue until 2000, when a vote by Chechen citizens will be held on the question of independence from Russia. Chechnya still considers itself an independent state, while Russia continues to treat Chechnya as part of the Russian Federation.

2 ● LOCATION

Chechnya is located inside the Russian Federation, along the border with Georgia. The mountainous terrain has long been strategically important for Chechnya, and it also supports sheep farming, the traditional Chechen occupation. The flatter territories of Chechnya accommodate other industries.

It is difficult to know how many Chechens now live in Chechnya. During the war, many fled as refugees to other areas of the Caucasus, especially Ingushetia.

3 ● LANGUAGE

The Chechen language is unique to the Caucasus region, and not related to any languages outside of this region. Until 1991, Chechnya had two official languages, Chechen and Russian. After 1991, Chechen nationalism and rising anti-Russian sentiment resulted in movements to rid the Chechen language of Russian words. A new school curriculum to increase the teaching of the Chechen language was developed, and Chechens tried to increase the number of publications and media broadcasting in the native language.

Union. By August 1991, with the collapse of the Soviet system and rise of Russian president Boris Yeltsin, ideas of national independence gained widespread support in Chechnya.

In November 1991, the Chechens formed a government under leader Dzhokhar Dudaev and declared Chechnya an independent state. Yeltsin immediately challenged the declaration and refused to negotiate with Dudaev. Tensions between Russia and Chechnya increased, and in November 1994 Russia launched an air attack on Chechnya. Although severely outnumbered, the Chechens managed to prevent Russia from gaining control in Chechnya. The war lasted for nearly two years, with massive casualties on both the Chechen and Russian sides. Much of Chechnya was destroyed.

4 ● FOLKLORE

Because the Chechens did not develop a widely used written language until the early twentieth century, folklore was passed on orally from generation to generation. Traditional folktales are similar to those found throughout the Caucasus. Such tales feature stories of heroism, hardship, and sacrifice, reinforcing values of bravery and personal or family honor. The Chechens used these folktales to present historical events.

5 ● RELIGION

Islam is the traditional Chechen religion. Despite efforts of the atheistic Soviet government to get rid of Islam, the Chechens continued to adhere strongly to their religion throughout the years of Soviet power. However, because the practice of Islam was not permitted during these years, many observances (such as public prayers) were not maintained.

Islam remained a strong force among Chechens. The religious freedoms granted during the late 1980s intensified the public expression of religion.

6 ● MAJOR HOLIDAYS

During the years of Soviet power, the celebration of religious or national Chechen holidays was discouraged. Soviet holidays such as the Day of the Revolution (October 7) and the Day of International Socialism (May 1), were officially recognized. New Year's Day, another holiday acceptable to Soviet power, was widely celebrated.

After the collapse of Soviet power and the Chechen declaration of independence in 1991, the Chechen government tried to create new holidays. In particular, November 9 was declared a national holiday in celebration of Chechen independence. Muslim religious holidays have regained popularity.

7 ● RITES OF PASSAGE

Even in modern Chechen society, the birth of a boy is viewed as an especially important occasion. Family and friends hold celebrations welcoming the new son. The festivities surrounding the birth of a daughter are much more modest.

In modern society, a child's first day of school, which begins in the first grade at the age of seven, is viewed as an important step toward greater maturity. Most young people spend some time in high school, and many go on to university, enabling them to enjoy some years of relative freedom before assuming adult roles. Even today, many young men are married by age twenty, and many girls marry at age seventeen or eighteen. Most young couples have children soon after marriage.

Rituals surrounding death are generally religious, although deaths are always registered with local authorities. The family of the deceased generally holds a large feast for mourners.

8 ● RELATIONSHIPS

Chechen men greet one another with handshakes. Women are expected to behave modestly in the company of men, keeping their eyes lowered. When a man enters the room, women stand in respect. At most social gatherings, men and women gather separately. Children remain with the women most of the time. Segregation by gender is not strictly observed in the workplace, although there is a tendency for men and women to spend most of their time in the company of their own gender.

In a Chechen home, guests can expect to receive the best food and the most pleasant accommodations that the hosts can afford. The younger generation today tends to have a much more casual and relaxed attitude toward the treatment of guests, which tends to irritate the older generation. Visiting is an important part of Chechen social life, and guests are expected to return invitations and extend hospitality to those who have entertained them in the past.

Dating is not usually part of Chechen social life. Marriages are sometimes arranged by families, as each family is seeking to marry into another family of at least equal, if not superior, wealth and social standing. Many young people choose whom they will marry, although they may ask for parental approval. Chechen parents exert considerable pressure on their children to marry other Chechens. This is particularly true for women, as married women are considered to belong to the culture of their husbands.

Chechens are among the few peoples of the Caucasus who still observe avoidance customs in everyday life. Avoidance customs limit the contact that an individual may have with his or her in-laws. For example, a son-in-law is not allowed to speak to, or even see, his mother-in-law. Similarly, relations between daughters-in-law and fathers-in-law are limited by avoidance customs. Because the daughter-in-law often lives with her husband's parents, she cannot always avoid her father-in-law. However, the two will often limit their contact and may speak to one another only indirectly through a third person.

9 ● LIVING CONDITIONS

Many Chechens, particularly the younger ones, have chosen to move to towns and cities. Most urban residents live in apartments. Chechen towns and cities also have a large number of small houses, set behind walls with their own small courtyards. Even in cities, people may keep some small livestock, such as chickens. Many towns, cities, and rural areas were destroyed during the 1994–96 war, and thousands of people were forced to flee their homes.

Food was always difficult to get in the former Soviet Union and, in Chechnya, food selection and variety were often poor. This problem was particularly bad for city dwellers, while people in the country were able to produce and store food more easily. Chechen farmland and reserves of food were destroyed during the war. Other basic essentials, such as medical supplies, became difficult to obtain after the war.

10 ● FAMILY LIFE

Many rural families still live in large family units. The additional labor provided by many family members helps increase the economic welfare of the whole family. In urban areas, few families live in the traditional, extended family groups. Married couples rarely live with the wife's family.

The youngest wife in the household is considered the lowest person in the family hierarchy. Therefore, she usually does the bulk of the work and unpleasant tasks. Many families (especially those in more isolated rural regions) continue to use dowries and bride prices to negotiate the marriage of their children, although these were declared illegal under Soviet law.

Polygyny (the practice of a man having multiple wives) was traditionally practiced among Chechens. According to Islamic restrictions, a man can have no more than four wives and he must provide equally for each. During the years of Soviet power, this practice was outlawed and it stopped. However, since the fall of Soviet power and the rise in Islamic tradition, interest in the practice has grown. Although polygyny is not widely practiced, some Chechen men take a second wife. A second wife is not only a means of bringing more children into the family, but also of displaying prestige and wealth.

The traditional role of women is to maintain the household and raise children. In earlier times, few women attended school or pursued careers. Today, women are obtaining higher education and have challenging careers. Chechen society remains quite traditional, placing a high value on a women's domestic duties.

11 ● CLOTHING

Chechen men and women wear Western-style clothing, although some men, particularly those in rural regions, continue to wear the traditional tall leather boots and loose-fitting trousers. Women almost always wear skirts or dresses that fall below the knee, and rarely dress in trousers or short skirts. Women in the cities wear jewelry and use cosmetics. Chechen men and women wear headcoverings. Older women often wear wool headscarves, usually in grey or black. The headcovering of younger women is often purely symbolic, usually consisting of a silk scarf, folded and wrapped around the head to resemble a thick headband. Men, especially middle-aged or elderly men, still wear traditional lambswool hats.

As Chechen nationalism has become a widespread and powerful force, more men have adopted the traditional headcovering. Sometimes, a colored band of cloth is sewn around the hats, most commonly green, the Chechen national color. With increasing awareness of their Islamic identity, some Chechens, especially young people, have adopted very conservative Islamic dress.

12 ● FOOD

Lamb and mutton are staples of the Chechen diet. Like all Muslims, Chechens do not eat pork or pork products. Tomatoes, red or green peppers, or eggplants are often stuffed with a ground lamb mixture and baked. Milk products, such as butter and cheese, are also an important part of the diet. Fruits, fresh in summer and dried in winter, are the most common dessert.

Traditionally, Chechen men and women dined separately. The men ate together in the dining room as the women cooked and served the food. Then the women and children ate in the kitchen. Larger, more traditional families, where many generations are dining together, often observe this segregation today. However, younger, more modern families tend to eat together rather than separately.

13 ● EDUCATION

Children continue to attend school until tenth grade. Universities and trade institutes offer further career training to high school graduates. Many high school graduates, particularly boys from cities and towns, choose to continue their education. Girls sometimes do not take advantage of higher education opportunities, choosing instead to marry and raise a family. People in rural areas often remain at home and work in the family farming business. During the recent war, most schools were not able to remain open, and many educational buildings and supplies were destroyed.

14 ● CULTURAL HERITAGE

Chechens express great pride in their culture and began in the late 1990s to publish collections of Chechen memoirs and folklore. Traditional music is very percussive and energetic, with drums and the accordion as the main instruments. European and North American classical and rock music are available in Chechnya, but Chechen music is still very popular, even among young people.

15 ● EMPLOYMENT

Traditionally, Chechens were sheep farmers, with men living a seminomadic life accompanying the herds through mountain pastures. In the twentieth century, opportunities for education and urban employment have grown, and many people chose to leave farming, obtain higher education, and work in the towns or cities. Oil refining has been an important part of the Chechen economy, drawing many workers. The process of urbanization was interrupted during the Soviet period by the deportations. In addition, many Chechens became unwilling to remain in agriculture.

After the collapse of Soviet power, the change from a government-driven to a market-based economy was difficult for some, who were unable to find new areas of employment. For others, the changes opened up new fields of work, such as the import/export field. Because many Chechens have links with other countries, particularly Muslim countries such as Turkey, import/export is a popular career choice. For the most part, Chechens have made a smooth transition to new economic conditions. Extended families are often involved in a single family business.

As the Chechen economy was beginning to develop, the war with Russia broke out. Much of the area's basic transportation and communication structure was destroyed, including oil refineries and pipelines. Because of closed borders, the import/export business became difficult. However, the current reconstruction of the country is underway, with great likelihood of economic recovery.

16 ● SPORTS

A popular traditional Chechen sport is horseback riding. Riding has always been part of the job of sheepherding, but is also enjoyed as a recreational sport. Recreational riding features daring tricks on horseback, and is common among young people in the countryside.

Wrestling is another popular sport. Boys start to wrestle at a young age and, as they get older, are often encouraged to pursue the sport seriously. During the Soviet years, many coaches and wrestlers on the Soviet national team were from Chechnya.

17 ● RECREATION

In Chechnya, entertainment centers around the family and the home. There are few cafes, restaurants, or theaters. Most people entertain at home. Guests are treated to elaborate and lengthy meals, and are expected to entertain their hosts in their own homes at a later date.

Some socializing also takes place at work or school. Often, people will invite the families of friends and coworkers to their homes. Young people, who may wish to get out of the family environment from time to time, may get together in groups and go for walks, especially in the early evenings.

Most Chechen homes have televisions, radios, and stereos, and watching television and listening to music are popular pastimes.

18 ● CRAFTS AND HOBBIES

Weaving and knitting are traditional folk arts among Chechens. Even in the 1990s, rural Chechen women continue to weave and knit, producing fine garments. Children may have opportunities to learn music and visual arts in school.

19 ● SOCIAL PROBLEMS

The most urgent social problems in Chechnya today are consequences of the 1994–96 war with Russia. Many people spent almost two years as refugees in neighboring territories, returning to disrupted lives and destroyed homes in their native region. Education was disrupted and opportunities for a normal social life and secure living environment have been delayed for young people of the late 1990s. Many youths were exposed to and involved in great violence. Many were orphaned, and some were badly injured.

20 ● BIBLIOGRAPHY

Bennigsen, A., and S. E. Wimbush. *Muslims of the Soviet Empire.* Bloomington: Indiana University Press, 1986.

Brown, Archie, Michael Kaser, and Gerald S. Smith, ed. *The Cambridge Encyclopedia of Russia and the Former Soviet Union.* Cambridge: University Press, 1994.

Kozlov, V. *The Peoples of the Soviet Union.* Trans. by P. M. Tiffen. Bloomington: Indiana University Press, 1988.

Murrell, Kathleen Berton. *Russia.* New York: Alfred A. Knopf, 1998.

Schomp, Virginia. *Russia: New Freedoms, New Challenges.* Tarrytown, N.Y.: Benchmark Books, 1996.

Wixman, Ron. *Language Aspects of Ethnic Patterns and Processes in the North Caucasus.* Chicago: University of Chicago Press, 1980.

WEBSITES

Chechen Republic Online. [Online] Available http://www.amina.com/chechens, 1998.

Interknowledge Corp. and Russian National Tourist Office. Russia. [Online] Available http://www.interknowledge.com/russia/, 1998.

World Travel Guide. Russia. [Online] Available http://www.wtgonline.com/country/ru/gen.html, 1998.

Chukchi

PRONUNCIATION: chook-CHEE
ALTERNATE NAMES: Lygoraveltlat; Chukchee
LOCATION: Russia (Chukchi peninsula in northeastern Siberia)
POPULATION: 15,000
LANGUAGE: Chukchi
RELIGION: Native form of Shamanism

1 ● INTRODUCTION

Several small and ancient Paleo-Siberian groups live in Russia's extreme northeastern section of Siberia. The Chukchi are an ancient Arctic people who chiefly live on the Chukchi peninsula, or Chukotka. The Koriak also inhabit the southern end of the Chukchi peninsula and the northern reaches of the Kamchatka peninsula. The Nivkhs inhabit the island of Sakhalin and the Amur River Valley. Some scholars believe that the Nivkhs may be related to the Koriaks and Chukchi of far northeastern Siberia, and perhaps some native peoples of Alaska. This article profiles the Chukchi, the largest of the three groups.

The Chukchi who live in the interior of the Chukchi peninsula have traditionally been herdsmen and hunters of reindeer; those who live along the coasts of the Arctic Ocean, the Chukchi Sea, and the Bering Sea have customarily hunted sea mammals such as seals, whales, walruses, and sea lions. The Chukchi call themselves the *Lygoravetlat* (singular: *Lygoravetlan*), which means "genuine people."

In 1729, Russia launched a series of vigorous military campaigns against the Chukchi. By the 1760s, the Russian government decided that the cost of getting rid of the Chukchi was too high in terms of money and troops. They ended the war on the condition that the Chukchi stop attacking Russian settlers and start paying the yearly tax that native Siberians paid in furs. In the 1930s, the Chukchi were forced into state-supervised economic collectives (group settlements where their work and pay were controlled by the government). Chukotka became a region of mines and gulags (concentration camps). The arrest of millions of Soviet citizens during the 1930s created a need for isolated areas in which to build prison camps. Later in the Soviet era, the Chukchi were the frequent subjects of ethnic stereotype jokes told by Russians.

2 ● LOCATION

The Chukchi presently number slightly over 15,000, all of whom live in the Russian Federation. Most Chukchi live in the Chukchi Autonomous District within the Magadan Region at the eastern tip of the country. The territory is mostly tundra (treeless arctic plains), with some taiga areas (plains with scattered trees) in the south. The climate is harsh, with winter temperatures sometimes dropping as low as –65°F (–54°C). The cool summers average around 50°F (10°C). Coastal regions, especially along the coast of the Arctic Ocean, are damp and foggy; the climate is drier the farther inland one goes.

3 ● LANGUAGE

The Chukchi language belongs to the Paleoasiatic language family. The speech of women differs slightly from that of men. The Chukchi did not have a written language until 1931. About 75 percent of the

Chukchi claim to have a fluent command of their people's language.

Until well into the twentieth century, most Chukchi had only one given name. The practice of using a surname came only after the government pressured people to adopt a family name (based on the father's given name) in order make school registrations and other bureaucratic paperwork easier. Some Chukchi personal names reflect natural occurrences at the time of the person's birth—for example, *Tynga-gyrgyn* ("sunrise"; male) and *Gyrongav* ("spring"; female). Other names, such as *Umqy* ("polar bear"; male) *Galgan-nga* ("duck"; female) are the names of animals native to Chukotka. Parents sometimes give their children names that reflect a quality that they hope the child will come to possess—for instance, *Omryn* ("robust fellow"; male) or *Gitingev* ("beautiful woman"; female). Some Chukchi use Russian first names.

4 ● FOLKLORE

Chukchi folklore includes myths about the creation of the earth, moon, sun, and stars; tales about animals; anecdotes and jokes about foolish people; stories about evil spirits that are responsible for disease and other misfortunes; and stories about shamans (tribal priests) with supernatural powers. The Chukchi also have many legends about ancient battles between them and the Koriaks and Eskimos.

In one Chukchi folktale, several shamans and the storyteller are traveling on the ocean when their boat develops a leak. The boat's owner succeeds in stopping the leak with the aid of seaweed-spirits. When they approach land, he tells the seaweed-spirits

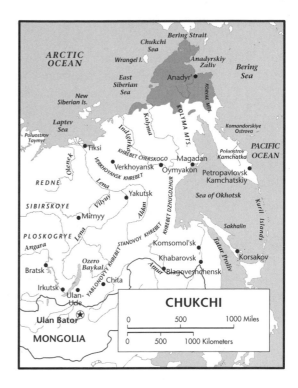

to depart; the leak re-appears, and he challenges the other shamans to stop it. Their powers are weaker than his, they are unsuccessful, and they drown. The shaman who was able to master the seaweed-spirits swims to safety together with the teller of the tale.

5 ● RELIGION

Chukchi religious beliefs and practices are best described as a form of shamanism. Animals, plants, heavenly bodies, rivers, forests, and other natural phenomena are considered to have their own spirits.

During their rituals, Chukchi shamans fall into trances (sometimes with the aid of hallucinogenic mushrooms), communicate with the spirits and allow the spirits to speak through them, predict the future, and cast spells of various kinds. Chukchi shamanism suffered less than other religions from the Soviet government's antireligious policies. Since most shamanist activity took place in the home, there was no religious organization to attack, and so it was relatively easy for shamanism to survive underground.

6 ● MAJOR HOLIDAYS

The most important traditional Chukchi holidays were festivals in which sacrifices were made to the spirits the Chukchi depended upon for their survival. These sacrifices took place in autumn for the reindeer-herding Chukchi and during the summer for the coastal Chukchi.

7 ● RITES OF PASSAGE

The birth of a Chukchi child has traditionally been surrounded by many rituals and rules, although these are probably performed less often today as a result of modernization. After a woman has discovered that she is pregnant, she must go outside every day as soon as she awakens, look at the rising sun, and circle her dwelling in the direction of the sun's movement. When the time comes for her to give birth, no men can enter the sleeping chamber where she is giving birth, as it is thought that bad luck may accompany them.

Death, too, has customarily been accompanied by a series of precise ceremonies. The deceased is placed in the sleeping chamber and is watched over for a day or so in case he or she comes back to life. At this time, it is forbidden to beat drums or make other loud noises. After the watch is completed, the corpse is washed, dressed in new clothing, given gifts of tobacco and a bow and arrow or spear (for men) or sewing and skin-dressing tools (for women). The corpse is then taken into the tundra for disposal either by cremation or exposure to the elements.

8 ● RELATIONSHIPS

Due to the harsh climate and difficulty of life in the tundra, hospitality and generosity are highly prized among the Chukchi. It is forbidden to refuse anyone, even a stranger, shelter and food. The community is expected to provide for orphans, widows, and the poor. Stinginess is considered the worst character defect a person can have.

9 ● LIVING CONDITIONS

The traditional Chukchi form of housing was the *yaranga*, a cone-shaped or rounded reindeer-hide tent. Inside was a box-shaped inner sleeping chamber made of fur that was large enough for several people. Some Chukchi still live in *yarangas*, but far more common are one-story wooden houses and prefabricated concrete apartment buildings typical of the former Soviet Union.

The coastal Chukchi traditionally used dogsleds and skin boats for transportation, while inland Chukchi rode in sleds pulled by reindeer. These traditional methods of transportation still survive, but are increasingly supplemented by air travel, motorboats, and snowmobiles.

Medicine was unknown among the Chukchi prior to Russian contact, most likely due to the lack of medicinal plants and minerals in the Chukchi lands. Not surprisingly, disease was widespread. Smallpox and influenza, brought by infected

Russians or those who had been in contact with them, were especially deadly because the Chukchi had no immunity to them. Western medicine became much more widespread during the Soviet period. Treatment was provided either free or at a very low cost; nevertheless, its availability and quality were, and still are, insufficient to meet Chukchi needs. As a result, tuberculosis and alcoholism are major problems in Chukchi communities.

One peculiar illness that is common among the Chukchi and other Arctic peoples is "Arctic hysteria." A person affected by Arctic hysteria is seized by sudden fits of rage, depression, or violence and often harms others or himself. Murder and suicide are sometimes committed in this state.

10 ● FAMILY LIFE

Families consisting of parents and unmarried children living in a single dwelling are now typical. Sexual activity usually begins before marriage. There is little shame attached to unwed motherhood.

Women's status in traditional Chukchi society was clearly inferior to that of men. The status of Chukchi women has improved in the twentieth century as a result of Soviet policies of sexual equality, and women now serve as administrators, teachers, and doctors.

11 ● CLOTHING

Chukchi women traditionally wore a *kerker*, a knee-length coverall made from reindeer or seal hide and trimmed with fox, wolverine, wolf, or dog fur. In addition to the kerker, women also wore robe-like dresses of fawn skins beautifully decorated with beads, embroidery, and fur trimmings. Men wore loose shirts and trousers made of the same materials. Both sexes wore high boots and leather undergarments. Children's clothing consisted of a one-piece fur coverall with a flap between the legs to allow the moss that served as a diaper to be easily changed. Present-day Chukchi wear Western clothing (cloth dresses, shirts, trousers, and underclothes) except on holidays and other special occasions.

12 ● FOOD

The staple foods of the inland Chukchi diet are products of reindeer breeding: boiled venison, reindeer-blood soup, and reindeer brains and bone marrow. One traditional dish, *rilkeil*, is made from semi-digested moss from a slaughtered reindeer's stomach mixed with blood, fat, and pieces of boiled reindeer intestine. Coastal Chukchi cuisine is based on boiled walrus, seal, and whale meat and fat, as well as seaweed. Both groups eat frozen fish and edible leaves and roots. Traditional Chukchi cuisine is now supplemented with canned vegetables and meats, bread, and other prepared foods purchased in stores.

13 ● EDUCATION

Most Chukchi children study in primary and secondary boarding schools, because their settlements are too small and far apart to allow a school to be built in each one. Literacy in the Russian language is now virtually universal, but because the Soviet government discouraged cultural differences, not everyone can read and write in the Chukchi language.

14 ● CULTURAL HERITAGE

Since the 1950s, the most famous Chukchi writer has been Yuri Rytkheu, whose poems, novels, and short stories are written in both Chukchi and Russian. Since the growth of freedom of speech and the press in the 1980s, Rytkheu has become a visible and outspoken critic of policies harmful to Russia's Arctic and Siberian peoples.

15 ● EMPLOYMENT

Although both sexes share responsibility for running the household, they have different tasks. Chukchi men drive their reindeer in search of vegetation and travel to the edge of the taiga to gather firewood, fish, and hunt sea mammals. Women's work includes cleaning and repairing the *yaranga* (the traditional tent-like house), cooking food, sewing and repairing clothing, and preparing reindeer or walrus hides. It is considered unseemly for a man to perform work usually done by women.

16 ● SPORTS

Traditional Chukchi sports are reindeer- and dog-sled races, wrestling, and foot races. Competitions of these types are often performed following the reindeer sacrifices of the inland Chukchi and the sea-spirit sacrifices of the coastal Chukchi. The coastal Chukchi, like the neighboring Eskimo, enjoy tossing each other high into the air on walrus-skin blankets.

17 ● RECREATION

Among children, foot races and playing with dolls (girls) and lassos (boys) are the most typical pastimes. Chukchi of all ages have traditionally enjoyed listening to folk-tales, reciting tongue-twisters, singing, and dancing. Ventriloquism is a common amusement.

18 ● CRAFTS AND HOBBIES

Sculpture and carving on bone and walrus tusk are the most highly developed forms of folk art among the Chukchi. Common traditional themes are landscapes and scenes from everyday life: hunting parties, reindeer herding, and animals native to Chukotka. In traditional Chukchi society, only men engaged in these arts, but there are now female sculptors and carvers as well. Chukchi women are also skilled at sewing and embroidering.

19 ● SOCIAL PROBLEMS

Pollution caused by Soviet-era mining and industry, poverty, poor diet and medical care, and widespread alcoholism have led to high rates of tuberculosis and other diseases among the modern Chukchi. In addition, pollution, weapons testing, strip mining, and overuse of industrial equipment and vehicles have greatly damaged Chukotka's environment and endangered its ability to support traditional Chukchi activities.

In the 1960s and 1970s, the Soviet government abolished many native settlements, dispersed their former inhabitants, and made Russian the language of instruction in Chukchi schools. During the 1980s, writers, teachers, and other concerned Chukchi began to criticize these policies and to participate in native-rights organizations. They have also begun to expand Chukchi-language teaching and publishing.

20 ● BIBLIOGRAPHY

Bartels, Dennis A., and Alice L. Bartels. *When the North was Red: Aboriginal Education in Soviet Siberia*. Montreal: McGill-Queen's University Press, 1995.

Forsyth, James. *A History of the Peoples of Siberia: Russia's North Asian Colony, 1581-1990*. Cambridge: Cambridge University Press, 1992.

Slezkine, Yuri. *Arctic Mirrors: Russia and the Small Peoples of the North*. Ithaca, N.Y.: Cornell University Press, 1994.

Sverdrup, Harald U. *Among the Tundra People*. Trans. Molly Sverdrup. San Diego: University of California Press, 1978.

Zharnitskaia, Maria. "The Chukchee." In *Encyclopedia of World Cultures. Vol. 6, Russia and Eurasia / China*. Ed. Paul Friedrich and Norma Diamond. Boston: G. K. Hall, 1994.

WEBSITES

Digaev, Albert. Chukchi. [Online] Available http://www.chukchi.com, 1998.

Embassy of Russia, Washington, D.C. Russia. [Online] Available http://www.russianembassy.org/, 1998.

Interknowledge Corp. and Russian National Tourist Office. Russia. [Online] Available http://www.interknowledge.com/russia/, 1998.

World Travel Guide. Russia. [Online] Available http://www.wtgonline.com/country/ru/gen.html, 1998.

Mordvins

PRONUNCIATION: MORD-vins
ALTERNATE NAMES: Erzias; Mokshas
LOCATION: Russia (Moksha and Sura rivers region)
POPULATION: 1.15 million
LANGUAGE: Mordvin (Moksha and Erzia); Russian

1 ● INTRODUCTION

There are many Finno-Ugric peoples living in Russia. These groups speak languages that are related to modern Finnish and/or Hungarian and include the Karelians, Komi, Maris, Mordvins, and Udmurts. These groups traditionally lived in the Middle Volga region of Russia and are culturally diverse. This article will focus on one of the largest Finno-Ugric groups, the Mordvins.

The modern Mordvins live in the Russian Federation. The Mordvins consider themselves to be two separate groups—the Erzias and the Mokshas. Before the Mongol conquest of the thirteenth century, the Mordvins were ruled by their own princes. After the withdrawal of the Mongols in the early fifteenth century, the Mordvins found themselves between the powerful Russian principality of Moscow and the Kazan khanate, a successor state of the Mongols. With the Russian defeat of Kazan in 1552, the Mordvin ethnic territory fell under Russia's control.

Under Russian rule, the Mordvins were gradually made into serfs (feudal peasants bound to a master's land) and became Christians. During the seventeenth, eighteenth, and nineteenth centuries, many

MORDVINS

0 500 1000 Miles

0 500 1000 Kilometers

Mordvins left their traditional homeland. These migrations dispersed the Mordvin population, and they gradually became more like ethnic Russians. By 1917, the Mordvins had become one of the most Russian-like of all the minorities in Russia.

In 1936, Soviet authorities granted the Mordvins a self-governing region, which came to be known as the Mordvin Autonomous Soviet Socialist Republic (ASSR), a part of the Soviet Union. During the Soviet period, the Mordvin ASSR was closed to foreigners, largely because there were many forced-labor camps located there.

2 ● LOCATION

The Mordvins are one of the largest ethnic minorities in Russia, with a population of over 1.15 million. The traditional homeland

of the Mordvins are the Moksha and Sura river valleys and their tributaries. The climate is like much of Europe; in January temperatures average about 16 to 18°F (−12 to −11°C) and in July temperatures average about 70°F (20°C).

Most Mordvins live outside their homeland republic, usually in neighboring districts, areas farther to the east, or even in the more distant region of Siberia. Outside of the Russian Federation, there are Mordvin communities in Kazakstan and Armenia.

3 ● LANGUAGE

The Mordvin language actually consists of separate but closely related languages called Moksha and Erzia. Speakers of Moksha and Erzia do not easily understand one another, making Russian the language of communication. Virtually all Mordvins are fluent in Russian, often at the expense of their native language.

4 ● FOLKLORE

The Mordvins have retained a rich body of oral literature and music, much of which was recorded in the Soviet era. Many Mordvin historical songs (which are actually long narrative poems) may be the remnants of a now-lost Mordvin national epic. These songs include narratives of the Russian conquest of Kazan.

5 ● RELIGION

Mordvin communities as a whole were converted to Russian Orthodox Christianity in the first half of the eighteenth century, although some had adopted the new religion even earlier. By the end of the eighteenth century, the Mordvins were one of the

Mordvins converted to Russian Orthodox Christianity in the first half of the eighteenth century, but they retained many of their native religious traditions.

region's most Christianized minorities. As Russian Orthodox and non-Orthodox Christianity took hold in the Mordvin communities, the Mordvins retained many of their native religious traditions along with the Christian traditions. Their activities included group prayers and animal sacrifices for various spirits. This aspect of Mordvin religious life survived the Soviet period and is still evident today.

6 ● MAJOR HOLIDAYS

The major holidays of the Mordvins correspond to the Russian Orthodox calendar, with the chief religious holidays being Orthodox New Year (January 6, by the Gregorian calendar) and Easter (in March or April on the Gregorian calendar). Traditionally, however, Mordvins observed most other Christian holidays and festivals as coinciding with the agricultural calendar. Important nonreligious holidays introduced during the Soviet period include New Year's Day (January 1), May Day (May 1), and Victory Day (May 9).

7 ● RITES OF PASSAGE

Birth rituals were typically performed by a religious specialist, usually an old woman, and included rituals to protect the newborn from harmful spirits. Although baptism was discouraged during the Soviet period, many Mordvins saw it more as a national custom than a religious ritual. The Mordvins have retained the pre-Christian tradition of funeral feasts for the dead, as well as the practice of holding group prayers and making offerings at the tombs of ancestors.

8 ● RELATIONSHIPS

Interpersonal relations among the Mordvins (such as greeting, body language, and gestures), do not differ substantially from those of Russians. In both Erzia and Moksha, the typical greeting upon seeing someone for the first time on a given day is *Shumbrat.*

9 ● LIVING CONDITIONS

Most Mordvins today live in villages, where houses tend to be made out of wood. Typically, the house forms part of a courtyard, to which is attached sheds, barns, and other outbuildings. In addition, nearly every house has its own sauna or bathhouse. Most villages have electric power, but very few houses have any indoor plumbing, and water is usually obtained from a well or a communal pump. Wages are usually very low, and there is little money available for consumer goods. Similarly, health care in rural areas is of poor quality and not always available. However, Mordvins often make use of herbal medicines and other traditional remedies.

10 ● FAMILY LIFE

Historically, women were more confined to the home and rarely traveled far from their village, so they were less likely to speak Russian or be exposed to Russian culture. As a result, Mordvin women played a large role in the preservation of the Mordvin languages, oral traditions, and customs. In traditional Mordvin society, when a girl married she would leave her home and move in with her husband's family. As a result, a Mordvin family had an interest in delaying a daughter's wedding as long as possible, so as not to lose her labor, and there was a corresponding interest in a son marrying as soon as possible so as to bring an extra worker (his wife) into the family. As a result, marriages sometimes involved eleven- or twelve-year-old Mordvin boys marrying twenty-five-year-old (or older) Mordvin women. During the Soviet period, this custom gradually disappeared, and today Mordvin marriage patterns are similar to those for Russia as a whole. A typical couple today will have only one or two children, whereas before World War II (1939–45), family sizes were much larger, and the infant mortality rate was also much higher.

11 ● CLOTHING

Traditional Mordvin festive clothing was typically white and decorated with elaborate embroidery. By the nineteenth century, Mordvin men were dressing in the Russian manner. Summer clothes were often woven out of linen. In winter, woolens and reversed sheepskin coats were common. Currently, everyday clothing is identical to the clothing typical of Russian society as a whole.

12 ● FOOD

The basis of the Mordvin economy was cereal agriculture, and the staples of the Mordvin diet were bread made from rye flour, as well as oats and barley. During the Soviet period, potatoes also came to form an important part of the Mordvins' diet. The main vegetables include cabbages, carrots, beets, and onions. The main types of meat are pork, chicken, and mutton. Beverages include tea, beer, and vodka.

13 ● EDUCATION

The language of instruction during the Soviet years was often Russian. Few Mordvins were educated in their native language, especially in the later Soviet period. Typically, Mordvins achieve the equivalent of a high school education.

14 ● CULTURAL HERITAGE

Beginning in the 1930s, the Soviet authorities created an official Mordvin national culture. A Mordvin national literature emerged in the Soviet style. Poetry, prose, and drama being produced and performed in the two Mordvin languages, and published both in magazines and as separate books. Similarly, Mordvin folk dance groups were created.

15 ● EMPLOYMENT

Mordvins have traditionally been farmers. During the Soviet period and since the collapse of the Soviet Union, Mordvin agriculture has been collectivized, with Mordvins either working as part of a group farm or collective *(kolkhoz)* or as paid employees on a state-owned farm *(sovkhoz)*. During the Soviet period many Mordvins peasants moved into urban areas for industrial work.

16 ● SPORTS

Numerous sports and games are played at the religious festivals of the Mordvins, especially foot races and horse races, and other contests. The most popular sports are soccer and hockey, which are not only spectator sports but are played by children and young adults alike.

17 ● RECREATION

The lack of recreational outlets in rural areas has limited the recreational opportunities of rural Mordvins. In larger urban areas, however, common recreational activities include the theater, movies, sports events, and television.

18 ● CRAFTS AND HOBBIES

Mordvins are skilled at woodcarving, and this forms an important element of their folk art. Another folk art that is especially well-developed is weaving. Beekeeping is a common money-making hobby.

19 ● SOCIAL PROBLEMS

Alcoholism is a severe problem among the Mordvins. The problem is especially severe in rural areas, where drinking alcohol is essentially the main form of recreation. In addition, the current economic crisis affecting all of the former Soviet Union is also a problem for Mordvins, who are suffering from low and erratic wages and a severely decreasing standard of living.

Another serious problem facing the Mordvins is Russification (legally forcing Russian language and culture in other ethnic groups). The isolation of the Mordvins and their lack of access to Russian education ensured the survival of the Mordvin language, at least before 1917. However, in the twentieth century, the integration of the Mordvins into Soviet society and the access to Russian education (combined with limited opportunities for Mordvin-language education) has resulted in a rapid absorption of Mordvins by Russian society. In fact, Russia's Mordvin population has gradually been declining.

20 ● BIBLIOGRAPHY

Vuorela, Toivo. "The Mordvinians" In *The Finno-Ugric Peoples.* Indiana University Uralic and Altaic Series, No. 39, Bloomington: Indiana University, 1964.

WEBSITES

Embassy of Russia, Washington, D.C. Russia. [Online] Available http://www.russianembassy. org/, 1998.

Interknowledge Corp. and Russian National Tourist Office. Russia. [Online] Available http://www.interknowledge.com/russia/, 1998.

World Travel Guide. Russia. [Online] Available http://www.wtgonline.com/country/ru/gen. html, 1998.

Nentsy

PRONUNCIATION: NEN-tzee
ALTERNATE NAMES: Yurak
LOCATION: Northcentral part of the Russian Federation
POPULATION: Over 34,000
LANGUAGE: Nenets
RELIGION: Native form of shamanism with elements of Christianity

1 ● INTRODUCTION

For thousands of years, people have lived in the harsh arctic environment in what is today northern Russia. In ancient times,

people relied exclusively on what nature provided and on what their ingenuity allowed them to use and create. The Nentsy (also known as the Yurak) are one of five Samoyedic peoples, which also include the Entsy (Yenisei), Nganasany (Tavgi), Sel'kupy, and Kamas (who became extinct as a group in the years following World War I [1914–1918]). Although many aspects of their lives have changed, the Nentsy still rely on their traditional way of life (hunting, reindeer herding, and fishing) as well as on industrial employment.

In the 1930s, the Soviet government began policies of collectivization, education for all, and assimilation. Collectivization meant turning over rights to land and reindeer herds to the Soviet government, which reorganized them into collectives *(kolkhozy)* or state farms *(sovkhozy)*. The Nentsy were expected to conform to the dominant Russian society, which meant changing the way they thought of themselves through education, new jobs, and close contact with members of other (mainly Russian) ethnic groups.

2 ● LOCATION

The Nentsy are generally divided into two groups, the Forest Nentsy and the Tundra Nentsy. (Tundra means treeless frozen plains.) The Tundra Nentsy live farther north than the Forest Nentsy. The Nentsy are a minority living among people (mostly Russians) who have settled in northcentral Russia near the coast of the Arctic Ocean. There are over 34,000 Nentsy, with over 28,000 living in rural areas and following a traditional way of life.

The climate varies somewhat across the vast territory inhabited by the Nentsy. Winters are long and severe in the far north, with the average January temperature ranging from 10°F (−12°C) to −22°F (−30°C). Summers are short and cool with frost. Temperatures in July range from an average of 36°F (2°C) to 60°F (15.3°C). Humidity is relatively high, strong winds blow throughout the year, and permafrost (permanently frozen soil) is widespread.

3 ● LANGUAGE

Nenets is part of the Samoyedic group of Uralic languages and has two main dialects: Forest and Tundra.

4 ● FOLKLORE

The Nentsy have a rich and varied oral history, which includes many different forms. There are long heroic epics *(siudbabts)* about giants and heroes, short personal narratives *(yarabts)*, and legends *(va'al)* that tell the history of clans and the origin of the world. In fairy tales *(vadako),* myths explain the behavior of certain animals.

5 ● RELIGION

The Nentsy religion is a type of Siberian shamanism in which the natural environment, animals, and plants are all thought to have their own spirits. The earth and all living things were created by the god Num, whose son, Nga, was the god of evil. Num would protect people against Nga only if they asked for help and made the appropriate sacrifices and gestures. These rituals were sent either directly to the spirits or to wooden idols that gave the animal-gods human forms. A second benevolent spirit, Ya-nebya (Mother Earth) was a special

friend of women, aiding in childbirth, for example. Worship of certain animals such as the bear was common. Reindeer were considered to represent purity and were accorded great respect. In some areas, elements of Christianity (especially the Russian Orthodox version) were mixed with the traditional Nentsy gods. Although it was forbidden to conduct religious rituals during the Soviet period, the Nenets religion seems to have survived and is enjoying a strong revival today.

6 ● MAJOR HOLIDAYS

During the Soviet years (1918–91), religious beliefs and practices were forbidden by the Soviet government. Holidays of special Soviet significance such as May Day (May 1) and Victory in Europe Day (May 9) were celebrated by Nentsy and all peoples throughout the Soviet Union.

7 ● RITES OF PASSAGE

Births were accompanied by sacrifices, and the *chum* (tent) where the birth took place would be purified afterward. Children were tended by their mothers until the age of about five. Girls would then spend their time with their mothers, learning how to take care of the *chum*, prepare food, sew clothing, and so on. Boys would go with their fathers to learn how to tend reindeer, hunt, and fish.

8 ● RELATIONSHIPS

Marriages were traditionally arranged by the heads of clans; marriages today are generally personal matters between adults. There are strict divisions between the activities of men and women in traditional Nenets society. Although women were generally considered less important, the strict division of labor between men and women in the arctic made relations more equal than not.

9 ● LIVING CONDITIONS

Reindeer herding is a nomadic occupation, requiring families to move with the herds across the tundra to find new pastures throughout the year. Herding families live in tents made from reindeer hides or canvas and take their personal possessions with them as they travel, in some cases as many as 600 miles (1,000 kilometers) in a year. Nentsy in non-traditional occupations live in Russian log houses or elevated apartment buildings.

Transportation in the tundra is often by sleds pulled by reindeer, although helicop-

ters, airplanes, snowmobiles, and all-terrain vehicles are also used, especially by non-natives. The Nentsy have different types of sleds for different purposes, including traveling sleds for men, traveling sleds for women, and freight sleds.

10 ● FAMILY LIFE

Today there are still approximately one hundred Nenets clans, and the clan name is used as the surname of each of its members. Although most Nentsy have Russian first names, they are one of the few native groups to have non-Russian surnames. Kinship and family units continue to be the main organizing features of society in both urban and rural settings. These family ties often serve the important function of keeping the Nentsy in the towns and in the country connected. Rules regarding appropriate behavior follow traditional guidelines handed down from elders to young.

Women are responsible for the home, food preparation, shopping, and child care. Some men follow traditional occupations, and others choose professions such as medicine or education. They might also take jobs as laborers or serve in the military. In towns and villages, women may also have non-traditional jobs as teachers, doctors, or store clerks, but they are still primarily responsible for domestic chores and child care. Extended families often include some individuals engaged in traditional occupations and some engaged in non-traditional work.

11 ● CLOTHING

Clothing is most often a combination of traditional and modern. People in towns and cities tend to wear modern clothes made of manufactured cloth, perhaps with fur coats and hats in winter. Traditional clothes are more common in rural areas because they are more practical. In the tundra, traditional clothing is generally worn in layers. The *malitsa* is a hooded coat made of reindeer fur turned inside-out. A second fur coat, the *sovik,* with its fur turned to the outside, would be worn on top of the *malitsa* in extremely cold weather. Women in the tundra might wear the *yagushka*, a two-layered open coat made with reindeer fur on both the inside and the outside. It extends almost to the ankles, and has a hood, which is often decorated with beads and small metal ornaments. Older winter garments that are wearing out are used for the summer, and today lighter-weight manufactured garments are often worn.

12 ● FOOD

Reindeer are the most important source of food in the traditional Nenets diet. Russian bread, introduced to the native peoples long ago, has become an essential part of their diet, as have other European foods. Nentsy hunt for wild reindeer, rabbits, squirrels, ermine, wolverine, and sometimes bears and wolves. Along the arctic coast, seal, walrus, and whales are hunted as well. Many foods are eaten in both raw and cooked forms. Meat is preserved by smoking, and is also eaten fresh, frozen, or boiled. In the spring, reindeer antlers are soft and grisly and may be eaten raw or boiled. A type of pancake is made from frozen reindeer blood dissolved in hot water and mixed with flour and berries. Gathered plant foods were traditionally used to supplement the diet. Beginning in the late 1700s, imported foodstuffs such as flour, bread, sugar, and butter became important sources of additional food.

13 ● EDUCATION

During the Soviet years, Nentsy children were often sent to boarding schools far from their parents and other relatives. The Soviet government believed that by separating children from parents, they could teach the children to live in more modern ways, which they would then teach their parents. Instead, many children grew up learning the Russian language rather than their own Nenets language and had difficulty communicating with their own parents and grandparents. Children were also taught that traditional ways of living and working should be abandoned in favor of life in a modern industrial society. Most small villages have nursery schools and "middle" schools that go up to eighth grade and sometimes tenth. After the eighth (or tenth) grade, students must leave their village to receive a higher education, and such a journey for fifteen- and sixteen-year-olds can be quite intimidating. Today, attempts are being made to change the educational system to include studies of Nentsy traditions, language, reindeer herding, land management, and so on. Educational opportunities at all levels are available to the Nentsy, from major universities to special technical schools where they can learn modern veterinary practices regarding reindeer breeding.

14 ● CULTURAL HERITAGE

Samoyedic peoples have long had some contact with Europeans. The Nentsy and other Samoyedic peoples did not willingly accept the interference of either imperial Russia or the Soviet government in their affairs, and beginning in at least the fourteenth century they often put up fierce resistance to attempts to conquer and control them.

15 ● EMPLOYMENT

Nentsy have traditionally been reindeer herders, and today reindeer are still a very important part of their lives. Today, sea-mammal hunting is secondary to reindeer herding in the overall economy of the Nentsy. Herding groups continue to be formed around a family core or group of related people. Reindeer herding among the northern Nentsy includes the year-round pasturing of reindeer under the supervision of herders and the use of herd dogs and reindeer-drawn sleighs. Seasonal migrations cover great distances, as much as 600 miles (1,000 kilometers). In winter, herds are grazed in the tundra and forest-tundra. In the spring, the Nentsy migrate north, some as far as the arctic coast; in the fall, they return south again.

The Nentsy who live to the south have smaller herds, usually twenty to thirty animals, which are grazed in the forest. Their winter pastures are only 25 to 60 miles (40 to 100 kilometers) from their summer pastures. In the summer, they turn their reindeer loose and the Nentsy fish along the rivers. In the fall, the herds are gathered back together and moved to winter grounds.

16 ● SPORTS

There is little information on sports among the Nentsy. Recreational activities such as bicycle riding occur in the villages.

17 ● RECREATION

Children in urban communities enjoy riding bicycles, watching movies or television, and other modern forms of recreation, but children in rural settings are more limited. In villages, there are bicycles, manufactured toys, televisions, radios, VCRs, and sometimes movie theaters. In the tundra, there might be radio and an occasional store-bought toy, but children also depend on their imaginations and the games and toys of their nomadic ancestors. Balls are made of reindeer or seal skin. Dolls made from felt with heads made from birds' beaks are not only toys but important items in Nentsy tradition.

18 ● CRAFTS AND HOBBIES

There is generally little spare time to devote to hobbies in Nentsy society. Folk arts are represented in the figurative art that adorns traditional clothing and some personal items. Other forms of expressive arts include carving on bone and wood, inlays of tin on wood, and wooden religious sculptures. Wooden sculptures of animals or humans as representations of gods took two basic forms: wooden sticks of various sizes with one or more crudely carved faces on their upper portions, and carefully carved and detailed figures of people, often dressed with real furs and skins. The ornamentation of women's clothing was especially widespread and continues to be important. Medallions and appliqués are made with furs and hair of different colors and then sewn onto the clothing.

19 ● SOCIAL PROBLEMS

The economic basis of Nentsy culture—the land and the reindeer herds—are threatened today by the development of natural gas and oil. Economic reforms and democratic processes in Russia today present both new opportunities and new problems for the Nentsy. Natural gas and oil are critical resources that Russia's economy desperately needs to develop. On the other hand, the reindeer pasture destroyed by resource development and the construction of pipelines is critical to the survival of the Nentsy culture. These two land-use strategies compete with each other.

Unemployment, inadequate health care, alcohol abuse, and discrimination all contribute to declining standards of living and higher disease and mortality rates among the Nentsy. Social welfare payments for children, old people, and the disabled are essential to the well-being of many families unable to support themselves entirely through jobs or traditional means.

20 ● BIBLIOGRAPHY

Hajdu, P. *The Samoyed Peoples and Languages.* Bloomington: Indiana University Press, 1963.

Krupnik, I. *Arctic Adaptations: Native Whalers and Reindeer Herders of Northern Eurasia.* Hanover, N.H.: University Press of New England, 1993.

Pika, A., and N. Chance. "Nenets and Khanty of the Russian Federation." In *State of the Peoples: A Global Human Rights Report on Societies in Danger.* Boston: Beacon Press, 1993.

Prokof'yeva, E. D. "The Nentsy." In *Peoples of Siberia.* Ed. M. G. Levin and L. P. Potapov. Chicago: University of Chicago Press, 1964. (Originally published in Russian, 1956.)

WEBSITES

Embassy of Russia, Washington, D.C. Russia. [Online] Available http://www.russianembassy.org/, 1998.

Interknowledge Corp. and Russian National Tourist Office. Russia. [Online] Available http://www.interknowledge.com/russia/, 1998.

World Travel Guide. Russia. [Online] Available http://www.wtgonline.com/country/ru/gen.html, 1998.

Wyatt, Rick. Yamalo-Nenets (Russian Federation). [Online] Available http://www.crwflags.com/fotw/flags/ru-yamal.html/, 1998.

Tatars

PRONUNCIATION: TAH-tars
ALTERNATE NAMES: Tartars
LOCATION: Russian Federation
POPULATION: 6.6 million
LANGUAGE: Tatar
RELIGIONS: Islam (Sunni Muslims, majority); Orthodox Christianity; Sufism; Old Believers; Protestantism; Judaism

1 ● INTRODUCTION

There are many Turkic-speaking ethnic groups living throughout the Russian Federation. These diverse groups lie scattered from the Caucasus and Ural mountains to eastern Siberia, and include the Tatars, Chuvash, Bashkirs, Sakha, Tuvans, Karachai, Khakass, Altays, and others. This article focuses on the largest Turkic group in the Russian Federation, the Tatars.

Historically, the Tatars lived farther west than any other Turkic nationality. As Mongolian control over the Volga River region weakened during the 1430s and 1440s, several successor states emerged. During the fifteenth and early sixteenth centuries, the Kazan khanate became the most prominent of these states, and its people became

TATARS

0   500   1000 Miles

0   500   1000 Kilometers

population found itself living outside the borders of Tatarstan.

In the 1920s, most Tatar leaders and intellectuals who wanted independence were eliminated through execution or exile. This policy against the Tatars continued to some extent until the early 1950s. Tatar culture was also affected until the 1970s through the policy of Russification, where the Russian language and culture were legally forced on the Tatars and other ethnic groups. During the Soviet era, economic hardship and job preference given to Russians in industrial areas caused many Tatars to leave their homeland.

In August 1990, the Tatar parliament declared Tatarstan's independent authority and in April 1991 declared that Tatar law had dominance over Russian law whenever the two were in conflict.

known as the Tatars. The Kazan Tatars were conquered by imperial Russian forces during the reign of Tsar Ivan IV in 1552, becoming the first Muslim subjects of the Russian Empire.

When the Russian Empire collapsed in 1917, the Tatars took advantage of the chaos and immediately formed their own homeland, the Idil-Ural State. The Soviet government, however, did not tolerate the independence movement and instead formed the Bashkir Autonomous Republic (Bashkortostan) and the Tatar Autonomous Soviet Socialist Republic (Tatarstan) on the same soil. When the Soviet government took over these regions, it redrew the boundaries and gave neighboring Russian provinces the best lands. By changing the boundaries, about 75 percent of the Tatar

2 ● LOCATION

The Tatars are a very diverse group, both ethnically and geographically. The Tatars formed the second largest non-Slavic group (after the Uzbeks) in the former Soviet Union. There are more than 6.6 million Tatars, of whom about 26 percent live in Tatarstan, an ethnic homeland that is located within the Russian Federation. Tatarstan, with about 4 million inhabitants, is about the size of Ireland or Portugal. It is considered the most northern frontier between Muslim and Orthodox Christian cultures. The capital of Tatarstan is Kazan, a city of more than 1 million people and the largest port on the Volga River.

After Russians and Ukrainians, the Tatars are the most populous ethnic group in

Jeannine Davis-Kimball

Some Tatars are still engaged in subsistence agriculture (growing just enough for their own use, with little left over), using simple tools and equipment.

the Russian Federation. About 15 percent of all Tatars live in Bashkortostan, another ethnic homeland in the Russian Federation that lies just east of Tatarstan. There are also smaller Tatar populations in Kazakstan, Kyrgyzstan, Tajikistan, Turkmenistan, and in the regions to the north and west of Tatarstan. Small Tatar communities are also scattered across Russia. A unique group of Tatars are the Krym (also called the Crimean Tatars), with a population of around 550,000. The Krym are from the Crimean peninsula of present-day Ukraine. The Tatars were one of the most urbanized or city-dwelling ethnic groups of the former Soviet Union, especially those who lived outside of Tatarstan.

3 ●LANGUAGE

In 922, the Tatars' predecessors, the Bulgars, converted to Islam, and the old Turkic script was replaced by the Arabic alphabet. A famous old Tatar saying is *Kilächägem nurlï bulsïn öchen, utkännärdän härchak ut alam*, which means "To make my future bright, I reach for the fire of the past." Another well-known Tatar proverb is *Tuzga yazmagannï soiläme*, which means, roughly, "If it's not written on salt, it's wrong to even mention it." The proverb refers to the

Jeannine Davis-Kimball

A Tatar family home, surrounded by a low fence to keep the family's animals in.

ancient method of keeping records on plaques made of wood and salt, and commends the practicality of keeping written records.

4 ● FOLKLORE

A Tatar legend about the city of Kazan tells of a rich man who was a beekeeper and would often take along his daughter to visit his hives in the woods near Jilan-Tau ("snake hill"). When his daughter got married, she lived in an older part of Kazan, where it was a long walk to get water. She complained about the poor planning of the town to the khan (ruler), and suggested that Jilan-Tau would be a better place for the city, because it was close to a river. The khan ordered two nobles to take one hun-

dered warriors to the site and to then open his sealed orders. According to the orders, they were to cast lots (draw straws) and bury the loser alive in the ground on the spot where the new city was to be built. However, when the khan's son lost, they buried a dog in his place. When the khan heard the news, he was happy for his son but said that it was a sign that the new city would one day be overtaken by the "unholy dogs"—a term referring to those of a different religion.

5 ● RELIGION

Most Tatars are Sunni Muslims, with the exception of the Kryashan Tatars, who are Christian. In Tatarstan, along with Islam and Russian Orthodox Christianity, there are some other religious communities such as Old Believers, Protestants, Seventh-Day Adventists, Lutherans, and Jews. Islam has played an important role in strengthening the Tatar culture, because the imperial Russian government repeatedly tried to limit the spread of Islam from the Tatars to other peoples. This approach, however, usually pushed Tatar Muslims closer to their faith, and there is generally a devout observance of rituals and ceremonies among Muslim Tatars.

6 ● MAJOR HOLIDAYS

Tatars typically observe some of the Soviet-era holidays and also Muslim holidays which, to a large degree, are the same as those elsewhere in the Muslim world. The Soviet celebrations include New Year's Day (January 1), International Women's Day (March 8), Labor Day (May 1), and Victory Day (May 9—commemorates the end of World War II). Since the Tatars are widely scattered across Russia and Central Asia, different communities have regional holidays as well.

The Islamic holidays include *Milad al-Nabi* (the birth of the Prophet Muhammad), *Eid al-Adha* (celebrating the story of Abraham offering his son for sacrifice), and *Eid al-Fitr* (celebrating of the end of the Ramadan month-long fast). The dates of these holidays vary due to the rotating nature of the lunar calendar. The Kryashan Tatars celebrate Christian holidays such as Easter and Christmas.

7 ● RITES OF PASSAGE

Circumcision and other rituals associated with birth, as well as those associated with death and marriage, and even certain Muslim dietary restrictions, are practiced by many Tatars today.

8 ● RELATIONSHIPS

For centuries, there was tension between ethnic Russians and Tatars. As a result, the Tatars suffered from discrimination, which affected how they came to interact with Russian society. The Tatars of today typically live in small communities and often rely on a network of friends and business contacts from within the Tatar community.

9 ● LIVING CONDITIONS

Living conditions are similar to those of neighboring populations (Russians, Bashkirs, and Ukrainians). Tatar houses are often surrounded by low fences to keep in their animals.

10 ● FAMILY LIFE

Tatars often encourage endogamy (marriage to other Tatars) out of the belief that it will help keep the Tatar identity from being lost. Family size is usually larger than that of neighboring populations and is often an extended family of three or more generations.

11 ● CLOTHING

Tatars, as one of the most urbanized minorities, wear Western-style clothing, and occasionally, mostly in rural areas, include fragments of traditional clothing such as the headscarf for women and skullcaps for men.

Recipe

Peremech (Meat Pie)

Dough ingredients

2 eggs
½ cup sour cream
6 Tablespoons of light cream or half-and-half
a pinch of salt
2½ cups flour

Filling ingredients

1 pound groundbeef chuck
1 onion, finely chopped
1 clove garlic
1 teaspoon salt
vegetable oil for frying

Directions

Make dough:

1. Beat eggs. Add sour cream, light cream, sugar, salt, and flour. Knead until smooth and pliable.
2. Wrap the dough in wax paper and chill overnight before making into pies.

Make pies:

1. Combine salt, garlic, chopped onion, and ground meat.
2. Remove about a quarter of the dough from the refrigerator at a time, keeping the rest of the dough chilled.
3. Roll each quarter of dough into a 12-inch cord.
4. Slice each cord into six pieces, rolling these smaller pieces between the palms of the hands to form balls. Flatten the balls slightly.
5. On a surface dusted with flour, roll each into a circle about 3½ to 4 inches in diameter.
6. Spread 1 tablespoon of the meat mixture on each circle of dough, leaving a 1-inch border around the edge. Gather the dough upward all the way around, forming a round, flat pastry. Leave a hole about 1-inch across on top.
7. Cover finished pies with a cloth to prevent dough from drying.
8. Heat about ½ inch of vegetable oil in a large skillet. Cook the pies, with the hole side down, in the oil. Cook a few at a time without crowding them in the skillet, for approximately 15 minutes, or until golden brown. Makes 24 pies.

12 ● FOOD

Lamb and rice play a prominent role in the traditional Tatar diet, as in those of many other central Asian peoples. The Tatars are known in particular for their wide array of pastries, especially their meat pies, which, besides beef or lamb and onions, may include ingredients such as hard-boiled eggs, rice, and raisins. Another traditional dish is *chebureki*, or deep-fried lamb dumplings. A recipe for the basic Tatar meat pie called *peremech* is included in this article.

13 ● EDUCATION

During the Soviet era, the required Russian language exam served to keep many Tatar youths out of institutions of higher learning.

14 ● CULTURAL HERITAGE

It is believed that Tatar prose dates back to the twelfth century, but scholars disagree about its origin. During the early part of the Soviet era and immediately after World War II (1939–45), Tatar literature was largely confined to praising communist ideology. Since the 1960s, however, Tatar literature has often emphasized the role of the artist in voicing the ideals of the Tatar people.

15 ● EMPLOYMENT

Traditional occupations of the Tatars include agriculture, hunting, fishing, crafts, and trade. Under Soviet rule, many jobs were in state-run agricultural and industrial collectives. The Tatars have held an increasing number of white-collar and professional jobs since World War II.

16 ● SPORTS

The Tatars enjoy many traditional and Western-style sports. Soccer became popular during the Soviet years and is perhaps the most widely played sport among young men. Horse racing is also very popular, as the horse has long been an important part of traditional Tatar culture.

17 ● RECREATION

Tatars enjoy many of the same leisure-time activities as neighboring populations in the former Soviet Union, such as watching television and visiting with friends and neighbors. Prominent among the traditional entertainments in rural areas is the week-long Festival of the Plow, or Sabantui, held in spring, which ends with a day of singing, dancing, and sporting events.

18 ● CRAFTS AND HOBBIES

The ancestors of the modern Tatars were skilled in crafting jewelry of gold, silver, bronze, and copper. They also were known for making pottery with engraved ornaments, as well as for crafting metal decorations and bronze locks in the shape of animals.

19 ● SOCIAL PROBLEMS

The Tatars in general suffered discrimination under the imperial Russian government, as well as during the Soviet era. Large deportations of Tatars fragmented the culture, and the loss of lives and property from those days still has an impact on modern Tatar society.

Problems with Crimean Tatars are much more complicated because of forced deportation from their homeland in the Crimean peninsula. Now that almost half of the Crimean Tatars have returned from Central Asia, they are facing problems with employment, housing, and schooling.

20 ● BIBLIOGRAPHY

Fisher, Alan W. *The Crimean Tatars.* Stanford, Calif.: Hoover Institution Press, 1978.

Rorlich, Azade-Ayse. *The Volga Tatars: A Profile in National Resilience.* Stanford, Calif.: Hoover Institution Press, 1986.

Shnirelman, V.A. *Who Gets the Past?: Competition for Ancestors among Non-Russian Intellectuals in Russia.* Washington, D.C.: Woodrow Wilson Center Press; Baltimore: Johns Hopkins University Press, 1996.

Smith, G., ed. *The Nationalities Question in the Post-Soviet States.* New York: Longman, 1996.

WEBSITES

Agi, Iskender. Tatar/Tatarstan FAQ with Answers. [Online] Available http://www.csl.sri.com/

~iskender/TMG/Tatar_FAQ.htm/#shs007, 1995–1996.

Embassy of Russia, Washington, D.C. Russia. [Online] Available http://www.russianembassy.org/, 1998.

Interknowledge Corp. and Russian National Tourist Office. Russia. [Online] Available http://www.interknowledge.com/russia/, 1998.

World Travel Guide. Russia. [Online] Available http://www.wtgonline.com/country/ru/gen.html, 1998.

Glossary

aboriginal: The first known inhabitants of a country.

adobe: A brick made from sun-dried heavy clay mixed with straw, used in building houses.

Altaic language family: A family of languages spoken in portions of northern and eastern Europe, and nearly the whole of northern and central Asia, together with some other regions.

Amerindian: A contraction of the two words, American Indian. It describes native peoples of North, South, or Central America.

Anglican: Pertaining to or connected with the Church of England.

animism: The belief that natural objects and phenomena have souls or innate spiritual powers.

apartheid: The past governmental policy in the Republic of South Africa of separating the races in society.

arable land: Land that can be cultivated by plowing and used for growing crops.

archipelago: Any body of water abounding with islands, or the islands themselves collectively.

Austronesian language: A family of languages which includes practically all the languages of the Pacific Islands—Indonesian, Melanesian, Polynesian, and Micronesian sub-families.

average life expectancy: In any given society, the average age attained by persons at the time of death.

Baha'i: The follower of a religious sect founded by Mirza Husayn Ali in Iran in 1863.

Baltic states: The three formerly communist countries of Estonia, Latvia, and Lithuania that border on the Baltic Sea.

Bantu language group: A name applied to the languages spoken in central and south Africa.

Baptist: A member of a Protestant denomination that practices adult baptism by complete immersion in water.

barren land: Unproductive land, partly or entirely treeless.

barter: Trade practice where merchandise is exchanged directly for other merchandise or services without use of money.

Berber: a member of one of the Afroasiatic peoples of northern Africa.

Brahman: A member (by heredity) of the highest caste among the Hindus, usually assigned to the priesthood.

bride wealth (bride price): Fee, in money or goods, paid by a prospective groom (and his family) to the bride's family.

Buddhism: A religious system common in India and eastern Asia. Founded by Siddhartha Gautama (c.563–c.483 BC), Buddhism asserts that suffering is an inescapable part of life. Deliverance can only be achieved through the practice of charity, temperance, justice, honesty, and truth.

Byzantine Empire: An empire centered in the city of Byzantium, now Istanbul in present-day Turkey.

cassava: The name of several species of stout herbs, extensively cultivated for food.

caste system: Heriditary social classes into which the Hindus are rigidly separated according to the religious law of Brahmanism. Privileges and limitations of each caste are passed down from parents to children.

Caucasian: The white race of human beings, as determined by genealogy and physical features.

census: An official counting of the inhabitants of a state or country with details of sex and age, family, occupation, possessions, etc.

Christianity: The religion founded by Jesus Christ, based on the Bible as holy scripture.

Church of England: The national and established church in England.

civil rights: The privileges of all individuals to be treated as equals under the laws of their country; specifically, the rights given by certain amendments to the U.S. Constitution.

coastal plain: A fairly level area of land along the coast of a land mass.

coca: A shrub native to South America, the leaves of which produce organic compounds that are used in the production of cocaine.

colonial period: The period of time when a country forms colonies in and extends control over a foreign area.

colonist: Any member of a colony or one who helps settle a new colony.

colony: A group of people who settle in a new area far from their original country, but still under the jurisdiction of that country. Also refers to the newly settled area itself.

commonwealth: A free association of sovereign independent states that has no charter, treaty, or constitution. The association promotes cooperation, consultation, and mutual assistance among members.

communism: A form of government whose system requires common ownership of property for the use of all citizens. Prices on goods and services are usually set by the government, and all profits are shared equally by everyone. Also, communism refers directly to the official doctrine of the former Soviet Union.

compulsory education: The mandatory requirement for children to attend school until they have reached a certain age or grade level.

Confucianism: The system of ethics and politics taught by the Chinese philosopher Confucius.

constitution: The written laws and basic rights of citizens of a country or members of an organized group.

copra: The dried meat of the coconut.

cordillera: A continuous ridge, range, or chain of mountains.

coup d'ètat (coup): A sudden, violent overthrow of a government or its leader.

cuisine: A particular style of preparing food, especially when referring to the cooking of a particular country or ethnic group.

Cushitic language group: A group of languages that are spoken in Ethiopia and other areas of eastern Africa.

Cyrillic alphabet: An alphabet invented by Cyril and Methodius in the ninth century as an alphabet that was easier for the copyist to write. The Russian alphabet is a slight modification of it.

deity: A being with the attributes, nature, and essence of a god; a divinity.

desegregation: The act of removing restrictions on people of a particular race that keep them socially, economically, and, sometimes, physically, separate from other groups.

desertification: The process of becoming a desert as a result of climatic changes, land mismanagement, or both.

Dewali (Deepavali, Divali): The Hindu Festival of Lights, when Lakshmi, goddess of good fortune, is said to visit the homes of humans. The four- or five-day festival occurs in October or November.

dialect: One of a number of regional or related modes of speech regarded as descending from a common origin.

dowry: The sum of the property or money that a bride brings to her groom at their marriage.

Druze: A member of a Muslim sect based in Syria, living chiefly in the mountain regions of Lebanon.

dynasty: A family line of sovereigns who rule in succession, and the time during which they reign.

Eastern Orthodox: The outgrowth of the original Eastern Church of the Eastern Roman Empire, consisting of eastern Europe, western Asia, and Egypt.

Eid al-Adha: The Muslim holiday that celebrates the end of the special pilgrimage season (hajj) to the city of Mecca in Saudi Arabia.

Eid al-Fitr: The Muslim holiday that begins just after the end of the month of Ramadan and is celebrated with three or four days of feasting.

emigration: Moving from one country or region to another for the purpose of residence.

empire: A group of territories ruled by one sovereign or supreme ruler. Also, the period of time under that rule.

Episcopal: Belonging to or vested in bishops or prelates; characteristic of or pertaining to a bishop or bishops.

exports: Goods sold to foreign buyers.

Finno-Ugric language group: A subfamily of languages spoken in northeastern Europe, including Finnish, Hungarian, Estonian, and Lapp.

fjord: A deep indentation of the land forming a comparatively narrow arm of the sea with more or less steep slopes or cliffs on each side.

folk religion: A religion with origins and traditions among the common people of a nation or region that is relevant to their particular life-style.

Former Soviet Union: Refers to the republics that were once part of a large nation called the Union of Soviet Socialists Republics (USSR). The USSR was commonly called the Soviet Union. It included the 12 republics: Russia, Ukraine, Belarus, Moldova, Armenia, Azerbaijan, Uzbekistan, Turkmenistan, Tajikistan, Kazakhstan, Kyrgizstan, and Georgia. Sometimes the Baltic republics of Estonia, Latvia, and Lithuania are also included.

fundamentalist: A person who holds religious beliefs based on the complete acceptance of the words of holy scriptures as the truth.

Germanic language group: A large branch of the Indo-European family of languages including German itself, the Scandinavian languages, Dutch, Yiddish, Modern English, Modern Scottish, Afrikaans, and others. The group also includes extinct languages such as Gothic, Old High German, Old Saxon, Old English, Middle English, and the like.

Greek Orthodox: The official church of Greece, a self-governing branch of the Orthodox Eastern Church.

guerrilla: A member of a small radical military organization that uses unconventional tactics to take their enemies by surprise.

hajj: A religious journey made by Muslims to the holy city of Mecca in Saudi Arabia.

Holi: A Hindu festival of processions and merriment lasting three to ten days that marks the end of the lunar year in February or March.

Holocaust: The mass slaughter of European civilians, the vast majority of whom were Jews, by the Nazis during World War II.

Holy Roman Empire: A kingdom consisting of a loose union of German and Italian territories that existed from around the ninth century until 1806.

homeland: A region or area set aside to be a state for a people of a particular national, cultural, or racial origin.

homogeneous: Of the same kind or nature, often used in reference to a whole.

Horn of Africa: The Horn of Africa comprises Djibouti, Eritrea, Ethiopia, Somalia, and Sudan.

human rights issues: Any matters involving people's basic rights which are in question or thought to be abused.

immigration: The act or process of passing or entering into another country for the purpose of permanent residence.

imports: Goods purchased from foreign suppliers.

indigenous: Born or originating in a particular place or country; native to a particular region or area.

Indo-Aryan language group: The group that includes the languages of India; also called Indo-European language group.

Indo-European language family: The group that includes the languages of India and much of Europe and southwestern Asia.

Islam: The religious system of Muhammad, practiced by Muslims and based on a belief in Allah as the supreme being and Muhammed as his prophet. Islam also refers to those nations in which it is the primary religion. There are two major sects: Sunni and Shia (or Shiite). The main difference between the two sects is in their belief in who follows Muhammad, founder of Islam, as the religious leader.

Judaism: The religious system of the Jews, based on the Old Testament as revealed to Moses and characterized by a belief in one God and adherence to the laws of scripture and rabbinic traditions.

khan: A sovereign, or ruler, in central Asia.

khanate: A kingdom ruled by a khan, or man of rank.

literacy: The ability to read and write.

Maghreb states: Refers to Algeria, Morocco, and Tunisia; sometimes includes Libya and Mauritania.

maize: Another name (Spanish or British) for corn or the color of ripe corn.

manioc: The cassava plant or its product. Manioc is a very important food-staple in tropical America.

matrilineal (descent): Descending from, or tracing descent through, the maternal, or mother's, family line.

Mayan language family: The languages of the Central American Indians, further divided into two subgroups: the Maya and the Huastek.

mean temperature: The air temperature unit measured by the National Weather Service by adding the maximum and minimum daily temperatures together and diving the sum by 2.

Mecca: A city in Saudi Arabia; a destination of Muslims in the Islamic world.

mestizo: The offspring of a person of mixed blood; especially, a person of mixed Spanish and American Indian parentage.

millet: A cereal grass whose small grain is used for food in Europe and Asia.

monarchy: Government by a sovereign, such as a king or queen.

Mongol: One of an Asiatic race chiefly resident in Mongolia, a region north of China proper and south of Siberia.

Moors: One of the Arab tribes that conquered Spain in the eighth century.

Moslem *see* **Muslim.**

mosque: An Islam place of worship and the organization with which it is connected.

Muhammad (or Muhammed or Mahomet): An Arabian prophet (AD 570–632), known as the "Prophet of Allah" who founded the religion of Islam in 622, and wrote the Koran, (also spelled Quran) the scripture of Islam.

mulatto: One who is the offspring of parents one of whom is white and the other is black.

Muslim: A follower of Muhammad in the religion of Islam.

Muslim New Year: A Muslim holiday also called Nawruz. In some countries Muharram 1, which is the first month of the Islamic year, is observed as a holiday, in other places the new year is observed on Sha'ban, the eighth month of the year. This practice apparently stems from pagan Arab times. Shab-i-Bharat, a national holiday in Bangladesh on this day, is held by many to be the occasion when God ordains all actions in the coming year.

mystic: Person who believes he or she can gain spiritual knowledge through processes like meditation that are not easily explained by reasoning or rational thinking.

nationalism: National spirit or aspirations; desire for national unity, independence, or prosperity.

oasis: Fertile spot in the midst of a desert or wasteland.

official language: The language in which the business of a country and its government is conducted.

Ottoman Empire: A Turkish empire that existed from about 1603 until 1918, and included lands around the Mediterranean, Black, and Caspian seas.

patriarchal system: A social system in which the head of the family or tribe is the father or oldest male. Ancestry is determined and traced through the male members of the tribe.

patrilineal (descent): Descending from, or tracing descent through, the paternal, or father's, family line.

pilgrimage: religious journey, usually to a holy place.

plantain: Tropical plant with fruit that looks like bananas, but that must be cooked before eating.

Protestant: A member of one of the Christian bodies that descended from the Reformation of the sixteenth century.

pulses: Beans, peas, or lentils.

Ramadan: The ninth month of the Muslim calender. The entire month commemorates the period in which the Prophet Muhammad is said to have recieved divine revelation and is observed by a strict fast from sunrise to sundown.

Rastafarian: A member of a Jamaican cult begun in 1930 that is partly religious and partly political.

refugee: Person who, in times of persecution or political commotion, flees to a foreign country for safety.

revolution: A complete change in a government or society, such as in an overthrow of the government by the people.

Roman alphabet: Alphabet of the ancient Romans from which alphabets of most modern European languages, including English, are derived.

Roman Catholic Church: Christian church headed by the pope or Bishop of Rome.

Russian Orthodox: The arm of the Eastern Orthodox Church that was the official church of Russia under the tsars.

Sahelian zone: Eight countries make up this dry desert zone in Africa: Burkina Faso, Chad, Gambia, Mali, Mauritania, Niger, Senegal, and the Cape Verde Islands.

savanna: A treeless or near treeless grassland or plain.

segregation: The enforced separation of a racial or religious group from other groups, compelling them to live and go to school separately from the rest of society.

Seventh-day Adventist: One who believes in the second coming of Christ to establish a personal reign upon the earth.

shamanism: A religion in which shamans (priests or medicine men) are believed to influence spirits.

shantytown: An urban settlement of people in inadequate houses.

Shia Muslim *see* Islam.

Shiites *see* Islam.

Shintoism: The system of nature- and hero-worship that forms the native religion of Japan.

sierra: A chain of hills or mountains.

Sikh: A member of a community of India, founded around 1500 and based on the principles of monotheism (belief in one god) and human brotherhood.

Sino-Tibetan language family: The family of languages spoken in eastern Asia, including China, Thailand, Tibet, and Myanmar.

slash-and-burn agriculture: A hasty and sometimes temporary way of clearing land to make it available for agriculture by cutting down trees and burning them; also known as swidden agriculture.

slave trade: The transportation of black Africans beginning in the 1700s to other countries to be sold as slaves—people owned as property and compelled to work for their owners at no pay.

Slavic languages: A major subgroup of the Indo-European language family. It is further subdivided into West Slavic (including Polish, Czech, Slovak and Serbian), South Slavic (including Bulgarian, Serbo-Croatian, Slovene, and Old Church Slavonic), and East Slavic (including Russian Ukrainian and Byelorussian).

sorghum: Plant grown for its valuable uses, such as for grain, syrup, or fodder.

Southeast Asia: The region in Asia that consists of the Malay Archipelago, the Malay Peninsula, and Indochina.

Soviet Union *see* **Former Soviet Union.**

subcontinent: A large subdivision of a continent.

subsistence farming: Farming that provides only the minimum food goods necessary for the continuation of the farm family.

Sudanic language group: A related group of languages spoken in various areas of northern Africa, including Yoruba, Mandingo, and Tshi.

Sufi: A Muslim mystic who believes that God alone exists, there can be no real difference between good and evil, that the soul exists within the body as in a cage, so death should be the chief object of desire.

sultan: A king of a Muslim state.

Sunni Muslim *see* Islam.

Taoism: The doctrine of Lao-Tzu, an ancient Chinese philosopher (c.500 BC) as laid down by him in the *Tao-te-ching.*

Third World: A term used to describe less developed countries; as of the mid-1990s, it is being replaced by the United Nations designation Less Developed Countries, or LDC.

treaty: A negotiated agreement between two governments.

tribal system: A social community in which people are organized into groups or clans descended from common ancestors and sharing customs and languages.

tundra: A nearly level treeless area whose climate and vegetation are characteristically arctic due to its northern position; the subsoil is permanently frozen.

untouchables: In India, members of the lowest caste in the caste system, a hereditary social class system. They were considered unworthy to touch members of higher castes.

Union of the Soviet Socialist Republics *see* Former Soviet Union.

veldt: A grassland in South Africa.

Western nations: General term used to describe democratic, capitalist countries, including the United States, Canada, and western European countries.

Zoroastrianism: The system of religious doctrine taught by Zoroaster and his followers in the Avesta; the religion prevalent in Persia until its overthrow by the Muslims in the seventh century.

Index

All culture groups and countries included in this encyclopedia are included in this index. Selected regions, alternate groups names, and historical country names are cross-referenced. Country chapter titles are in boldface; volume numbers appear in brackets, with page number following.

A

Abkhazians (Georgia) [3]214
Aborigines *see* Australian Aborigines (Australia)
Abyssinia *see* Ethiopia
Adjarians (Georgia) [3]218
Afghanis (Afghanistan) [1]3
Afghanistan [1]3
Africa, Horn of *see* Djibouti; Eritrea; Ethiopia; Somalia
Africa, North *see* Algeria; Chad; Egypt; Libya;
    Morocco; Sudan; Tunisia
Afrikaners (South Africa) [8]93
Afro-Brazilians (Brazil) [2]11
Ainu (Japan) [5]14
Aka (Congo, Republic of the) [2]215
Albania [1]19
Albanians (Albania) [1]19
Algeria [1]27
Algerians (Algeria) [1]27
Amerindian *see* Araucanians (Chile); Cunas (Panama);
    Garifuna (Belize); Guajiros (Venezuela); Kayapos
    (Brazil); Páez (Colombia); Sumu and Miskito
    (Nicaragua); Tenetehara (Brazil); Xavante (Brazil)
Amhara (Ethiopia) [3]133
Andalusians (Spain) [8]132
Andhras (India) [4]96
Andorra [1]35
Andorrans (Andorra) [1]35
Angola [1]39
Angolans (Angola) [1]39
Antigua and Barbuda [1]49
Antiguans and Barbudans (Antigua and Barbuda) [1]49
Arabs *see* Bahrainis (Bahrain); Bedu (Saudi Arabia);
    Druze (Syria); Emirians (United Arab Emirates);
    Iranians (Iran); Iraqis (Iraq); Marsh Arabs (Iraq);
    Moroccans (Morocco); Omanis (Oman);
    Palestinians (Israel); Qataris (Qatar); Saudis (Saudi
    Arabia); Syrians (Syria); Tunisians (Tunisia);
    Yemenis (Yemen)
Araucanians (Chile) [2]126
Argentina [1]57
Argentines (Argentina) [1]57
Armenia [1]65
Armenians (Armenia) [1]65
Asháninka (Peru) [7]113
Asian Indians *see* Indians (India)
Asmat (Indonesia) [4]139
Australia [1]73
Australian Aborigines (Australia) [1]80
Australians (Australia) [1]73

Austria [1]87
Austrians (Austria) [1]87
Aymara (Bolivia) [1]193
Azande (Congo, Democratic Republic of the) [2]197
Azerbaijan [1]95
Azerbaijanis (Azerbaijan) [1]95

B

Baganda (Uganda) [9]98
Bahamas [1]101
Bahamians (Bahamas) [1]101
Bahrain [1]107
Bahrainis (Bahrain) [1]107
Bakongo (Congo, Republic of the) [2]221
Balinese (Indonesia) [4]143
Balkans *see* Bosnia and Herzegovina; Croatia;
    Macedonia
Baltic nations *see* Estonia; Latvia; Lithuania
Baluchi (Pakistan) [7]35
Bangladesh [1]113
Bangladeshis (Bangladesh) [1]113
Banyankole (Uganda) [9]105
Barbadians (Barbados) [1]133
Barbados [1]133
Basques (Spain) [8]138
Bedoin *see* Bedu (Saudi Arabia)
Bedu (Saudi Arabia) [8]41
Belarus [1]139
Belarusans (Belarus) [1]139
Belgians (Belgium) [1]145
Belgium [1]145
Belize [1]159
Belizeans (Belize) [1]159
Bemba (Zambia) [9]215
Bengalis (Bangladesh) [1]121
Benin [1]173
Beninese (Benin) [1]173
Berbers *see* Algerians (Algeria); Moroccans (Morocco);
    Tunisians (Tunisia)
Bhutan [1]179
Bhutanese (Bhutan) [1]179
Bolivia [1]185
Bolivians (Bolivia) [1]185
Bosnia and Herzegovina [1]201
Bosnians (Bosnia and Herzegovina) [1]201
Brahui (Pakistan) [7]41
Brazil [2]1
Brazilians (Brazil) [2]1
Bretons (France) [3]181

British *see* English (United Kingdom)
Brittany *see* Bretons (France)
Bulgaria [2]31
Bulgarians (Bulgaria) [2]31
Burkina Faso [2]39
Burkinabe (Burkina Faso) [2]39
Burma *see* Myanmar
Burman (Myanmar) [6]67
Burundi [2]51
Burundians (Burundi) [2]51

C

Cambodia [2]61
Cameroon [2]77
Cameroonians (Cameroon) [2]77
Canada [2]83
Canadians (Canada) [2]83
Cape Coloreds (South Africa) [8]100
Cape Verde [2]101
Cape Verdeans (Cape Verde) [2]101
Caribbean *see* Antigua and Barbuda; Bahamas;
    Barbados; Cuba; Dominica; Dominican Republic;
    Grenada; Haiti; Jamaica; St. Kitts and Nevis; St.
    Lucia; St. Vincent and the Grenadines; Trinidad and
    Tobago
Castilians (Spain) [8]144
Catalans (Spain) [8]150
Central African Republic [2]105
Central Africans (Central African Republic) [2]105
Central America *see* Belize; Costa Rica; El Salvador;
    Guatemala; Honduras; Nicaragua; Panama
Central Americans *see* Belizeans (Belize); Costa Ricans
    (Costa Rica); Cunas (Panama); Garifuna (Belize);
    Guatemalans (Guatemala); Hondurans (Honduras);
    Nicaraguans (Nicaragua); Panamanians (Panama);
    Salvadorans (El Salvador); Sumu and Miskito
    (Nicaragua)
Central Asia *see* Afghanistan; Azerbaijan; Kazakstan;
    Tajikistan; Turkmenistan; Uzbekistan
Chad [2]113
Chadians (Chad) [2]113
Chagga (Tanzania) [9]19
Chakmas (Bangladesh) [1]127
Cham (Vietnam) [9]191
Chechens (Russia) [7]199
Chechnya *see* Chechens (Russia)
Chewa and other Maravi Groups (Malawi) [5]205
Chile [2]119
Chileans (Chile) [2]119
China [2]131
Chinese (China) [2]132
Chukchi (Russia) [7]206
Colombia [2]177

Colombians (Colombia) [2]177
Coloreds, Cape (South Africa) [8]100
Congo, Democratic Republic of the [2]189
Congo, Republic of the [2]209
Congolese (Congo, Democratic Republic of the) [2]189
Congolese (Congo, Republic of the) [2]209
Costa Rica [3]1
Costa Ricans (Costa Rica) [3]1
Cote d'Ivoire [3]7
Creoles of Sierra Leone (Sierra Leone) [8]67
Croatia [3]13
Croats (Croatia) [3]13
Cuba [3]21
Cubans (Cuba) [3]21
Cunas (Panama) [7]64
Cyprus [3]29
Czech Republic [3]37
Czechoslovakia *see* Czech Republic; Slovakia
Czechs (Czech Republic) [3]37

D

Dahomey *see* Benin
Danes (Denmark) [3]43
Denmark [3]43
Dinka (Sudan) [8]181
Djibouti [3]51
Djiboutians (Djibouti) [3]51
Dominica [3]57
Dominican Republic [3]63
Dominicans (Dominica) [3]57
Dominicans (Dominican Republic) [3]63
Dong (China) [2]141
DROC *see* Congo, Democratic Republic of the
Druze (Syria) [8]219
Dutch *see* Netherlanders (The Netherlands)

E

Ecuador [3]69
Ecuadorans (Ecuador) [3]69
Efe and Mbuti (Congo, Democratic Republic of
    the) [2]201
Egypt [3]83
Egyptians (Egypt) [3]83
El Salvador [3]91
Emirians (United Arab Emirates) [9]117
England *see* English (United Kingdom)
English (South Africa) [8]105
English (United Kingdom) [9]123
Equatorial Guinea [3]99
Equatorial Guineans (Equatorial Guinea) [3]99
Eritrea [3]107
Eritreans (Eritrea) [3]107

Eskimos *see* Inuit (Canada)
Estonia [3]113
Estonians (Estonia) [3]113
Ethiopia [3]121
Ethiopians (Ethiopia) [3]121
Ewenki (Mongolia) [6]46

F

Fiji [3]157
Fijians (Fiji) [3]157
Filipinos (Philippines) [7]125
Finland [3]167
Finns (Finland) [3]167
Flemings (Belgium) [1]151
France [3]175
French (France) [3]175
French Canadians (Canada) [2]89
French Guiana *see* French Guianans (France)
French Guianans (France) [3]185
French Somaliland *see* Djibouti
Frisians (The Netherlands) [6]122
Fulani (Guinea) [4]46

G

Gabon [3]189
Gabonese (Gabon) [3]189
Galicians (Spain) [8]155
Gambia, The [3]195
Gambians (Gambia, The) [3]195
Garifuna (Belize) [1]166
Georgia [3]205
Georgians (Georgia) [3]205
Germans (Germany) [4]1
Germany [4]1
Ghana [4]9
Ghanaians (Ghana) [4]9
Gikuyu (Kenya) [5]50
Gonds (India) [4]102
Greece [4]17
Greek Cypriots (Cyprus) [3]29
Greeks (Greece) [4]17
Grenada [4]25
Grenadians (Grenada) [4]25
Guajiros (Venezuala) [9]170
Guaranís (Paraguay) [7]98
Guatemala [4]31
Guatemalans (Guatemala) [4]31
Guinea [4]39
Guineans (Guinea) [4]39
Gujaratis (India) [4]107
Gusii (Kenya) [5]60
Guyana [4]51

Guyanans (Guyana) [4]51
Gypsies *see* Roma (Romania)

H

Haiti [4]57
Haitians (Haiti) [4]57
Han (China) [2]148
Hausa (Nigeria) [6]176
Hazaras (Afghanistan) [1]10
Hiligaynon (Philippines) [7]136
Hill Tribespeople (Cambodia) [2]70
Hondurans (Honduras) [4]67
Honduras [4]67
Horn of Africa *see* Djibouti; Eritrea; Ethiopia; Somalia
Hungarians (Hungary) [4]75
Hungary [4]75
Hutu (Rwanda) [8]7

I

Iatmul (Papua New Guinea) [7]79
Iceland [4]81
Icelanders (Iceland) [4]81
Igbo (Nigeria) [6]181
Ilocanos (Philippines) [7]142
India [4]87
Indians (India) [4]88
Indo-Fijians (Fiji) [3]163
Indonesia [4]129
Indonesians (Indonesia) [4]129
Inuit (Canada) [2]94
Iran [4]161
Iranians (Iran) [4]161
Iraq [4]169
Iraqis (Iraq) [4]169
Ireland [4]181
Irish (Ireland) [4]181
Israel [4]189
Israelis (Israel) [4]189
Italians (Italy) [4]207
Italy [4]207
Ivoirians (Cote d'Ivoire) [3]7
Ivory Coast *see* Cote d'Ivoire

J

Jamaica [4]215
Jamaicans (Jamaica) [4]215
Japan [5]1
Japanese (Japan) [5]1
Javanese (Indonesia) [4]149
Jivaro (Ecuador) [3]77
Jordan [5]21
Jordanians (Jordan) [5]21

K

Kalenjin (Kenya) [5]67
Kammu (Laos) [5]125
Kampuchea *see* Cambodia
Karakalpaks (Uzbekistan) [9]153
Karens (Myanmar) [6]75
Kayapos (Brazil) [2]17
Kazaks (Kazakstan) [5]29
Kazakstan [5]29
Kenya [5]39
Kenyans (Kenya) [5]39
Khmer (Cambodia) [2]61
Kittitians and Nevisians (St. Kitts and Nevis) [8]11
Korea, Republic of [5]91
Kurds (Turkey) [9]78
Kuwait [5]99
Kuwaitis (Kuwait) [5]99
Kyrgyz (Kyrgystan) [5]107
Kyrgyzstan [5]107

L

Lao (Laos) [5]115
Laos [5]115
Lapps *see* Sami (Norway)
Latvia [5]133
Latvians (Latvia) [5]133
Lebanese (Lebanon) [5]139
Lebanon [5]139
Lesotho [5]149
Liberia [5]159
Libya [5]167
Libyans (Libya) [5]167
Liechtenstein [5]175
Liechtensteiners (Liechtenstein) [5]175
Lithuania [5]181
Lithuanians (Lithuania) [5]181
Luhya (Kenya) [5]74
Luo (Kenya) [5]81
Luxembourg [5]189
Luxembourgers (Luxembourg) [5]189

M

Ma'dan (Iraq) [4]176
Maasai (Tanzania) [9]25
Macedonia [5]193
Macedonians (Macedonians) [5]193
Madagascar [5]199
Maghreb states *see* Algeria; Libya; Mauritania; Morocco; Tunisia
Malagasy (Madagascar) [5]199
Malawi [5]205
Malays (Malaysia) [5]213

Malaysia [5]213
Mali [5]221
Malians (Mali) [5]221
Malinke (Liberia) [5]159
Man (China) [2]153
Manchus *see* Man (China)
Maori (New Zealand) [6]133
Mapuches see Araucanians (Chile)
Marathas (India) [4]112
Maravi Groups *see* Chewa and other Maravi Groups (Malawi)
Maronites (Lebanon) [5]145
Marsh Arabs *see* Ma'dan (Iraq)
Masai *see* Maasai (Tanzania)
Mauritania [6]1
Mauritanians (Mauritania) [6]1
Maya (Mexico) [6]13
Melanesians (Papua New Guinea) [7]71
Melpa (Papua New Guinea) [7]84
Mexicans (Mexico) [6]7
Mexico [6]7
Miao (China) [2]157
Micronesia [6]21
Micronesians (Micronesia) [6]21
Middle East *see* Bahrain; Cyprus; Iran; Iraq; Israel; Jordan; Kuwait; Lebanon; Oman; Qatar; Saudi Arabia; Syria; United Arab Emirates; Yemen
Miskito *see* Sumu and Miskito (Nicaragua)
Moldavia *see* Moldova
Moldova [6]25
Moldovans (Moldova) [6]25
Monaco [6]33
Monégasques (Monaco) [6]33
Mongolia [6]39
Mongols (Mongolia) [6]39
Mordvins (Russia) [7]211
Moroccans (Morocco) [6]53
Morocco [6]53
Mossi (Burkina Faso) [2]43
Motu (Papua New Guinea) [7]89
Mozambicans (Mozambique) [6]61
Mozambique [6]61
Myanmar [6]67

N

Namibia [6]91
Namibians (Namibia) [6]91
Nentsy (Russia) [7]216
Nepal [6]99
Nepalis (Nepal) [6]99
Netherlanders (The Netherlands) [6]115
Netherlands, The [6]115
New Zealand [6]127

New Zealanders (New Zealand) [6]127
Newly Independent States (former Soviet republics) *see* Armenia; Azerbaijan; Belarus; Georgia; Kazakstan; Kyrgyzstan; Moldova; Russia; Tajikistan; Turkmenistan; Ukraine; Uzbekistan
Nicaragua [6]145
Nicaraguans (Nicaragua) [6]145
Niger [6]157
Nigeria [6]171
Nigerians (Nigeria) [6]171
Nigeriens (Niger) [6]157
Ni-Vanuatu (Vanuatu) [9]159
Nomads *see* Bedu (Saudi Arabia); Mongols (Mongolia)
North Africa *see* Algeria; Chad; Egypt; Libya; Morocco; Sudan; Tunisia
Norway [7]1
Norwegians (Norway) [7]1
Nyamwezi (Tanzania) [9]34
Nyasaland *see* Malawi

O

Oman [7]17
Omanis (Oman) [7]17
Oriya (India) [4]117
Oromos (Ethiopia) [3]141

P

Páez (Colombia) [2]183
Pakistan [7]25
Pakistanis (Pakistan) [7]25
Palestine *see* Palestinians (Israel)
Palestinians (Israel) [4]198
Pamiri [9]7
Panama [7]57
Panamanians (Panama) [7]57
Papua New Guinea [7]71
Paraguay [7]93
Paraguayans (Paraguay) [7]93
Pashtun (Afghanistan) [1]13
Pemon (Venezuala) [9]174
Persians *see* Iranians (Iran)
Peru [7]105
Peruvians (Peru) [7]105
Philippines [7]125
Poland [7]149
Poles (Poland) [7]149
Polynesia see Polynesians (New Zealand)
Polynesians (New Zealand) [6]139
Portugal [7]157
Portuguese (Portugal) [7]157
Portuguese East Africa *see* Mozambique
Punjabis (Pakistan) [7]46

Pygmies *see* Aka (Congo, Republic of the); Efe and Mbuti (Congo, Democratic Republic of the)

Q

Qatar [7]165
Qataris (Qatar) [7]165
Quechua (Peru) [7]119

R

Rajputs (India) [4]122
Rhodesia *see* Zimbabwe
Roma (Romania) [7]178
Romania [7]171
Romanians (Romania) [7]171
Russia [7]187
Russians (Russia) [7]187
Rwanda [8]1
Rwandans (Rwanda) [8]1

S

St. Kitts and Nevis [8]11
St. Lucia [8]17
St. Lucians (St. Lucia) [8]17
St. Vincent and the Grenadines [8]23
St. Vincentians (St. Vincent and the Grenadines) [8]23
Salvadorans (El Salvador) [3]91
Sami (Norway) [7]9
Sammarinese (San Marino) [8]29
Samoa *see* Western Samoa
Samoans (Western Samoa) [9]197
San Marino [8]29
Saudi Arabia [8]33
Saudis (Saudi Arabia) [8]33
Scandinavia see Denmark; Finland; Iceland; Norway; Sweden
Scotland *see* Scots (United Kingdom)
Scots (United Kingdom) [9]130
Senegal [8]49
Senegalese (Senegal) [8]49
Seychelles [8]61
Seychellois (Seychelles) [8]61
Shambaa (Tanzania) [9]39
Shans (Myanmar) [6]83
Sherpas (Nepal) [6]107
Sierra Leone [8]67
Sinhalese (Sri Lanka) [8]161
Slovakia [8]73
Slovaks (Slovakia) [8]73
Slovenes (Slovenia) [8]81
Slovenia [8]81
Somalia [8]87
Somaliland, French *see* Djibouti

Somalis (Somalia) [8]87
Songhay (Mali) [5]227
Sotho (Lesotho) [5]149
South Africa [8]93
South Asia *see* Afghanistan; Bangladesh, Bhutan, India, Pakistan, Sri Lanka
South Koreans (Korea, Republic of) [5]91
South West Africa *see* Namibia
Southeast Asia *see* Brunei Darussalam; Cambodia; Indonesia; Laos; Malaysia; Thailand; Vietnam
Soviet Union (former) *see* Armenia; Azerbaijan; Belarus; Georgia; Kazakstan; Kyrgyzstan; Moldova; Russia; Tajikistan; Turkmenistan; Ukraine; Uzbekistan
Spain [8]125
Spaniards (Spain) [8]125
Sri Lanka [8]161
Sudan [8]175
Sudanese (Sudan) [8]175
Sumu and Miskito (Nicaragua) [6]152
Sundanese (Indonesia) [4]155
Suriname [8]185
Surinamese (Suriname) [8]185
Swahili (Tanzania) [9]45
Swaziland [8]189
Swazis (Swaziland) [8]189
Sweden [8]195
Swedes (Sweden) [8]195
Swiss (Switzerland) [8]205
Switzerland [8]205
Syria [8]213
Syrians (Syria) [8]213

T

Tajikistan [9]1
Tajiks [9]1
Tamils (Sri Lanka) [8]169
Tanganyika *see* Tanzania
Tanzania [9]13
Tanzanians (Tanzania) [9]13
Tatars (Russia) [7]221
Thai (Thailand) [9]51
Thailand [9]51
Tibet *see* Tibetans (China)
Tibetans (China) [2]163
Tigray (Ethiopia) [3]149
Tonga (Zambia) [9]221
Trinidad and Tobago [9]59
Trinidadians and Tobagonians (Trinidad and Tobago) [9]59
Tuareg (Niger) [6]164
Tunisia [9]65
Tunisians (Tunisia) [9]65

Turkmenistan [9]85
Turkey [9]71
Turkmens (Turkmenistan) [9]85
Turks (Turkey) [9]71
Tutsi (Burundi) [2]57

U

UAE *see* United Arab Emirates
Uganda [9]91
Ugandans (Uganda) [9]91
Uighurs (China) [2]168
Ukraine [9]111
Ukrainians (Ukraine) [9]111
United Arab Emirates [9]117
United Kingdom [9]123
Upper Volta *see* Burkina Faso
Uruguay [9]143
Uruguayans (Uruguayans) [9]143
USSR *see* Soviet Union (former)
Uzbekistan [9]147
Uzbeks (Uzbekistan) [9]147

V

Vanuatu [9]159
Venezuela [9]163
Venezuelans (Venezuela) [9]163
Vietnam [9]181
Vietnamese (Vietnam) [9]181

W–X–Y–Z

Wales *see* Welsh (United Kingdom)
Walloons (Belgium) [1]155
Welsh (United Kingdom) [9]136
West Africa *see* Benin
Western Sahara *see* Morocco
Western Samoa [9]197
Wolof (Senegal) [8]56
Xavante (Brazil) [2]22
Xhosa (South Africa) [8]110
Yemen [9]201
Yemenis (Yemen) [9]201
Yoruba (Nigeria) [6]186
Zaire *see* Congo, Democratic Republic of the
Zambia [9]209
Zambians (Zambia) [9]209
Zanzibar *see* Tanzania
Zhuang (China) [2]173
Zimbabwe [9]227
Zimbabweans (Zimbabwe) [9]227
Zulu (South Africa) [8]117